VICKERS/BAC
VC10

1962 to 2013 (all marks and models)

COVER IMAGE: **Vickers/BAC VC10 K Mk 2.**
(Mike Badrocke)

First published in October 2016

A catalogue record for this book is available
from the British Library.

ISBN 978 0 85733 799 3

Library of Congress control no. 2015948109

Published by Haynes Publishing,
Sparkford, Yeovil,
Somerset BA22 7JJ, UK.
Tel: 01963 440635
Int. tel: +44 1963 440635
Website: www.haynes.com

Haynes North America Inc.,
861 Lawrence Drive, Newbury Park,
California 91320, USA.

Printed in Malaysia.

Copy editor: Michelle Tilling
Proof reader: Penny Housden
Indexer: Peter Nicholson
Page design: James Robertson

VICKERS/BAC
VC10

1962 to 2013 (all marks and models)

Owners' Workshop Manual

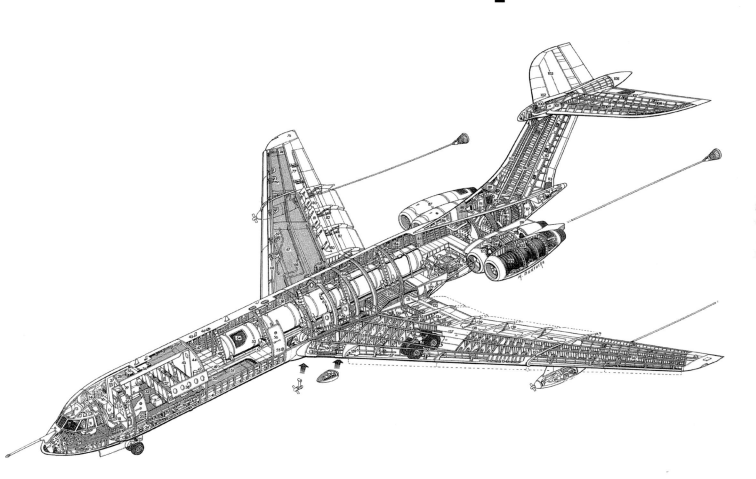

Insights into the design, construction, operation and maintenance of the VC10 in civil and military service

Keith Wilson

Contents

BELOW During the service life of the VC10 with the British Overseas Airways Corporation (BOAC), a number of special paintings were commissioned by the airline for use in connection with promotional activities. This particular piece was created by the famous aviation artist Frank Wootton. *(BAE SYSTEMS Image Ref WCN1015)*

THE B·O·A·C VC10

ABOVE All of the remaining RAF VC10 C.1 aircraft were converted to C.1K two-point tankers by Flight Refuelling at Hurn. XV101 was one of the first aircraft converted and returned to 10 Squadron in its 'shiny' colour scheme. It was photographed over the North Sea refueling a pair of Tornado F3s (ZG733/BK and ZE834) from 29 Squadron, Coningsby. *(Keith Wilson)*

Acknowledgements

A project of this nature requires the help and support of many people who have contributed in different ways to make the book possible. The author would like to offer his sincere thanks to the following:

Gary Spoors at GJD Services, Bruntingthorpe, for providing unlimited access to ZD241, along with all of the other VC10 airframes and components at Bruntingthorpe; and to his lovely wife Aine for the never-ending supply of tea!

To the ZD241 Preservation Group at Bruntingthorpe – a tremendous team of enthusiastic and knowledgeable individuals – and for allowing me to share in your passion for all things VC10. My individual thanks must go to Ollie Pallett, Steve Jones, Phil Juffs, Chris Haywood, Andy Townshend, William Rowe, Richard Faint and Ollie Suckling.

To the staff at the Brooklands Museum, Weybridge, for allowing photographic access to their VC10 A4O-AB; along with access to the test fuselage and to G-ARVM.

To the team at Dunsfold who maintain K.3 ZA150 on behalf of the Brooklands Museum – especially to Paul Robinson and Bob Cooper.

To David Garside and Chris Giles at the Duxford Aviation Society for allowing special photographic access to G-ASGC, as well as providing a number of useful diagrams.

To Howard Mason and Barry Guess at the BAe Heritage Centre at Farnborough for access to their excellent archive and for their help with images and information.

To the Brooklands Museum for providing various images and illustrations. However, very special thanks are due to Abigail 'Abi' Wilson, whose patience and cooperation went way beyond the call of duty!

To Zoe Watson and Linda Coote at the Bristol Aero Collection Trust for providing images and information.

To Jim Davies and Paul Jarvis at the BA Heritage Collection for access to the Speedbird Heritage archives and supplying images.

To Melissa White at Cobham plc for providing images and information. To Charles Polidano; for assistance with data on the VC10.

To Paul Newman for contributing information on the VVIP activities at 10 Squadron during his time at Brize Norton. To Darren Speechley ('Bag Man') who kindly put me in touch with a number of key VC10 people during my research for this book.

To the various photographers who have kindly provided images to this book including: Lee Barton, Patrick Bunce, Cpl Adam Cooper, Philip Dawes, Peter R. Foster, Jelle Hieminga, Geoffrey Lee, Andrew Long, Peter R. March, Paul Robinson, Kev Slade, Gary Spoors, Philip Stevens, Andy Townshend, Richard Vandervoord, Chris Williams, Ken Williams and Ollie Wilson.

To Sebastian Cox at the Air Historical Branch, RAF Northolt, for providing the Branch's support with access to the collection of images – along with his encouragement and sense of humour.

My thanks must also go to Lee Barton at the Air Historical Branch for his unwavering enthusiasm, vision and attention to detail during the image selection process. Due credit must be given for his research skills – unearthing new information and responding to the never-ending stream of questions.

To Ollie Pallett an RAF technician with a wealth of knowledge and experience on the VC10. Ollie leads the team of enthusiastic volunteers who keep ZD241 'live' at Bruntingthorpe. He gave of his time and support freely, and nothing seemed too much of a problem. Ollie operated the flight engineer's position during the high-speed run at Bruntingthorpe on 16 March 2016.

To Chris Haywood; an RAF flying instructor and experienced VC10 pilot who has provided descriptions of so many of his first-hand experiences of flying the VC10. Chris was in the right-hand seat during the high-speed run at Bruntingthorpe on 16 March 2016.

To John B. Williamson, a retired former BOAC, EAA, Gulf Air and British Airways flight engineer, who related many of his happy 'experiences' on the VC10 in airline service. John is now a volunteer at both the Cornwall Heritage Centre and the ZD241 Preservation Group at Bruntingthorpe.

To Andy Townshend, an RAF pilot who obligingly lent me his vast collection of VC10 manuals and documentation to aid my research. In addition, Andy generously allowed me to join his team in the cockpit of ZD241 during the high-speed run at Bruntingthorpe on 16 March 2016. While it all happened far too quickly, the acceleration and noise in that short space of time brought so many happy memories of earlier VC10 flights flooding back.

At Haynes Publishing, I would like to thank Jonathan Falconer, Michelle Tilling and James Robertson for their considerable input at key stages during the book's production and for keeping me on track whenever I wavered.

Finally, sincere thanks to my wife Carol and sons Sam and Oliver. Thank you for your patience and support throughout the project. I couldn't have done it without you.

Introduction

When the first Vickers Type 1100, also known as the Model VC10, made its maiden flight from Brooklands on 29 June 1962, Vickers had already completed 50 years of aviation history. All of the knowledge and experience that had been accumulated over the years had been built into the big jet. The graceful VC10 would go on to become known as the 'Queen of the Skies'. It embodied all the aerodynamic and engineering sophistication that had advanced aeronautics to the threshold of knowledge at the time of its design. Further progress would eventually project air transport into the supersonic age.

On that memorable day at Brooklands, G-ARTA made its take-off from a 4,500ft runway and the distance to unstick was just 2,150ft. The first landing at the test airfield at Wisley was on to a 6,000ft runway, although the aircraft stopped 3,600ft from the runway threshold, after a ground run of just 2,550ft. That first flight at Brooklands, in the hands of Vickers' chief test pilot G.R. 'Jock' Bryce, his deputy Brian Trubshaw and flight engineer Bill Cairns, was witnessed by the 8,000 people who had constructed the prototype.

In Brian Trubshaw's autobiography *Test Pilot*, he described the changes made at Brooklands to facilitate the first flight:

The runway at Brooklands was lengthened by 400ft for the first flight but, because of the position of the monument to Lord Brabazon at the north end, it was not possible to re-site the runway in the proper manner. This produced an extension at a slight angle to the main strip and a taxiway was built around Lord Brabazon's monument so that the take-off run could at least start at the beginning of the extension. It meant that at the very low take-off

BELOW **After completing a ground resonance programme lasting around four weeks, the prototype VC10, G-ARTA commenced engine trials at Weybridge on 15 June 1962. A Callum Detuner (silencer) was positioned to reduce the noise to neighbouring residents but the following day one detuner unit was torn from its mountings and blown a distance of about 150ft. Engine runs continued without it.** *(BAE SYSTEMS Image Ref WCN178)*

BELOW A model of the Vickers V.1000 where its resemblance to the Vickers Valiant is apparent. Although similar in some respects to the Comet, the V.1000 featured an advance wing along with a curved and swept fin and tailplane. Sadly, the project was cancelled by the British government when it was around 80% complete. Despite its unfortunate cancellation, the V.1000 played an integral part in the ultimate VC10 story. (BAE SYSTEMS)

weight for flights out of Brooklands, the aircraft came around the corner doing about 100 knots. This half-baked arrangement did permit the raising of the nosewheel to check elevator response and putting it back on the runway in time to stop. This is what was done before the first flight.

The VC10 offered exceptional short-field performance combined with transatlantic non-stop range, a high cruise speed coupled with a low approach speed, and all with a high level of passenger safety and comfort. Full-load take-off was possible from some of the most exacting airfields in the world – including those with 'hot and high' issues – along with relatively short runways all across the Far East and Africa on what were called BOAC's 'Empire' routes. The choice of four 21,000lb static thrust Rolls-Royce Conway 42 engines installed in paired pods at the rear of the aircraft further enabled the full-span clean wing to incorporate high-lift devices.

The standard VC10 was designed to accommodate up to 151 passengers with a maximum cruise speed around 600mph. The exceptionally low compressibility drag of the clean wing, together with the power available from the four Conway engines, provided a high attainable cruise speed.

By modern standards, the VC10 was very noisy, but at the time, the high bypass ratio Rolls-Royce Conway 42 engine was considered quiet. Along with a steep climb-out, the VC10 was able to operate within most airports' noise abatement requirements. Sadly, this situation would not last.

From a passenger perspective, the rear-engine design offered the quietest, smoothest ride. Passengers also enjoyed cabin air-conditioning and a higher standard of service than had previously been achieved.

Vickers V.1000 and a VC7

The story of the VC10 goes back to 1951 when the Ministry of Supply (MoS) approached Vickers to design a military transport based

on the Valiant bomber. The British Overseas Airways Corporation (BOAC) also expressed an interest in the type as it was seeking a jet airliner suitable for its transatlantic routes. At the time, those routes were being served by piston-engined aircraft such as the Lockheed Constellation and the Douglas DC-7C, while the turboprop-powered Bristol Britannia – although at that time not yet in service – did offer potentially shorter crossing times.

The MoS specification called for an aircraft able to carry 120 passengers for 2,100 nautical miles. In September 1952 the ministry ordered a single prototype powered by four Rolls-Royce Conway engines. The military serial XD662 was allocated to the aircraft.

The aircraft was to be called the V.1000 in military guise and VC7 for the civilian variant. The V.1000 bore some similarity with the Valiant bomber but was substantially larger, with a fuselage 146ft (44.5m) long, a low-mounted wing of 140ft (42.67m) span, four engines located in the wing roots, along with a conventional tailplane arrangement. Production continued on the new aircraft at Weybridge and was around 80% complete when the government dropped a bombshell!

ABOVE After the Second World War, transatlantic travel was becoming popular. Aircraft available at the time may have provided a luxurious crossing, but tended to be a little on the slow side and lacking in range. Boeing 377 Stratocruiser G-AKGH joined BOAC in June 1948 and flew transatlantic services with the airline until it returned to the USA in August 1958. *(Speedbird Heritage Collection/BOAC image 6891)*

Short-sighted government

On 29 November 1955, the Conservative government cancelled the V.1000, stating: 'The Minister of Supply has indicated that he could not devote money to the development of an aircraft without a home market, and that since BOAC does not require this aircraft, no home market exists.' At the time BOAC was deemed to be 'happy' with the Bristol Britannia.

The RAF had been forced to make budget cuts and so cancelled their order for six V.1000 aircraft, replacing them with an order for Bristol Britannia aircraft to be assembled at the Shorts factory in Belfast, an area of high unemployment.

As a consequence of the announcement, work on the prototype XD662 was immediately stopped. The airframe was used for destructive testing before being cut up for scrap.

At the time, Vickers managing director, Sir George Edwards CBE, remarked that it was 'a decision we shall regret for many years'. There followed a huge wave of criticism and protest in the House of Commons, the aviation media and by a number of bodies including the Air League; but all to no avail.

The V.1000/VC7 was a design with significant potential and would have been able to carry 120 passengers across the Atlantic, entering service ahead of the Boeing 707 and Douglas DC-8, thereby placing Britain at the head of the lucrative jet airliner race – not trailing way behind, as was to become the case.

On 24 October 1956, less than a year after cancellation of the VC7, BOAC were given permission by the British government to order 15 Boeing 707s, as there was no equivalent British type available! The government had taken the step of speaking with Sir George Edwards to see if the VC7 could be resurrected, but as the prototype had been cut up and the tooling destroyed, they had few options.

Enter the VC10

Government approval for the BOAC order for Boeing 707s had been permitted on the strict understanding that no more dollars would be made available for American aircraft and that any additional aircraft ordered would have to be British-built. Having purchased the Boeing 707 for transatlantic operations, BOAC sought

a smaller design to operate its African and Far Eastern 'Empire' routes, so it issued a requirement for a jet airliner to service them.

The VC10 was designed to an exceptionally severe set of requirements, written by and exclusively for BOAC. Early versions of the Boeing 707 and Douglas DC-8 were underpowered and required very long runways in order to take off and for this reason alone the 707 could not serve many of BOAC's 'Empire' routes, where short runways and 'hot and high' conditions were commonplace.

To meet the exacting BOAC specifications, the VC10 had excellent short-field performance but was heavier and higher-powered than its competitors. However, by supporting a fellow British company it would severely restrict the world market that the VC10 *may* have been able to otherwise achieve.

Satisfied with the design, BOAC placed an order in January 1958 for 35 139-seat VC10s, with options for a further 20. Between 1960 and 1962, a number of significant changes were made to this order, which will be covered in more detail in Chapter One.

First military orders

The Royal Air Force carefully considered the design of the VC10 as they required an aircraft to operate in three principal roles – passenger

BELOW XR806, the first VC10 C.1 for the RAF, making its first flight from a chilly Weybridge on 26 November 1965. XR806 was damaged beyond repair in a refuelling accident at Brize Norton on 18 December 1997 and was withdrawn from service and broken up. *(BAE SYSTEMS Image Ref WCN1802)*

transport, freight and casualty evacuation – at RAF bases across the globe. In September 1961, the RAF placed an order for five aircraft, increasing the order to eleven a year later. Following problems with the BOAC order, the government further increased it – in July 1964 – to 14 aircraft.

The aircraft was to become the VC10 C.1 variant and its role would also involve many VIP flights. These included a significant number for members of the royal family, for which the aircraft featured a very special VIP interior fit.

'Poffler' and 'sniffer'

As early as February 1960, the RAF had already held discussions with the Ministry of Aviation regarding the VC10 as a natural follow-on to the Comet. However, from information gleaned from documents made available under the Freedom of Information Act, the RAF were also very keen to discuss a 'poffler' version of the aircraft – that is, a nuclear deterrent version usually capable of carrying four, but up to eight, Skybolt weapons on underwing hard points. According to a memo from the Deputy Chief of the Air Staff (DCAS) dated 29 February 1960:

> . . . we have already had discussions about the VC10, both as a successor to the Comet and as a Skybolt carrier. With regard to the latter, Vickers is doing a feasibility study to determine how many weapons could be carried and the most suitable point of attachment. Pending further information on the modifications required to make the VC10 into a Skybolt carrier, I think we should assume that the first few aircraft to replace the Comet will be purely passenger and light freight aircraft.

The full extent of this prospective deterrent role, as well as a number of other variants that did not progress beyond the drawing board, is discussed in more detail in Chapter Eight.

Later in its RAF career, the VC10 also took on the role of air sampling – often referred to as 'sniffing' – a capability that has currently been lost to the RAF when the last K.3 variant was withdrawn from service in 2013. This role involved the option to fit sampling pods in place of the wing-mounted Mk. 32 air-to-air refuelling

pods plus a smaller pod under the nose of the aircraft. This is covered in more detail in Chapter Five (see pp. 104 to 105).

Blind landing capabilities

No 10 Squadron took delivery of the first VC10 C.1 aircraft; initially at RAF Fairford but shortly afterwards they moved to Brize Norton. Here, they shared facilities with 53 Squadron who were operating the Shorts Belfast C.1. Interestingly, both aircraft possessed blind landing capabilities with the necessary equipment to carry them out. While the ground equipment required to permit this capability was slow to be installed across the globe, RAF Brize Norton was one of the first. As a direct consequence, both squadrons benefitted significantly from the ability to arrive back at their home base in minimum weather conditions, rather than having to divert elsewhere and thereby incurring significant time and financial penalties.

Soviet imitation

It is often said that imitation is the greatest form of flattery – the almost identical Ilyushin Il-62 appeared from the Soviet Union in 1962. Unlike its inspirational Western counterpart, the Il-62 achieved only modest civilian success with absolutely no military orders.

The Super VC10

The Super VC10 came about as a result of BOAC's realisation that while the Standard VC10 would meet the requirements of its 'Empire' routes, it was not going to be as economic on a seat-per-mile basis on the North Atlantic routes, especially when compared to the later Boeing 707 models. The fact that the Standard VC10 was *never* meant to be used on those routes is a moot point!

Long before G-ARTA took to the air, Vickers and BOAC had discussions on a stretched version that would make the design more economically viable. By 1959, the Vickers design team had drawn up the Super VC10 specification, which was for an aircraft that would mainly be used on long-sector, prestige routes between sea-level airports with long runways in moderate climate conditions. This variant proposed a 212-seat arrangement with small changes to the wing

and fuel tanks, transforming the VC10 into a true transatlantic airliner.

BOAC's reaction to the proposal was somewhat surprising. Although the stretch had added extra seating capacity that was valuable in financial terms, it impinged on the trade-off between performance and range. As a result of BOAC's concerns over the range, they asked Vickers to produce a smaller stretch that would

ABOVE The first flight of Super VC10 G-ASGA was made at Weybridge on 7 May 1964. Here it is seen taking off from Wisley during a later test flight, equipped with the 'spare' engine pod located under the leading edge of the starboard wing. *(BAE SYSTEMS Image Ref MP22891)*

still be an improvement in economic terms, yet maintain the range and runway performance, which would permit the aircraft to also operate

LEFT Unfortunately, the US location and date of this image are not known, but it shows all three of BOAC's transatlantic assets – Super VC10 G-ASGD, Boeing 707-465 G-ARWE and Bristol Britannia 312 G-AOVL side by side on the ramp. In the background can be seen a pair of TWA Convair 880s, a Boeing 707 and 727, along with a National Airways Douglas DC-8. *(BAE SYSTEMS)*

on the African routes. Having asked Vickers to provide a true transatlantic aircraft – a requirement that was admirably met by Vickers – BOAC then altered that requirement. BOAC appeared to want to preserve a dual ability that was completely at odds with the Atlantic-range stretch model it had requested in the first place!

With a 13ft fuselage extension providing 163 seats, with a lower seat-per-mile cost for its owners, the Super VC10 – designated Model 1151 – was born.

Despite all of this effort, BOAC preferred to order additional Boeing 707 aircraft at the expense of the VC10. However, Britain's lack of foreign currency reserves ensured the government dug their heels in and the Super VC10 order remained in place. The first aircraft (G-ASGA) entered service at the beginning of 1966 with the final aircraft (G-ASGR) being delivered in 1969.

Other airline customers

Having been designed specifically for the African and Far Eastern routes, it is of little surprise that the few orders obtained for the VC10 came from operators in these sectors. British United Airways (BUA) initially ordered four, and then halved the order, before acquiring a pair of second-hand aircraft. The two new BUA aircraft (G-ASIX and G-ASIW) were the first to feature the large forward freight door providing the airline with an excellent mixed capability for passenger and cargo, especially on developing routes.

Ghana Airways became the first export customer when they ordered three standard VC10s in February 1961, although this was later reduced to two.

East African Airways ordered three Super VC10s and later increased the order to five. Their final aircraft (5H-MOG) was the very last VC10 off the Weybridge production line in February 1970.

Other operators of the VC10 included British Caledonian, which acquired the aircraft when they merged with BUA in November 1970; and Middle East Airlines (MEA) who initially leased an aircraft from Ghana Airways and later leased the prototype (G-ARTA) from Sir Freddie Laker.

Five former BOAC (which had merged with British European Airways in April 1974 and now operated as British Airways) VC10s were initially leased to Gulf Air, before the airline purchased them outright. The three ex-BUA aircraft were eventually sold on to the Sultan of Oman (A4O-AB) as a VIP transport, Air Malawi (7Q-YDH) and finally, the Royal Aircraft Establishment (RAE) at Boscombe Down (XX914).

Chinese interest

Such was the interest in the VC10 from Beijing that a British Aircraft Corporation (BAC) sales team left for China in October 1972 to discuss a purchase of VC10s by the Chinese government, which was dissatisfied with its Soviet-built Ilyushin Il-62 aircraft. After the visit, BAC offered a proposal for the reopening of the production line for an order of 20 aircraft, with a further undertaking of licence production in China. Such a deal was strewn with pitfalls and, sadly, never came to fruition.

Retired from British Airways

British Airways started to withdraw their three remaining standard VC10s from service in 1974. Initially, they were placed into storage at Heathrow. G-ARVB, -E and -H were later scrapped at Heathrow and the final remains had been cleared by 1976.

By the late 1970s only British Airways and Ghana Airways were still operating the VC10 commercially. The first British Airways aircraft to be withdrawn was G-ASGC, which was flown to Duxford for preservation in April 1980. Subsequently, all remaining British Airways Super VC10s were withdrawn and flown to Prestwick for storage pending sale. The end of commercial operations came in March 1981. The following year it was announced that the RAF had acquired the entire fleet, including spares. The aircraft were flown from Prestwick to Abingdon where they were placed into storage awaiting their eventual fate – which was to follow ten years later.

J.R. Finnimore was BOAC's aircraft development manager from the VC10's inception in 1958 until 1970, before continuing as the British Airway's general manager supplies in the Boeing 747 era. In 1989, he was quoted as saying:

When the VC10s were retired from [British Airways] service, it was an appropriate time to consider their contribution: they were late in the market-place; they were heavy; and they were expensive to buy. But they were not the lame ducks some had predicted: they were reliable; they made money; they had passenger appeal; they were safe; and they were loved by crew and staff. Their loss was almost a bereavement.

Tanker conversions

In the late 1970s, the RAF was considering how it could replace its ageing Victor tanker fleet. Five former Gulf Air VC10s along with the four surviving East African Airways Super VC10s were purchased by the RAF between 1977 and 1978 for conversion into three-point flight-refuelling tankers. Weybridge completed the design work, which was then undertaken at the former BAC facility at Filton. The standard VC10s became K.2s while the Super VC10s

were designated K.3s. After conversion, all joined 101 Squadron at Brize Norton.

In 1981, after the Super VC10s had been withdrawn from British Airways service, the 15 remaining airframes were purchased by the RAF. Initially, all were flown to and stored at RAF Abingdon. Serial numbers ZD230 to ZD243 were allocated and some airframes had the serial hand-painted on to the fuselage. Ten years later, five of these airframes were flown to Filton and converted to three-point tankers with the designation K.4. The remaining aircraft at Abingdon were broken up for spares.

BELOW ZA141, the first VC10 K.2 tanker conversion undertaken by British Aerospace at Filton, comes in to land after a flight test ahead of its delivery to 101 Squadron at Brize Norton. The unusual grey/green camouflage was only applied to this aircraft and was replaced with the standard 'hemp' colours shortly after delivery. *(BAE SYSTEMS Image Ref A6753B via Bristol Aero Collection Trust)*

As part of the same (K.4) contract, the RAF's remaining VC10 C.1 aircraft were converted to two-point tankers at Hurn by Flight Refuelling. The work involved the addition of a pair of Mk. 32 underwing refuelling pods and the modified aircraft were designated C.1K. The conversions were carried out between 1991 and 1997.

Into theatre

Aside from playing a key transport and trooping role during peacetime, the RAF VC10s were used in a number of conflicts. These included the evacuation of almost 5,000 dependant civilians from Malta in 1972 following Prime Minister Dom Mintoff's proposed hike in annual rental for the RAF base at Luqa. His actions were compounded by the Libyan leader Colonel Gaddafi's willingness to get involved in supporting Malta's economy once the British forces had been removed.

The VC10 provided valuable trooping capabilities into and out of the Falkland Islands as well as during the First Gulf War.

BELOW Out with the old and in with the new. When the remaining VC10 C.1K, K.3 and K.4 variants were retired from service with 101 Squadron in September 2013, they were replaced by a fleet of Airbus A330 Voyager KC.2 and KC.3 aircraft equipping Nos 10 and 101 Squadrons. On 24 September 2013, a 10 Squadron Voyager KC.2, ZZ331, along with a VC10 K.3, were photographed in formation over the North Sea. At the end of the sortie, VC10 K.3 ZA150/J landed at Dunsfold where, after 47 years of service in the RAF, she has taken up residence with the Brooklands Museum. ZZ331 was later damaged when the aircraft struck a hangar at St John's, Newfoundland, while taxiing on to the ramp after landing. It has since been repaired and has been returned to service. *(Geoff Lee/Planefocus image GHL-132569)*

The RAF tanker capabilities have seen active service during the Bosnian conflict, Operation Telic (the security and protection of Iraq and Afghanistan) and more recently during the troubles in Libya.

Finally, a VC10 had been positioned on the Falkland Islands, supporting the resident Tornado – and more recently Typhoon – aircraft in the protection of the islands.

Retirement from the RAF

The VC10 continued to soldier on in RAF service until 2013 when the last of the fleet was finally withdrawn from 101 Squadron service at Brize Norton. The very last flight by the type was made on 25 September 2013, when a team from 101 Squadron flew K.3 ZA147/F into Bruntingthorpe. Signatures from all of the crew involved in that final flight adorn the cockpit and passenger compartment of the aircraft. The airframe is still sitting at Bruntingthorpe, having had its engines and some equipment removed, although its ultimate fate is looking distinctly uncertain.

Personal interest

At this point in proceedings I must nail my VC10 colours firmly to the mast! I am a big fan of the graceful aircraft. I thoroughly enjoyed flying in the aircraft and was fortunate enough to experience numerous trips in all of the military variants – C.1, K.2, K.3, C.1K and K.4.

My first ever trip on board a VC10 was a 10 Squadron C.1 trip on XV102 from Brize Norton to Washington/Dulles Airport on the 'Washington Trooper' scheduled service. While conducting their scheduled routes around the globe, 10 Squadron operated just like an airline, right down to the airline-style check-in facilities in the main terminal at Brize Norton. All flight and cabin crew wore smart RAF uniforms. Two slight differences that I recall were the rearward-facing seating (a military safety feature) and the VIP pods carried on board, on what was largely a regular diplomatic service into the US capital.

Later, I flew on a large number of tanker sorties with 101 Squadron on a variety of trails across the globe and tow lines around the UK. On numerous occasions I witnessed the spectacular air-to-air refuelling (AAR) skills of both tanker and receiver crews alike. Such amazing coordination was ably demonstrated by all involved during the crucial phases of the peacetime trips. Now, please take a moment to try to imagine just how difficult AAR was in a theatre of war, at night, in radio silence and with the adrenalin pumping. To all involved, I salute you!

VC10 fan clubs

The VC10 had a great following while in service – both civilian and military – and still has; even though all aircraft have been withdrawn. Today, a number of dedicated websites honour the aircraft and provide VC10 aficionados with an excellent source of background data and information. Similarly, a number of airframes and cockpit sections have been retained for display in museums, while two aircraft (ZA150/J and ZD241/N) are being maintained by restoration groups in a 'live' condition at Brooklands and Bruntingthorpe respectively, allowing them to taxi under their own engine power. Both are available to the public on special open days, so the 'roar' of the VC10 should be with us for many years to come, although it is most unlikely that one will ever return to the air. Dare we hope?

51 years of service

Only 54 VC10s were eventually built, all at the Brooklands factory at Weybridge. Although it was a great engineering achievement, the VC10 failed to penetrate world markets and sadly was a costly financial failure for Vickers-Armstrong.

It could have been so different! Had the politicians not intervened and cancelled the Vickers Type 1000 project, Britain may have had a jet airliner crossing the Atlantic non-stop way before the Boeing 707 and Douglas DC-8 competition. The VC10 would still have followed the Vickers Type 1000/VC7 and had it been designed for all of the international airlines – rather than a specific marketplace – it may then have attracted significant orders from around the world. Sadly, it was not to be.

After 51 years of service, the 'Queen of the Skies' will be sadly missed!

Keith Wilson
Ramsey, Cambridgeshire, July 2016

Chapter One

History of the VC10

As a relative newcomer to commercial airliner design towards the end of the Second World War, Vickers-Armstrong had a lot of ground to cover if they were successfully to compete against established US manufacturers. Between 1945 and 1957 the team at Vickers produced a range of propeller-, turbine- and jet-powered aircraft for both military and commercial use. All of this experience was directed into the innovative VC10 concept – later to become known as the 'Queen of the Skies'.

OPPOSITE On 29 June 1962 the prototype Vickers-Armstrong Type V.1100 (model VC10) G-ARTA made its first flight from Brooklands Airfield, Weybridge, at 5.25pm. After a take-off run of just 2,150ft, G-ARTA lifted off and the uneventful flight was watched by an assembled crowd of airline personnel, manufacturers and government staff; along with a large number of press representatives. *(BAE SYSTEMS/Brooklands Museum)*

ABOVE The largely
completed fuselage of
the Ministry of Supply-
funded Vickers-
Armstrong Type V.1000
prototype XD662 at
Weybridge shortly
after the project had
been cancelled. It
was later cut into
sections for transport
to Shoeburyness. (BAE
SYSTEMS Image Ref
MP5324)

Vickers Type 716, Model V.1000

In order to appreciate the history of the
VC10, we must first look back to the political
wrangling surrounding Vickers-Armstrong's
earlier design, the model V.1000. It was
developed from 1951 as a jet-powered
replacement for the Handley Page Hastings
then in service with RAF Transport Command.

The decision to develop such an aircraft
was taken at an Air Staff meeting on 19 May
1951. The new aircraft was to be based on
an existing design and to enter service in

1956. Initial requirements demanded a cruising
speed of 450 knots, pressurisation, the ability
to carry a payload of at least 12,000lb (but up
to 20,000lb would be preferable) over 3,000
miles, a strengthened floor for heavy loads and
the ability to operate from 2,000yd runways
under both normal and tropical (hot and high)
conditions – something American aircraft
manufacturers of the time worried little about.
Cargo loading was to be by the preferred
method of end loading, or via a 6ft-square side
door. It was a tall order!

Vickers' initial design for what was to
become known as the V.1000, or the Type 716,
used the wings, tail unit and undercarriage of

RIGHT Designed
in parallel with the
military Vickers Type
V.1000, the Model
VC7 concept was
submitted to BOAC
in October 1955.
The four-engine
airliner was to seat
100–150 passengers
and have a cruising
speed of more than
500mph. However, it
was cancelled by the
Ministry of Supply
before the end of the
year. (BAE SYSTEMS)

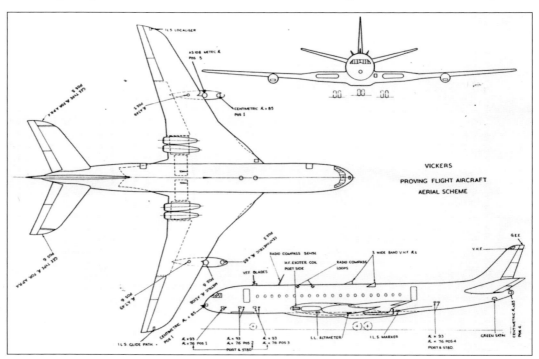

the Valiant bomber, married to a new fuselage. The wing was moved to a low position to provide an unobstructed cabin, while loading would be achieved by a powered lift in the rear fuselage. Four Rolls-Royce R.Co.3 Conway bypass engines would power the design, which was expected to meet – and probably even exceed – the required cruising speed.

Later, the Ministry of Supply's Controller of Aircraft (CA), Air Chief Marshal Sir John Baker, held a meeting with representatives of the British Overseas Airways Corporation (BOAC) to investigate potential civilian use. Some changes would need to be made, including reducing the cabin floor strength and removing the cargo lift, which would cut the basic weight of the aircraft by an estimated 4,250lb.

After further deliberations, the Air Ministry would prepare and issue their Operational Requirements (OR) in cooperation with BOAC. Consequently OR.315 for a 'Long-Range Jet Transport' was issued to Vickers on 8 December 1952. The intention was to promote the design of an aircraft suitable for both military and civilian use, and which therefore would meet British Civil Airworthiness Requirements (BCAR). The document called for an aircraft whose primary role was the movement of personnel and equipment from one theatre to another; with a typical task being envisaged 'to support the move of Wing of Canberra bombers from the UK to Singapore'. The aircraft's cruise performance was to be the same as the Valiant bomber, an aircraft it would be expected to support in theatre.

Shortly after the issue of the formal OR, the Ministry of Supply placed a contract for a single Vickers V.1000 prototype, with the serial XD662 being allocated. At the time BOAC had expressed an interest in the civilian design, designated the VC-7. Prolonged discussions continued between Vickers and BOAC while construction of the Vickers V.1000 prototype continued. On 12 August 1954, a contract Intention to Proceed (ITP) was issued for the construction of a further six V.1000 aircraft for Transport Command, with the serial numbers XH255–60 being allocated, although the paperwork described them as 'V.1001' aircraft.

The VC-7 version of the V.1000 was conceived in very close cooperation with BOAC.

It was the first airliner with what was to become the universal standard in the first generation of big jets – six-abreast seating with a centre aisle – and a large-diameter fuselage for those days. To meet the exacting demands of BOAC it had to have excellent capabilities at hot and high airfields, particularly those on the African routes.

Politics rears its ugly head!

So far, so good. Now politics reared its ugly head! On 11 November 1955, with the prototype V.1000 just six months from completion, the programme was cancelled for short-term political reasons; ostensibly because the RAF needed more large transport aircraft capacity quicker than the V.1000 programme could provide and also there were Bristol Britannia aircraft available that were going to be manufactured in politically attractive Northern Ireland.

According to Sir George Edwards OM, CBE, FRS, the Chief Designer of Vickers-Armstrong from 1945, 'the cancellation was, in my view, the most serious setback that the British aircraft industry suffered since the end of the Second World War because it came at precisely the moment when long-range jet operation was about to become big business'.

Shortly afterwards, BOAC abandoned any interest in the design. XD662 was broken up and sent to Shoeburyness for 'vulnerability trials'.

Statements made in the House of Commons at the time of the cancellation were rather pathetic, with one member stating 'BOAC was quite content that it was going to manage the North Atlantic route with propeller-turbines throughout the 1960s' and 'there was no question of needing a jet aeroplane'. The reality was quite the opposite, especially when less than a year after the cancellation of the V.1000, the British Ministry of Transport and Civil Aviation (MTCA) announced government approval for BOAC to purchase the Boeing 707, powered by the Conway and thereby enjoying the prestige of the Rolls-Royce tag. However, before the order was sanctioned, the government had gone through the political motions of asking if the VC-7 programme could be resurrected by Vickers for BOAC; unfortunately, however, the V.1000 prototype, jigs and tools had already been scrapped.

Jet airliners for BOAC

In 1952, BOAC became the first airline in the world to operate a commercial jet when they introduced the de Havilland Comet I into service. In 1956, BOAC was undergoing changes in its top management structure and experiencing more than a little difficulty with its aircraft fleet, particularly following the demise of the Comet I in 1954 and the continuing late delivery of the Britannia. It did, however, have the Comet 4. BOAC revamped the aircraft and opened up a jet service across the Atlantic in October 1958, just ahead of Pan American Airlines' first Boeing 707. The Comet 4 could only make it across the Atlantic utilising a one-stop strategy, while the Boeing 707 did not begin a non-stop service until August 1959, with the Douglas DC-8 following two years later.

Vanjet

Meanwhile, following cancellation of the V.1000, Vickers continued to build the jet-powered Valiant and turbine-powered Viscount, but it was a jet-powered version of the latter which was to have a significant influence on the VC10. Among many designs considered by Vickers in the 1950s was the Vanjet, a jet version of the Viscount and Vanguard. In its final version, the Vanjet featured three Rolls-Royce Avon engines – two engines mounted on small stub wings at the rear, with a third buried in the rear of the fuselage – much like the Trident and Boeing 727 that came almost a decade later.

Somewhat interestingly, the Vanjet's in-house project code was 'VC-10' (VC for Vickers Commercial and 10 as it was the tenth commercial project under consideration). While the design did not enter production, much was learned from the project, which proved to be influential in the later VC10 design.

No more dollars

Approval for the BOAC order for Boeing 707 aircraft came with the caveat that no more dollars would be available for further American aircraft and all additional aircraft ordered would have to be British-built. BOAC viewed the Boeing 707 as primarily for the transatlantic services and sought a smaller aircraft for its African and Far Eastern routes, thus issuing a requirement for a jet airliner suitable for operations on these routes.

In March 1957, BOAC issued a specification outlining requirements for an aircraft to operate routes to Africa and Australia, carrying a payload of around 35,000lb nearly 4,000 miles in still air. Vickers entered into serious negotiations with BOAC over the VC10, which was designed and built to the most exacting demands laid down by the airline – particularly those stipulations for hot and high operations at airfields including Kano and Nairobi. From that point on, the aircraft was designed specifically to BOAC's requirements alone. In many ways, this decision by Vickers precluded sales to airlines outside the very specific design marketplace and, perhaps, had a significant influence on the lack of commercial success later shown by the aircraft.

New VC10

To meet this new BOAC requirement, Vickers did not merely resurrect the older V.1000/VC7 design; instead they started with a blank sheet of paper and included a number of (for the time) very innovative features.

BELOW Vickers had set up the Advanced Project Office at Weybridge in the 1950s and it was busy during the initial design stages of the VC10. This included some early wind tunnel testing undertaken at the site ...
(BAE SYSTEMS Image Ref MP7504)

RIGHT ... although certain aspects of the tested 'design' did not make their way into final production. Later in the programme, more detailed wind tunnel testing was undertaken.
(BAE SYSTEMS Image Ref MP7499)

These included the rear-mounted, four-engine
set-up; a T-tail; and a large, clean wing –
unencumbered with engines and mountings
– allowing for leading-edge slats and trailing-
edge flaps that would provide the key to the
aircraft's excellent performance. This wing also
permitted lower approach and landing speeds,
as well as improved control characteristics,
an impressive runway performance, low
cabin noise and vibration levels (providing
a significantly improved level of passenger
comfort), a reduced fire hazard (in the event of
a crash) with the fuel tanks located in the wings
and superior ditching characteristics identified
during extensive trials conducted on behalf of
Vickers by Saunders Roe.

The VC10 became the very first aircraft to
use the supercritical peaky wing design theory,
the work of distinguished aerodynamicist H.H.
Pearcey of the National Physics Laboratory
(NPL) at Teddington and Barry Haines of the
Aircraft Research Association (ARA) wind tunnel
establishment at Bedford. Their aerodynamic
design concept provided a two-dimensional
transition from supersonic to subsonic flow
without creating a strong shock wave, as
was apparent with more conventional aerofoil
sections. This provided significant benefits in
terms of reduced drag and buffet.

Work now had to be done to convert
the two-dimensional theory into a three-
dimensional reality in the actual working
wing for the VC10. Here, Vickers turned to
the work of Dr Maria Weber of the Royal
Aircraft Establishment (RAE) Farnborough.
Working with Dr Weber's theories, the Vickers
Weybridge aerodynamics team – in conjunction
with the RAE – completed the design work.
Interestingly, at the time, the RAE was using
an early Pegasus analogue computer to assist
with calculations; perhaps one of the first
occasions for which computer power assisted
such complex work.

First orders

Declaring themselves 'highly satisfied'
with the design, BOAC placed an order
in January 1958 for 35 139-seat VC10s, with
options on a further 20, in a formal signing
ceremony attended by Sir Basil Smallpiece of

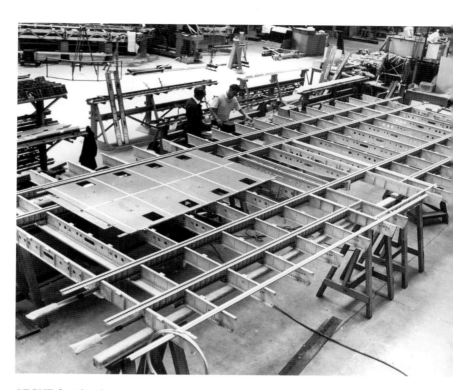

ABOVE Another item that underwent early structural testing was the
fuselage flooring, which featured thick floor cross-beams. *(BAE SYSTEMS
Image Ref MP12078 via Brooklands Museum)*

BELOW The structural integrity of the fuselage is apparent in this view taken
in September 1960. At the time of its construction, no other airliner in the world
boasted a structure built quite like it. *(BAE SYSTEMS Image Ref MP12347)*

BOAC and Sir George Edwards representing Vickers. Unfortunately for Vickers, BOAC would later renege on a large proportion of this order!

In June 1960 BOAC converted these 20 options into an order for 10 Super VC10s – the 212-seat version with sufficient range to cross the Atlantic. This projected 212-seat Super VC10 was to feature significantly uprated Conway engines and a fuselage stretch of 28ft (8.53m) to raise the passenger seating number. This was a larger capacity than the Boeing 707 and it was created with the intention of considerably reducing seat operating costs.

During 1961, the order was once again

altered; this time to just 15 standard VC10s (fitted with four Conway 42a engines producing 21,000lb each) and 30 Super VC10s (powered by four Conway 43 engines of 22,500lb each). However, as BOAC had serious doubts about filling 212 seats on the Super VC10, the specification was amended to include a 13ft (3.96m) stretch accommodating up to 174 passengers.

This order was further reduced in January 1962 to just 12 standard (Type 1101) VC10s and 30 (Type 1151) Super VC10s; eight of the Supers were to be in a passenger/freight ('Combi') combination, featuring a large forward

fuselage freight door along with a strengthened fuselage floor. The order for Super VC10s was later reduced to just 17 (Type 1151) with the 'Combi' version being cancelled.

Roll out and first flight

Work on the definitive VC10 commenced in early 1957. Vickers recruited for the drawing office and planned a major increase in staff for the beginning of the production run.

The prototype (Type 1100) VC10 – now registered G-ARTA – was rolled out at Brooklands on 15 April 1962, and was followed by a period of ground testing including extensive systems checks, resonance tests and engine running.

With the Brooklands runway so short, serious consideration was given to fitting the

LEFT At 8.30am on a bitterly cold and cloudy Sunday morning, the prototype VC10 G-ARTA was rolled out for the first time and posed for photographs, including this image taken from a Westland Widgeon helicopter. (BAE SYSTEMS Image Ref WHP25499)

runway with arrester gear, and the prototype aircraft with an arrester hook, but this idea was later abandoned.

The team chosen to make the first flight was Jock Bruce (pilot), Brian Trubshaw (co-pilot) and Bill Cairns, a Vickers pilot acting as flight engineer. Looking resplendent in BOAC livery,

G-ARTA made its first flight from Brooklands at 5.25pm on 29 June 1962, in front of a large audience including most of the workers from the factory who had designed and built her. Also present was a large contingent from the press.

For the maiden flight, the aircraft was very lightly loaded and used only 2,150ft of the available 4,200ft runway. It landed at the Wisley Flight Test Centre, which was only 3 miles from Brooklands, but Wisley featured a more generous 6,700ft runway. G-ARTA then commenced the flight test programme, although the interior of the aircraft didn't so much resemble an airliner as a mobile laboratory – with more than 10 tons of flight test equipment carried in the fuselage.

Less than three months after its maiden flight, G-ARTA appeared at the 1962 SBAC show at Farnborough, where it made a favourable impression on the crowd.

G-ARTA was shortly joined in the flight test programme by a number of production

BELOW G-ARTA arrives over the numbers at Wisley after its maiden flight on 29 June 1962 (having originated at Weybridge). Most of the VC10's test flying was completed from the Wisley Flight Test Centre, as it had a significantly longer runway (6,700ft) than that at Weybridge (4,200ft). (BAE SYSTEMS)

examples from the BOAC order including G-ARVA, -B, and -C, while G-ARVF carried out more than 1,000 hours of route-proving flights.

Early in the flight test programme, Vickers discovered that the aircraft's drag was greater than calculated, which would ultimately reduce its range and performance. They immediately commenced a programme to alleviate it. G-ARTA flew with aerodynamic 'tufting' fitted to the rear of the fuselage and around the engine mountings. It helped to identify the modifications which would be required to the rear of the engine nacelles and their pitch, to the leading-edge slats and to the wingtips. The modifications to the rear of the engines and between the nacelles were given the nickname 'beaver tail fairing' as the shape of the insert between the pair of engines now resembled that part of the animal!

G-ARVE, which made its first flight from Brooklands to Wisley on 15 April 1963, was the first aircraft to incorporate these modifications although all of the remaining aircraft had the modifications retrofitted before delivery.

Almost lost

On 31 December 1963, G-ARTA took off to conduct a series of stall tests and was almost lost during the flight. While recovering from one of the stalls, an elevator bracket broke, causing

ABOVE A photograph taken at Wisley shortly after the arrival of G-ARTA, following its first flight. Here we see E.E. Marshall (chief project engineer), Ken Lawson (chief aerodynamicist) and Sir George Edwards (managing director) by the aircraft. *(BAE SYSTEMS Image Ref MP15194)*

BELOW On 25 August 1962, the first air-to-air photographs were taken by Ian Macdonald from an Empire Test Pilots' School (ETPS) Meteor. Interestingly, at the time the aircraft was flying with tape over the retracted leading-edge slats and many of the photographs from the shoot could not be used for publicity purposes without retouching. In this view, the black tape is barely discernible. *(BAE SYSTEMS Image Ref WHP23514)*

violent flutter so bad that Brian Trubshaw, who was in command, thought it might break up. As the characteristics were so alarming, the decision was taken to jettison the crew escape parachute door (fitted only to G-ARTA for flight test purposes) at full cabin differential pressure. As a consequence, the cabin floor had to withstand this differential pressure instantaneously because the freight bays were not vented. This resulted in the escape chute being crushed and much of it was torn from the aircraft.

In his autobiography, Trubshaw wrote of the incident:

I was just recovering from a clean stall when at about 250 knots all hell broke loose as G-ARTA started shaking violently. There was a shout from the Senior Observer, Chris Mullen, who was looking at the tail through his periscope, 'Right Inner Elevator'. I was quite certain that G-ARTA was going to come apart and it nearly did, so I fired the escape hatch door and ordered the crew to bale out. The flight engineer, Roy Mole, could not get out of his seat and the same applied to the co-pilot, Captain Peter Cane of BOAC, while the crew in the back could not hear me above the general racket. I managed to reduce speed to about 160 knots which put me very close to the pre-stall buffet, whereupon the violent vibrations and oscillations calmed down to a smaller amount. The escape chute which went through the front forward hold had collapsed and gone out when the door had jettisoned,

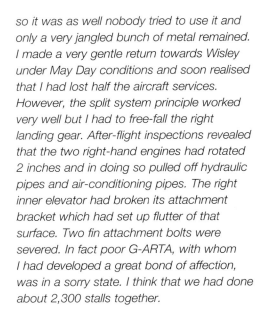

BELOW G-ARTA and G-ARVA, the prototype VC10 and the first production example for BOAC, seen at Wisley. In the foreground G-ARTA had not yet received the so-called 'beaver tail' drag-reducing modifications to the engine nacelles, while -VA does. The Gloster Javelin XA778 was normally based at Boscombe Down and used for ASI pressure correction readings. *(BAE SYSTEMS Image Ref WCN462)*

so it was as well nobody tried to use it and only a very jangled bunch of metal remained. I made a very gentle return towards Wisley under May Day conditions and soon realised that I had lost half the aircraft services. However, the split system principle worked very well but I had to free-fall the right landing gear. After-flight inspections revealed that the two right-hand engines had rotated 2 inches and in doing so pulled off hydraulic pipes and air-conditioning pipes. The right inner elevator had broken its attachment bracket which had set up flutter of that surface. Two fin attachment bolts were severed. In fact poor G-ARTA, with whom I had developed a great bond of affection, was in a sorry state. I think that we had done about 2,300 stalls together.

Thankfully, the aircraft made a slow return to Wisley where it landed safely. Repairs were immediately started and following these, the aircraft was back in the air on 7 February 1964.

Certification

Despite the setback to G-ARTA and the drag problem, the certification programme remained on schedule and the VC10 received its Type Certificate on 23 April 1964.

Route proving

In January 1964, BOAC's VC10 development pilot, Captain A.P.W. Cain, along with a small team of senior captains who had already been trained to fly the new aircraft, set out to complete a 1,000-hour flight development programme, before the new type received its full Certificate of Airworthiness (C of A) and entered revenue-earning passenger service.

The fifth production aircraft – G-ARVF – was selected to undertake most of the flying over the routes VC10s would initially operate in commercial service. This exercise allowed a smooth entry into revenue-earning service for the VC10.

Into service

After having received its Type Certificate, BOAC introduced it on regular passenger services on 29 April 1964, on their route from London to Lagos. It then began to take over other services

to other parts of Africa and to the Middle and Far East.

BOAC try to cancel Super VC10 order

At this stage you might think that BOAC would be pleased with the situation. However, in 1964, Sir Giles Guthrie became chairman of BOAC and endeavoured to cancel the entire Super VC10 order, instead wishing to purchase further Boeing 707s, which the airline stated were cheaper to operate. This information was soon in the public domain, adversely affecting possible VC10 sales to other airlines. BOAC were called before a Parliamentary Select Committee and implied that it had been 'forced' to purchase the VC10, which had not been designed for transatlantic routes. The British Aircraft Corporation's (BAC) managing director, Sir George Edwards, insisted on appearing in front of the committee to set the record straight. He clearly established that the aircraft had been designed for African and Far Eastern routes at BOAC's specific instigation. He further confirmed to the committee that in no way were BOAC forced to 'buy British'.

Government intervention ensured that BOAC

accepted the 12 standard VC10s and 17 of the 30 Super VC10s, while the RAF order for 11 was increased to 14.

At that point, rather than accepting the situation, BOAC demanded government subsidies to operate the VC10 while at the same time refusing to reveal its true operating costs! Once again, this action worked against the aircraft and its competitors were not slow in using this against the VC10 . . . again inevitably having a further negative impact on sales.

In service, BOAC found that the VC10 may have had slightly higher operating costs than the Boeing 707, but it possessed much greater passenger appeal, suffered fewer fatigue cracks or corrosion and had lower maintenance costs. On transatlantic routes the passenger appeal of the BOAC Super VC10s was evident and they achieved a 71.6% load factor, the market average being 52.1%. Anecdotal evidence indicated that many passengers elected to fly on the VC10 even in preference to the Boeing 747 'Jumbo Jet'.

Perhaps most interestingly, BOAC's 1975 annual report stated that 'the VC10's revenue performance was the best in the fleet, superior to the Boeing 707 and 747'.

ABOVE One of the two large assembly hangars at Weybridge in January 1970. At the far end of the hangar is 5H-MOG, a Super VC10 for East African Airways, and the final VC10 produced. Also in view are three Hurn-built aircraft in for refurbishment; Cambrian Airways BAC One-Eleven G-AWOE, former Autair One-Eleven G-AWXJ and a PLUNA Viscount 745 CX-BHA. *(BAE SYSTEMS Image Ref WCN3202)*

Chapter Two

Anatomy of the VC10

A successful airliner must combine two qualities: it must offer a significant design advance on the previous generation of aircraft, and it must also be based on a firm foundation of proven engineering. The VC10 was a classic in this tradition of aviation progress.

OPPOSITE VC10 production under way at Brooklands in late 1963. In the foreground is BOAC's standard VC10 G-ARVK, with British United Airways Type 1103 example G-ASIW, complete with large main deck cargo door. The remaining two BOAC standard VC10 aircraft were unidentified but are probably G-ARVL and G-ARVM. *(BAE SYSTEMS Image Ref WCN1224)*

RIGHT The fuselage of the prototype VC10, G-ARTA, under construction in the huge hangar at Brooklands, known locally as 'Cathedral City'. In the background is a Vanguard fuselage, and in the immediate foreground a Vanguard wing. The image is undated but was probably taken around mid- to late 1961. (BAE SYSTEMS)

BELOW An early Vickers-Armstrong diagram shows the extent of the VC10 machined from solid metal (either light alloy or steel) and – in the case of the engine support beam – S.99 high-tensile steel. (BAE SYSTEMS Image Ref MP16632)

Design changes

When BOAC announced in May 1957 that it had decided to enter into negotiations with Vickers for a fleet of 35 VC10s, the aircraft had a design weight of 247,000lb, a maximum payload of 38,000lb (of which 30,000lb could be carried between Karachi and Singapore), and was powered by four Rolls-Royce RCo.10 Conway bypass turbojets each producing 16,500lb of thrust. The weight later increased to 260,000lb when it was decided to enlarge the fuselage diameter by 12in to improve the comfort of six-abreast seating.

The size of the aircraft was dictated not by the amount of fuel to be carried, but by the wing area needed to obtain the field performance with the specific payloads. The 31° swept wing actually had space for 120,000lb of fuel, although no more than 107,000lb was required for any of the sectors on the 'Empire' routes. This fact provides the clue to the Atlantic-capability stretching of the VC10; the difference between capacity available and capacity required for the Atlantic was so small that it make the stretch possible – by a small increase in wing area and thickness – without any adverse effect on the middle-range performance.

In detail, the modifications proposed – and accepted by BOAC before the end of 1957 – were: an increase in wing sweepback of 1½° to 32½°; an increase in wing area of 70ft² to 2,800ft² and in wingspan of 2ft 6in to 140ft; an increase in aspect ratio from 6.93 to 7; and an increase of 16,000lb in fuel capacity.

For Atlantic operations, the VC10 weight increased to 299,000lb and by this time the project was based upon the Rolls-Royce RCo.15 engines of 18,500lb each. The increased power largely compensated for the increased take-off weight; but in any case, long runways were already available at the major Atlantic terminals. On the 'Empire' routes,

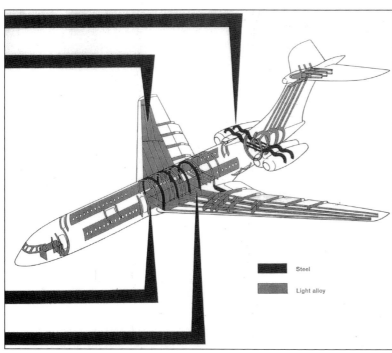

Steel

Light alloy

however, where the full fuel load need not be carried, the airfield performance was in no way impaired and there was virtually no economic penalty – at ranges over 1,000 miles or so, the cost curve is almost a straight line.

BOAC finally signed the contract for 35 VC10s on 14 January 1958, with an option to purchase a further 20. The 1958/59 BOAC *Annual Report and Accounts* showed that the contractual commitment in respect of future capital expenditure on the VC10 was £89.3 million, a figure which later rose to £95 million when spares and ground equipment were added to the contract.

Work on the definitive VC10 began early in 1957. Vickers recruited heavily for both drawing office staff as well as production staff to meet the demands of full-scale VC10 production.

The clean wing

The clean wing was the key to the VC10's performance, and the rest of the design followed almost inevitably once the location of the engines had been decided. To appreciate the impact of an uncluttered wing, it can best be recognised from the fact that, on a typical four-engine commercial aircraft design, around 20% of the total area is rendered ineffective as far as leading-edge and trailing-edge flaps are concerned. Without wing-mounted engine pods, maximum effective use of the leading and trailing edges can be made to improve the low-speed characteristics. In addition, there is also a general freedom of design without the complication of drag-producing pylon-wing intersections to be considered.

Slats were chosen as the most effective leading-edge device for the VC10. These were full-span, in four portions on each side and operated simultaneously with the large (30% chord) Fowler-type flaps. The latter were in five sections on each side and had three positions – 20° for take-off, 35° for approach and 45° for landing.

Development of the wing section for the best long-range cruise economy was one of the major design tasks on the VC10. The section was designed to maintain an entirely subsonic flow distribution at Mach 0.84, and much wind-tunnel testing was necessary to determine the correct camber along the wing. At the wing root, the camber is negative, and there are four changes along the wing as the camber becomes progressively more positive.

Tailplane

With the engines positioned on the rear fuselage, the tailplane had to be located somewhere on the fin. The top of the fin was chosen as it provided the optimum control over the required centre of gravity (CofG) range, while remaining clear of jet efflux and wing downloads. The engine nacelles themselves contributed to the longitudinal stability and helped to keep the size of the tailplane down.

ABOVE Super VC10 G-ASGA demonstrates the high-lift wing to good effect on take-off at Farnborough in September 1964. The wing leading-edge slats can be seen deployed, along with the trailing-edge flaps from outboard of the fuselage all the way across to the ailerons. *(BAE SYSTEMS Image Ref MP20798)*

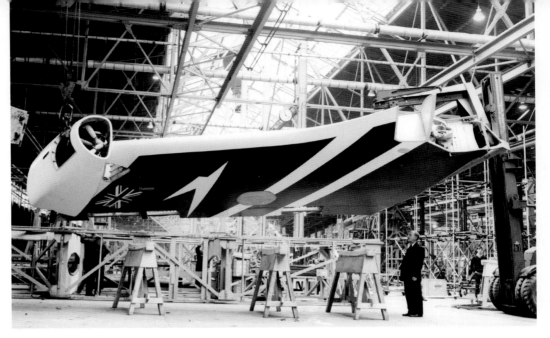

Engine mounts

As mentioned previously, the decision to locate the engines at the rear of the fuselage was undoubtedly the most momentous in determining the VC10's configuration. The advantages gained from this were:

- Elimination of the jet noise nuisance to passengers in the rear half of the fuselage.
- The elimination of potential jet fatigue problems on the wing and rear fuselage.
- The wings were left clear for the installation of the most powerful and effective high-lift devices.
- The wings were freed from interference effects at high Mach numbers, thus enabling the high-speed design of the wing to be developed with maximum efficiency.
- It reduced the fire hazard by removing the engines from the vicinity of the fuel tanks.
- It considerably reduced the possibility of engine damage due to ingestion of small stones and debris from runways.
- It almost entirely eliminated the aircraft handling problems under asymmetric thrust conditions due to engine failure (so considerable with power plants mounted far out on the wing).

The thrust reverser installation presented a problem, too. When a jet selects reverse thrust on landing, the jets blow downward and forward on to the runway allowing small stones and debris to be blown around, with the potential that they could be sucked back into the engine intake. Similarly, the hot gases from the reversed jet may be reingested, and might cause heating of the lower part of the aircraft.

Rolls-Royce helped significantly in overcoming the potential problems by designing the lower reverser to split into two parts, the major portion was inclined forward and

outboard, while the remainder had a small inclination forward. The upper reverser outlet was inclined forward.

Control systems

The keynote of the VC10 design philosophy had always been 'safety'. In the case of the flying controls, this was combined with the need for adequate controllability and pleasant handling characteristics at all times. These qualities themselves go a long way to improving safety by reducing pilot fatigue and therefore also minimising the likelihood that he might make errors of judgement or technique.

Each major control surface is divided – ailerons and elevators into two, and rudder into three – with each section actuated by its own adjacent power unit and jack. This arrangement ensured that a 'run-away' by one power control unit could be neutralised by one of the remaining sections of the control, leaving at least 50% (ailerons and elevators) or 33% (rudder) of normal power available until the faulty unit could be isolated.

Electrical and hydraulic power supply systems were split and each had four power sources, one on each engine, this being part of the safety philosophy of the design of these systems.

Aileron power was supplemented by the

three-section spoilers (see the photograph on p. 137) on each wing, which hinged upwards to a maximum angle of 50° where they operated symmetrically. The spoilers were of the 'vented' type, and could be selected from the cockpit (see the photograph on p. 138 for actuation levers) to act as air brakes or 'lift dumpers' during the landing. They could also operate differentially with the ailerons to supplement lateral control. As the ailerons lost effectiveness at higher speeds, the spoilers became relatively more effective in the control role. Like the other control surfaces, the

(see the photograph on p. 137)

LEFT During the early flight test programme carried out on the prototype VC10, unacceptable levels of drag and buffet were experienced. One of a number of modifications that were identified, and subsequently fitted to all production aircraft, was the 'beaver tail', to reduce backflow and drag issues around the engines. Here it is on VC10 K.3 ZA150 at Dunsfold. *(Keith Wilson)*

LEFT A diagram indicating the flying controls, hydraulic and electrical services on the VC10. The design had two almost-identical hydraulic systems, effectively ensuring that in the event of damage or failure in one system, the other could maintain complete control of the aircraft. Similarly, the electrical system had built-in redundancy capabilities. *(BAE SYSTEMS)*

	HYDRAULIC	
SYSTEM A		1 Windshield wipers parking unit
		2 Nose undercarriage and steering
		3 Slats
		4 Spoilers/airbrakes
		5 Flaps
SYSTEM B		6 Main undercarriage
		7 Tailplane incidence control
		8 Hydraulic pumps (System A)
		9 Hydraulic pumps (System B)
		10 Extreme emergency ram air turbo-pump

ELECTRICAL	
CIRCUIT 1	11 Left outer aileron
CIRCUIT 2	12 Left inner aileron
	13 Right inner aileron
	14 Right outer aileron
	15 Bottom rudder
	16 Middle rudder
	17 Top rudder
	18 Left outer elevator
	19 Left inner elevator
	20 Right inner elevator
CIRCUIT 3	21 Right outer elevator
	22 Electric generator (Circuit 1)
CIRCUIT 4	23 Electric generator (Circuit 2)
	24 Electric generator (Circuit 3)
	25 Electric generator (Circuit 4)
	26 Extreme emergency ram air turbo-generator

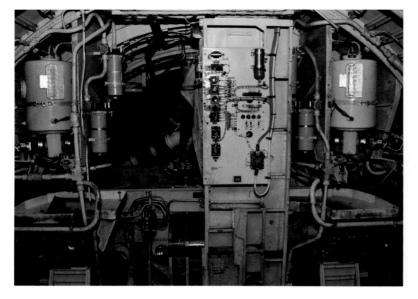

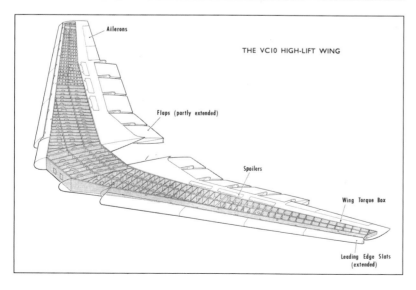

LEFT Located at the rear of the VC10 fuselage is the hydraulic services bay. Access on the K.3 variant is gained through a zipped, soft bulkhead. This image is of ZA150/J at Dunsfold. As ZA150 is maintained in a 'live' condition, the hydraulic services must be kept in full working order. *(Keith Wilson)*

CENTRE The ELRAT (electrical ram air turbine) (right) and the HYRAT (hydraulic ram air turbine) (left), deployed under the centre of the fuselage of the prototype VC10, G-ARTA. The HYRAT was only fitted to the prototype aircraft, while all other production VC10s had an ELRAT fitted under the fuselage. Interestingly, these two components were originally described by Vickers-Armstrong in early technical material as the 'Extreme emergency ram air turbo-generator' and the 'Extreme emergency ram air turbo-pump' respectively. *(BAE SYSTEMS Image Ref MP15152)*

spoilers were sectioned, with individual hydraulic jacks. As a further safety measure, operation of the flying control surfaces was divided between hydraulic and electrical systems.

While the elevators, ailerons and rudder were electro-hydraulically operated, the variable-incidence tailplane and the spoilers were operated hydraulically. Power for emergency purposes was provided by an ELRAT (Electrical Ram Air Turbine) which fell into the slipstream (see the photograph to the left) from under the centre-section fuselage when a lock was withdrawn mechanically from the cockpit.

Wing structure

The wing structure was derived from Vickers' experience with the Vanguard, in the light of

LEFT A schematic drawing of the VC10 high-lift wing. Without engines being hung from the wing, the Vickers-Armstrong team were able to design and develop a very high-performance wing featuring both leading-edge slats (running virtually the whole length of the forward wing) and trailing-edge flaps occupying most of the trailing edge (other than the space utilised by the ailerons). It was this amazing wing design that provided the VC10 with its sparkling performance, especially in 'hot and high' conditions. *(BAE SYSTEMS)*

THE VC10 HIGH-LIFT WING

Ailerons

Flaps (partly extended)

Spoilers

Wing Torque Box

Leading Edge Slats (extended)

which the choice of a multi-web box structure with machined panels was natural. Whereas the Vanguard wing only had three webs, the VC10 had four over the inner sections, reducing to three towards the wingtip. Closely spaced ribs provided integral bracing.

The machined skins, with integral stiffening stringers, were up to 35ft in length and 32in wide. At the time, they were among the largest produced for any aircraft application. To provide a fail-safe structure, the skin was divided chord-wise into seven sections at the wing root, reducing in number along the span.

Maintaining the proper aerofoil section, with its four changes along each wing, posed a major problem with the machined panels. This was solved by modifying the wing sections slightly and allowing the skins to be pulled down to shape on the ribs.

The entire wing was assembled in three sections – the centre-section torsion box and the port and starboard mainplanes. Each mainplane had two chord-wise manufacturing joints and contained two integral fuel tanks. In addition, fuel was carried in a tank in the wing centre section, which was unpressurised.

Fuselage

Conventional construction techniques were used in the fuselage, which had closely spaced hoop frames, stringers and flush-riveted skin. An unusual feature, however, was the use of machined panels along the window line in place of the more usual built-up structure around the

window and emergency exit cut-outs, as well as over the centre fuselage, where there were heavy sheer loads. The large cut-out for the wing centre section and the main undercarriage wells were bridged by a massive built-up keel member in the fuselage, between the forward and rear freight bays.

Because of the extra weight of the engines on the fuselage, there was a case for supporting the fuselage, as well as the wing, by the undercarriage.

ABOVE The hydraulically operated starboard leading-edge slat, seen deployed here on a BOAC VC10 on the production line at Brooklands. *(BAE SYSTEMS Image Ref MP19189)*

BELOW The first Type 1103 VC10 for British United Airways (BUA) taking shape at Brooklands. The large forward fuselage main deck cargo door is prominent in this view – a facility that later provided excellent cargo/passenger flexibility for BUA on both its African and South American routes. *(BAE SYSTEMS)*

Vickers/BAC VC10 K Mk 2 cutaway drawing.

(Mike Badrocke)

1 In-flight refuelling probe
2 Radome
3 Glide slope aerial
4 Radar tracking mechanism
5 Front pressure bulkhead
6 Windscreen wipers
7 Windscreen panels
8 Instrument panel shroud
9 Rudder pedals
10 Taxiing lamp
11 Pilot's seat
12 Cockpit eyebrow windows
13 Co-pilot's seat
14 Flight engineer's station
15 Closed-circuit television display (CCTV)
16 Refuelling control panel
17 Observer's seat
18 Navigator's station
19 Signal cartridge stowage
20 Air system safety and discharge valves
21 Nosewheel doors
22 Twin nosewheels
23 Landing lamp
24 Electronics cooling air ducting
25 Emergency exit door
26 Navigator's instrument rack
27 Stowage locker
28 Overhead stowage rack
29 Toilet compartment
30 Galley
31 10-man dinghy
32 Main cabin floor level
33 Emergency radio beacon
34 26-man dinghy
35 Upper VHF/UHF aerials (two)
36 IFF aerial
37 Aft-facing seating, 18 seats
38 Machined cabin window panel
39 Air conditioning system ducting
40 Underfloor electrical and avionic bay
41 Flight refuelling delivery pipe run
42 Spare drogue containers on aft face of bulkhead (3)
43 Doorway to rear cabin
44 Cabin bulkhead
45 TACAN aerial
46 Anti-collision light
47 Fuselage frame and stringer construction
48 A-frame crash restraint member
49 Fuel tank mounting rails
50 Starboard freight hold door
51 Underfloor freight hold
52 Fuselage fuel tank mountings
53 Double-skinned fuel tank container
54 Inner bag tank
55 Wing inspection light
56 Main cabin doorway (inoperative)
57 ADF loop aerials
58 Blanked-off cabin windows

59 Air conditioning system evaporators
60 Wing centre section carry-through structure
61 Forward emergency exit window
62 Aft emergency exit window (inoperative)
63 Fuel system vent piping
64 Wing attachment fuselage main frames
65 Wing tank boost pumps
66 Fuel system piping
67 Starboard wing integral fuel tanks
68 Leading-edge slat drive shaft
69 Slat rails and jacks
70 Wind driven fuel pump turbine
71 Flight Refuelling Mk 32 wing pod
72 Wing fence
73 Starboard leading-edge slat segments, open
74 Vent surge tank
75 Starboard navigation light
76 Wingtip fairing
77 Aileron hydraulic jacks
78 Two-segment ailerons
79 Fuel jettison pipe
80 Starboard spoilers, open
81 Spoiler twin hydraulic jacks
82 Flap screw jacks
83 Starboard slotted flaps, down position
84 Unfurnished fuselage interior
85 Rear service door (inoperative)
86 Fin root fillet
87 Starboard engine cowlings
88 Starboard thrust reverser (outboard engine only)
89 HF notch aerials
90 Ram air intake
91 Air system intercooler
92 Intercooler exhaust grille
93 Fin spar attachment joints
94 Tailfin construction
95 Bleed air leading-edge de-icing
96 Starboard refuelling hose
97 Drogue unit
98 Aft glide slope aerial
99 VOR localiser aerial

100 Tailplane actuator screw jack
101 Tailplane pivot fixing
102 Fin/tailplane bullet fairing
103 Starboard tailplane
104 Two-segment elevators
105 Tailplane bullet fairing
106 Tail navigation light
107 Elevator honeycomb panels
108 Hydraulic elevator jacks
109 Port tailplane construction
110 Bleed air leading-edge de-icing
111 Three-segment rudder construction
112 Rudder hydraulic jacks
113 Honeycomb trailing-edge panels
114 Rolls-Royce/Turboméca Artouste Mk 520 APU
115 Extended tailcone
116 Centre refuelling hose and drogue unit
117 Aft pressure bulkhead
118 Sloping fin frames
119 Engine pylon fairing
120 Exhaust nozzle tail fairing
121 Thrust reverser, outboard engine only
122 Machined engine mounting beams
123 Rolls-Royce Conway Mk 550B turbofans
124 Bleed air system compressor, inboard engines only
125 Engine mounting beams
126 Flight Refuelling Mk 17B hose drum unit (HDU)
127 HDU drogue fixed fairing (with engine nacelle floodlights in rear end)
128 Retractable air-inlet door for hose drum unit
129 Trailing-edge wing root fillet
130 Pressure floor above wheel bay
131 Main undercarriage wheel well
132 Inboard slotted flaps
133 Flap honeycomb skin panels
134 Flap shroud ribs
135 Main undercarriage leg pivot fixing
136 Hydraulic retraction jack
137 Machined wing stringer/skin panels
138 Port spoilers

139 Flap track fairings (with fuselage floodlights in inboard fairing each side)
140 Port outer slotted flaps
141 Flap down position
142 Fuel jettison pipe
143 Port refuelling hose
144 Port aileron construction
145 Omega navigation aerial (port wing only)
146 Port navigation light
147 Wing rib construction
148 Leading-edge slat guide rails
149 Flight Refuelling Mk 32 wing pod (with wing floodlights on each side)
150 Hose drum unit

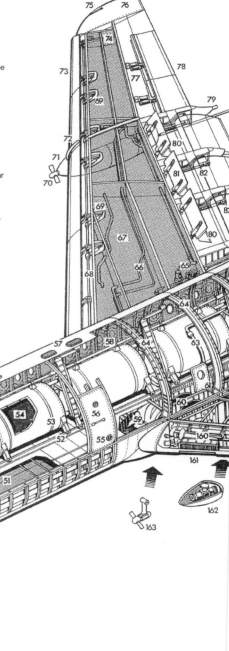

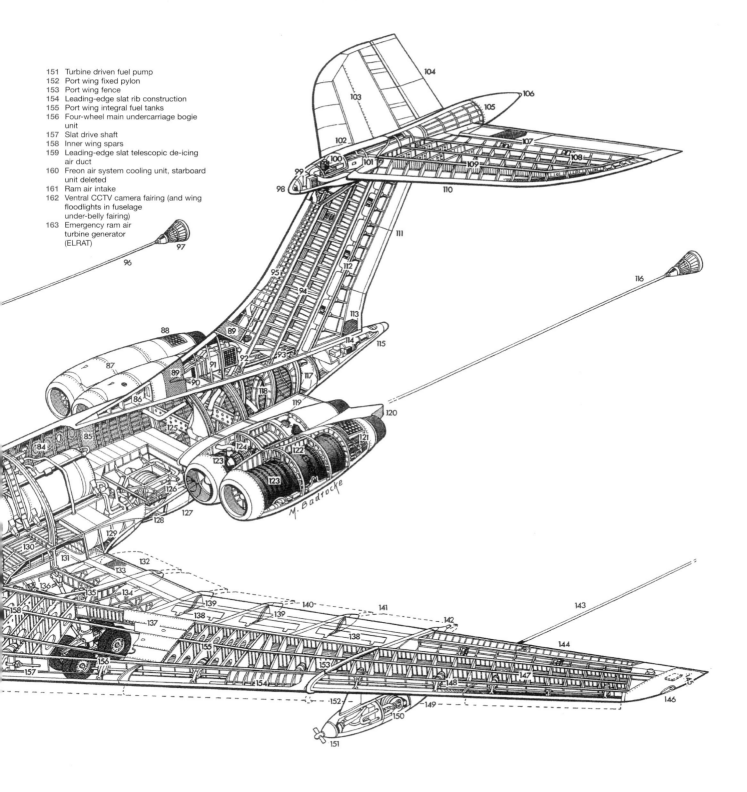

M. Badrocke

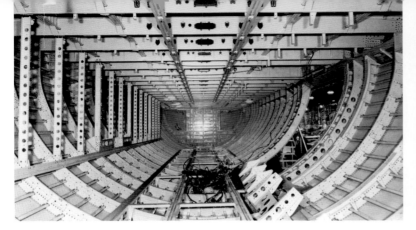

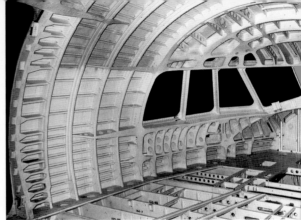

ABOVE BOAC fuselage production at Weybridge. Unusually at the time, some sections of the fuselage were milled from solid aluminium to ensure its structural integrity. It should be considered that these complex structures were designed and drawn by hand, then constructed when Computer Numerical Control (CNC) was in its infancy and long before Computer Aided Design (CAD) had even been invented! *(BAE SYSTEMS Image Ref MP16632)*

ABOVE The forward fuselage and cockpit section of BOAC's first VC10, G-ARVA. Once again, some sections of the outer skin were milled from a solid light alloy with others machined from solid steel. No other airliner boasted a structure constructed in this manner. *(BAE SYSTEMS Image Ref MP14475)*

The main chassis units were fixed both to the wing structure (at the rear web) and to a one-piece beam which connected the rear web and the fuselage. The mainwheels – with large-diameter, low-pressure tyres – were stowed within the under fuselage behind the wing centre section.

In addition to two freight holds and an air-conditioning bay, the fuselage underfloor area contained an equipment bay (see the photograph on p. 41) for radio, navigation and electrical services, accessible through a small hatch in the forward cabin area to permit in-flight servicing, if required. This entrance also provided access to the nose undercarriage assembly.

RIGHT Another Vickers-Armstrong schematic, this time of the VC10 equipment bay showing the locations of the various radio and navigational equipment carried. This view is towards the nosewheel of the aircraft. *(BAE SYSTEMS via Bristol Aero Collection Trust)*

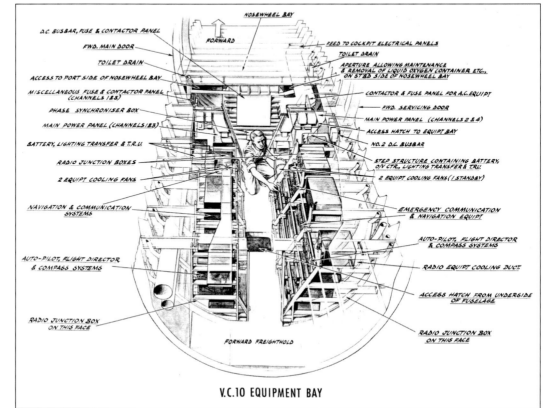

V.C.10 EQUIPMENT BAY

It was convenient to divide the fuselage into four sections, both for ease of manufacture and structural design. These were: flight deck area; forward fuselage; centre section; and rear fuselage including the engine nacelle.

Undercarriage – designed for smooth landings

At first sight, the most unusual feature of the main undercarriage was that the oleo leg was raked backwards approximately 10° in the ground attitude. This was something of a design compromise, since a vertical leg would have involved a reduction in the flap chord. Interestingly, when in the landing configuration, the trailing pair of main undercarriage legs contacted the ground ahead of the front pair, and a two-stage air compressor cushioned the landing impact.

The undercarriage design also provided for an emergency 'free-fall' lowering with automatic locking in the event of a power failure, but emergency hand-winding was also provided.

A straightforward design was possible with the nose undercarriage and a straight-up-

ABOVE The starboard side of the equipment bay facing rearwards. Beyond the open doorway is the forward baggage bay on VC10 K.4 ZD241 at Bruntingthorpe. *(Keith Wilson)*

BELOW LEFT The starboard main undercarriage on a Super VC10 seen here with the aircraft on jacks. The Vickers-designed gear gave the VC10 a characteristically smooth landing, despite its apparent simplicity. When in the landing configuration (seen here), the trailing pair of main undercarriage legs contacted the ground ahead of the front pair, and a two-stage air compressor cushioned the landing impact. Full gear retraction took just 9.5 seconds. *(BAE SYSTEMS Image Ref MP22461)*

BELOW A schematic diagram of the VC10's highly effective main undercarriage assembly that enabled the aircraft to gain a strong reputation for smooth landings. *(British Aircraft Corporation via Paul Robinson)*

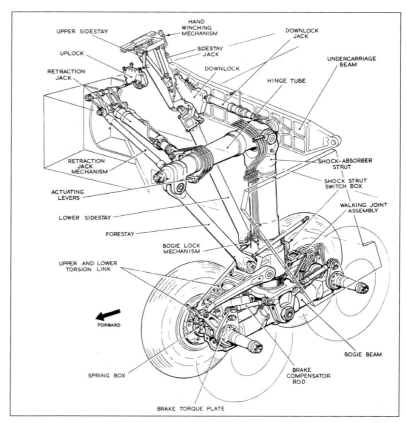

RIGHT The nose undercarriage leg, wheels and bay as seen on the prototype VC10, G-ARTA, in the Assembly Hall at Brooklands on 5 February 1962. (BAE SYSTEMS Image Ref MP14349)

ABOVE The nosewheel assembly on VC10 K.4 ZD241 at Bruntingthorpe. Note the additional lips on the outside of the tyres, which were added to increase the effectiveness of removing runway water from the treads, thereby improving braking effectiveness. (Keith Wilson)

and-down oleo was the result. Power steering throughout +/-70°, and retraction were achieved by hydraulic jacks.

Flight deck and cabin

The VC10 was designed to be operated with a crew of four, although five seats were provided to allow for a supernumerary crew member. The normal arrangement consisted of two pilots, a flight engineer and a navigator.

The flight engineer had all of the engine and systems instrumentation, along with a set of engine control throttles (the other set of throttles was located on the centre console between the two pilots). The flight engineer also had

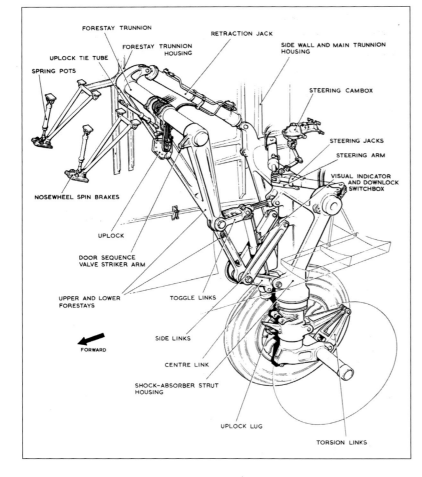

FORESTAY TRUNNION
FORESTAY TRUNNION HOUSING
RETRACTION JACK
SIDE WALL AND MAIN TRUNNION HOUSING
UPLOCK TIE TUBE
SPRING POTS
STEERING CAMBOX
STEERING JACKS
STEERING ARM
VISUAL INDICATOR AND DOWNLOCK SWITCHBOX
NOSEWHEEL SPIN BRAKES
UPLOCK
DOOR SEQUENCE VALVE STRIKER ARM
UPPER AND LOWER FORESTAYS
TOGGLE LINKS
SIDE LINKS
CENTRE LINK
SHOCK-ABSORBER STRUT HOUSING
UPLOCK LUG
TORSION LINKS
FORWARD

LEFT A schematic diagram of the VC10's nosewheel assembly. (British Aircraft Corporation via Paul Robinson)

LEFT The flight deck of standard VC10 A4O-AB, now displayed at the Brooklands Museum. During its conversion to a VVIP role, it had new navigation equipment added to the centre of the console, permitting the two pilots to undertake the navigation of the aircraft and thereby making the navigator's position redundant. While navigational equipment was retained in this position, the aircraft only carried a flight crew of three (first pilot, second pilot and flight engineer). See also the photograph on p. 46 for details of the new navigational equipment added to the flight deck. *(Keith Wilson)*

BELOW An early schematic diagram showing the proposed positions of various pieces of equipment on the flight deck of the standard VC10. Note item 37, the all-important foldaway pencil sharpener (see the photograph on p. 45) fitted to all production VC10 aircraft! *(BAE SYSTEMS via Bristol Aero Collection Trust)*

1 Weather radar
2 Chart tables
3 Visors
4 Escape rope stowage
5 Nosewheel steering control
6 Oxygen mask stowage
7 Document stowage
8 Electrical distribution panel (starboard only)
9 Rudder pedals
10 Control column
11 Crew seats
12 Windshield wipers
13 Glare shields
14 Side curtains
15 Engineer's document stowage
16 Emergency breathing apparatus
17 Sextant mounting station
18 Air conditioning louvre
19 Loudspeaker
20 Canopy windows
21 Lighting
22 Centre console
23 Engineer's table
24 Engineer's throttles
25 Engineer's panels
26 DV windows
27 Headset stowage
28 Briefcase stowage
29 Lights
30 Louvres
31 Fire switches
32 Instrument panel
33 Stowage
34 Smoke goggles (port only)
35 Mic. selector
36 Pitot static changeover switch
37 Pencil sharpener
38 Pilot's roof panel
39 PA microphone
40 Fire extinguisher
41 Life jacket stowage
42 Engineer's light
43 Starter panel
44 Fuse and CB location chart
45 Strip light
46 Grille

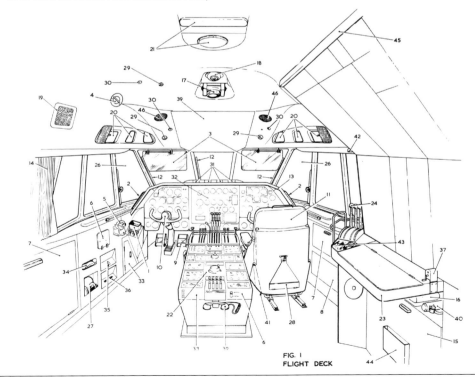

FIG. I
FLIGHT DECK

ABOVE The pilot's overhead panel appears to have been an addition from the earlier schematic diagram on p. 43. Once again, this is A4O-AB and the central panel contains the indicators for the aileron, elevator and rudder trimmers along with the position indicators for the leading-edge slats. *(Keith Wilson)*

LEFT The centre console on A4O-AB at the end of its service life; not significantly different from the early diagram on p. 43. *(Keith Wilson)*

BELOW LEFT The right-hand panel on the flight engineer's position on Super VC10 G-ASGC is seen here preserved in its original form at Duxford. An amazing collection of gauges, dials, switches, fuses and circuit-breakers! The left-hand panel controlled anti-icing as well as internal domestic services such as the water heating in the toilets. The right-hand panel controlled the aircraft's oxygen system, with the main switches being marked in bright red and green. *(Keith Wilson)*

BELOW The flight engineer's panel on A4O-AB, preserved at the Brooklands Museum and accessible to the public. Aside from a small extra panel controlling the ground supply to the aircraft (added since the aircraft was placed on display), it is almost identical to the day it left the factory at Weybridge back in 1964. *(Keith Wilson)*

the engine-starting systems located under a moveable Perspex panel on his desk. Once all four engines were running satisfactorily, the cover could be lowered and used as part of the working surface. On all production aircraft built at Weybridge, the flight engineer also had a pencil sharpener built into his desk, which folded underneath when not in use!

The radio controls were located in the centre console between the pilots, while both pilots had a standard flying panel in front of them, with all of the engine instrumentation located on the panel between them. Nosewheel steering was to the left of the first pilot and to the right of the co-pilot. Similarly, the weather radar screens were located adjacent to the nosewheel steering controls on both seats.

When the VC10 first entered airline service, the navigator's aft-facing position was permanent, although later in the VC10's airline career, when certain navigational equipment was upgraded, the control panels were located in the main pilot's panel, thereby rendering the navigator redundant. That said, the RAF always operated with a four-man (or woman) crew, where the navigator was a

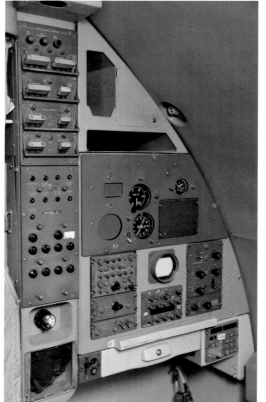

permanent feature, right up until the aircraft was retired from service in 2013.

The flight deck was a spacious, comfortable and well-lit environment for the flight crew, with an excellent field of view. This was just as well,

since some sectors flown by the aircraft were lengthy affairs.

Engines and fuel systems

The Rolls-Royce RCo.42 Conway engine was adopted by Vickers and BOAC as the basic engine for the VC10. It generated 20,370lb of thrust and was, at the time, the most powerful turbojet proposed for civilian use. The engine used in the Super VC10 was the RCo.43 producing 21,800lb each. Some writers have intimated that the VC10 was the first airliner to be over-powered, and remains the only one ever to be so.

The engines were hung from two steel 'half-spectacle' beams, which carried the loads into the strong rear fuselage structure (see the photograph on p. 25). Each engine nacelle cowling provided quick and easy access to the power units through hinged and removable panels in the top surfaces, and the entire engine could be lowered or raised through doors in the underside, without interfering with the nacelle structure.

On the standard VC10, thrust reversers were fitted to the inner engines only, although they were fitted to all four on the Super VC10.

The danger of main-engine turbine vane/disc failure is much greater when the engines are located next to each other. Rolls-Royce gave considerable thought to the issue of how to stop an adjacent engine being taken out by an explosion in a neighbour. Their solution was a compressor casing capable of containing a blade failure. The low-pressure stage was wrapped in a flanged steel case while the stage-4 position had a magnesium cladding added to it.

That said, some additional design work was required after the incident on 4 December 1969 involving Super VC10 G-ASGK at 6,500ft over Reading when a low-pressure turbine blade was catastrophically shed from No 3 (the starboard-inner) Conway engine penetrating the No 4 engine, causing it to catch fire. Both engines were shut down and the aircraft returned safely to Heathrow, although it landed at a gross weight of 327,000lb – some 90,000lb over the design limit landing weight. The aircraft had a full fuel load for the London to New York sector, and there was insufficient time to jettison any of it. The undercarriage was lowered manually. Two tyres deflated on landing – the fusible plugs blew – but there were no injuries among the 58 passengers and 11 crew.

Each of the four main wing tanks is of approximately equal capacity and supplies fuel to its particular engine; the centre-section tank serves as a transfer tank, delivering fuel into the wing tanks by way of the refuel/defuel system. Each outer wing tank is divided into two sections, of such capacity as to cater for the CofG shift conditions due to the length of the tanks and the swept wing.

Production

Production of the VC10 was handled at Vickers' main plant at Weybridge. A new pre-flight hall (later nicknamed the 'Cathedral' because of its high roof able to accommodate the height of a fully assembled VC10) was specially constructed to permit final assembly of the type, including the very high-mounted tail and fin that could not be assembled in the existing areas of the factory.

System testing

Ahead of production, test rigs of the six major systems of the aircraft were built. They were used to prove the design of the system and also to carry out tests which would not have been practical or safely done in flight.

A full-size replica of the aircraft powered flying control systems was created and control run function trials carried out. All components of the system had the same relative positions in the rig as they would later have in the aircraft. The rig was designed to simulate flight conditions as closely as possible and resistive loads were applied to control surfaces corresponding to those that would be experienced in flight. The rig was used for a series of intensive trials, including continuous running on simulated flights, as well as failure investigations by deliberately sabotaging parts of the system.

An Autopilot Test Rig was created and situated adjacent to the powered flying control systems rig so that the two could be integrated and compatibility scenarios examined. Additionally, the aircraft aerodynamic and inertia

ABOVE **A spare Rolls-Royce Conway engine being mounted on the leading-edge wing carrying point. This ability was demonstrated by the first Super VC10, G-ASGA, at Farnborough in September 1965. In service, this facility was used occasionally by BOAC and later, British Airways, on their Super VC10 aircraft. At the time it was considered somewhat innovative but was later replicated by Boeing on their 747.** *(BAE SYSTEMS Image Ref MP21732)*

BELOW **One complete aircraft excluding the cockpit was manufactured on the production jigs and tooling under the construction number 802. It was used exclusively for structural testing in these purpose-built test frames at Wisley. Proof load tests were conducted ahead of the first flight of G-ARTA and these were followed by a series of fatigue tests designed to simulate representative flights and gust loads. In this view the wing is undergoing simulated bending way beyond its designed limitations to ensure the fail-safe properties of the structure. Later, some members of the structure were deliberately severed to confirm the strength and integrity of the overall design.** *(BAE SYSTEMS)*

ABOVE Vickers constructed a fuel system test rig at Weybridge featuring a full-size replica VC10 left and centre-section wing, pivoted about a single point to provide pitch and roll attitudes. The dummy wing was constructed of steel while internally was an exact copy of the real wing. If the right wing was required for testing, drum tanks of an equivalent volume were used. The tests ran for almost three years and provided considerable data. *(BAE SYSTEMS Image Ref MP14879)*

characteristics were reproduced by an analogue computer – perhaps the first occasion when computerisation has played such an important function in aviation safety testing.

A Hydraulic System Test Rig was constructed utilising the majority of the designed systems and was coupled to the landing gear, flap and slat mechanisms and cockpit controls. The rig was used to test functionality, fatigue and fault-finding of the final design.

The Electrical System Test Rig was used with Westinghouse 40KVa brushless alternators, driven through Sundstrand constant speed units. Normally, the power would have been generated from the aircraft engines but electrical motors were used to simulate engine characteristics of speed and acceleration.

A full-size Full Test Rig was created utilising the left and centre-section wing, pivoted about one point to simulate pitch and roll attitudes.

An Air-Conditioning Test Rig was also completed, with all the ducting installed together with a mock-up cabin section. Interestingly, the effects of tobacco smoke on the system, particularly on the filters, were also investigated.

A forward fuselage section was constructed using production jigs and tooling and was placed in a water tank for pressurisation testing. The fatigue properties were then examined by continuous cycling of the pressure application on a simulated flight basis in the stratosphere chamber where the effects of temperature and altitude could be reproduced to provide realistic and representative test conditions.

Finally, a large Structural Test Rig for a complete aircraft was built. Inside, the second airframe constructed using the production jigs and tooling was installed to allow proof load tests to be applied ahead of the first flight. These were followed by a series of fatigue tests which were programmed to simulate a sequence of representative flights and gust loads. The effects of take-off, landing, fuel loads, flaps and air brakes were all included in the programme flight cycle. Once sufficient data had been achieved from the first stage of the testing, the specimen was used

LEFT The aircraft underwent extensive ditching trials with Saunders Roe. The T-tail and clean wings provided excellent ditching characteristics. *(Westland Aircraft, Saunders Roe Division Image Ref E1778/D via Brooklands Museum)*

RIGHT Not so much an airliner, more a flying laboratory. The interior of G-ARTA used a raft of testing equipment to ensure that all required testing information was gained and to make certain that the aircraft met, or exceeded, its designed performance parameters. *(BAE SYSTEMS Image Ref MP16314 via Brooklands Museum)*

to demonstrate the fail-safe properties of the structure by deliberately severing members and by exerting loads way in excess of design limitations.

The test programme provided much data and, more importantly, confirmation of the design integrity ahead of the VC10s first flight. The VC10 was a tough aeroplane.

LEFT Another test carried out ahead of the first flight was the examination of the strength of the flight deck screens. Objects were forced out of the wind tunnel, aimed straight at the waiting screen. *(BAE SYSTEMS Image Ref MP20240)*

LEFT The end of the line. An East African Airways (EAA) VC10 Type 1154 on the production line at Brooklands in March 1966. It is thought to be 5X-UVA, which made its first flight on 3 September 1966 and was delivered to EAA on the 30th of the same month. This was one of five aircraft ordered by EAA and represented the final VC10 production at Brooklands. *(BAE SYSTEMS Image Ref WCT1927)*

Chapter Three

VC10 in airline service

'On 1 April, BOAC moves six years ahead of any other airline. The BOAC Super VC10 takes off for London. Triumphantly swift, silent, serene.'

It wasn't an April fool's joke but a BOAC advertisement aimed at the US market in early 1965. The airline's London–New York route started operating with Super VC10s on 1 April 1965, with G-ASGD flying the inaugural crossing. Routes to the West Indies and Canada, with onward services to California, quickly followed.

OPPOSITE Photographed at Düsseldorf in March 1978, just four years after the BOAC/BEA merger, Super VC10 G-ASGG looks resplendent in the red, white and blue livery of British Airways. *(Dietrich Eggert)*

Route proving

Following the first flight of the prototype VC10, G-ARTA, from Brooklands on 29 June 1962, Vickers made significant efforts to obtain the type's Airworthiness Certificate as quickly as possible. BOAC contributed to this by permitting production aircraft destined for the airline to be used in the flight test programme, with G-ARVA, -B, and -C participating.

Meanwhile, G-ARVF was undertaking a series of route-proving flights to a variety of destinations – both hot and cold. These included Salisbury, Rhodesia, on 29 January 1962 and Lagos on 9 March 1964, just a month ahead of the start of the airline's regular service to this destination. In total, around 1,000 hours of route-proving flights were made by -VF ahead of the type formally entering service with the airline on 29 April 1964. This proved significantly beneficial to the airline as the VC10's entry into service ultimately went smoothly.

BOAC commences services

On 29 April 1964, only six years after signing the order for the aircraft, the first VC10 formally entered service with BOAC when G-ARVJ departed London Airport (it wasn't renamed Heathrow until 1966) en route to Lagos and Kano. The following day, G-ARVI followed on the London–Lagos–Kano–Lagos–London route.

Within just a few months, VC10s flew to all of the 'hot and high' destinations for which

the aircraft had been designed. The outcome was a gradual phasing out of service of both the Bristol Britannia and de Havilland Comet 4 aircraft. By 1966, Singapore, Karachi, Calcutta, Delhi and the Orient routes were all operated by the VC10. Shortly afterwards Hong Kong and Tokyo were served by the VC10, while the early standard model VC10s were also finding their way to New York, Toronto and a number of Central American cities.

As the only operator of the VC10 on all of these routes, the aircraft and their crews had to operate autonomously; self-sufficiency was definitely the order of the day. Thankfully, the aircraft had an excellent maintenance record although they owed much to the cache of spare parts held along the routes and to the engineers who flew with them. BOAC flight engineers were given the engineering authority to replace/rectify a long list of aircraft components and many of these interventions kept the aircraft flying down-route and significantly assisted in achieving the VC10's enviable reliability record and passenger appeal (more about this can be read in Chapter Six). By early 1970, BOAC had used the VC10 to build up its Middle East routes to great effect and it became the premier European airline serving the region. As late as 1973, the standard VC10 was still opening up Africa. From the beginning of February, BOAC VC10 aircraft commenced services from Bole Airport, Addis Ababa, where the runway was very hot and 7,625ft above sea level, making it one of the highest on the 'Empire' routes network. Previous attempts had been made to take the VC10 into Addis Ababa but the old runway had not been up to the task and an East African Airways' (EAA) Super VC10 had sunk into the tarmac. The runway had to be rebuilt as a consequence!

Such was the success of the VC10 on the 'Empire' routes, that load factors on many were well in excess of 70% and it became the passengers' preferred choice – just as the Super VC10 would later become the Atlantic business travellers' preferred choice.

BUA/BCAL

In the early 1960s, British United Airways (BUA) called for a Britannia replacement capable of carrying economic payloads out

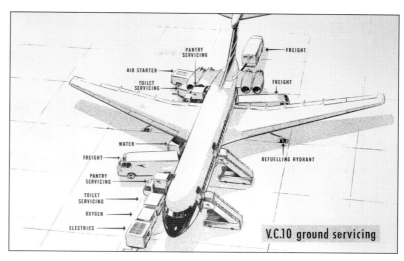

V.C.10 ground servicing

of difficult destinations on their route network. Unfortunately, the Type 1101 VC10 did not meet the needs of the diverse nature of payloads carried by BUA. Vickers responded with the Type 1103, which featured a large freight door in the forward fuselage permitting the airline flexibility in passenger/freight combinations. At the time, BUA were attempting to enter the African market and the VC10 would certainly assist them with their aims.

BUA placed an order for two aircraft in 1961 and when G-ASIW and -IX were delivered in

BELOW An early BOAC publicity shot for the VC10 that was also used on the airline's first-class menu shows the level of service offered in the airline's first-class cabin area. It is little wonder the aircraft was so popular with its passengers. *(BOAC Image Ref 65406 via BAE SYSTEMS)*

ABOVE British United Airways' (BUA) standard VC10 G-ASIW (a Type 1103 with construction number 819) was exhibited at the Farnborough Air Show in September 1964 with its large main deck cargo door wide open, showing a Rolls-Royce car on board. G-ASIW was one of three Type 1103s built for BUA. *(BAE SYSTEMS)*

BELOW After completing its flight test programme, the prototype VC10 G-ARTA was converted into a Type 1103 with a large main deck cargo door. Initially, it was purchased by Freddie Laker and leased to Middle East Airlines (MEA) in 1968–69, before being sold to BUA in April 1969. After the merger with British Caledonian Airways (BCAL), G-ARTA was repainted in their colours, as seen here at Gatwick Airport. Unfortunately, the aircraft was written off after a heavy landing at Gatwick on 28 January 1972. This image was taken after the incident at Gatwick and some of the damaged areas where the external fuselage skin was badly wrinkled has been covered. A possible repair was considered but was unfortunately proved uneconomical and the aircraft was broken up at Gatwick in early 1973. *(Richard Vandervord)*

September and October 1964, they began operating the African routes on 1 October and shortly afterwards to Caracas. With the addition of the South American routes, it became apparent to BUA that additional capacity was required and BUA quickly accepted the third aircraft destined for Ghana Airways as G-ATDJ. The modified prototype G-ARTA was also acquired, to supplement the success of the other three aircraft.

BUA's parent company – British and Commonwealth Shipping – sold the airline to the Scottish charter airline British Caledonian Airways (BCAL) in November 1970. The two airline operations were merged under the BCAL flag, although the four VC10 aircraft did not fit into BCAL's long-term plans. Instead, they preferred the Boeing 707-320 and already had a number on order. They allowed the VC10 fleet to be run down for eventual sale. G-ATDJ was sold to the Royal Aircraft Establishment for blind landing trials as XX914; G-ARTA had been broken up at Gatwick in 1973 following a heavy landing incident at the airport in January 1972; G-ASIW was sold to Air Malawi as 7Q-YKH; while the final aircraft, G-ASIX, was sold to the Sultan of Oman as A4O-AB.

Ghana Airways

Ghana Airways ordered three Type 1102 standard VC10s in 1961, one in an all-passenger configuration, with the other two featuring the large forward freight door

developed for BUA. All too soon, Ghana Airways realised they were purchasing more capacity than their network required, so they sold their final production position to BUA as G-ATDJ (see above). The first aircraft, 9G-ABO, was delivered to the airline in January 1965 and the aircraft spent virtually all of its working life shuttling between London and Accra, while sometimes calling at Rome.

The second aircraft, 9G-ABP, was delivered in June 1965 but was under-utilised and placed up for sale. In mid-1967 it was leased to Middle East Airlines (MEA) in the airline's colours but retained the Ghana Airways registration. It was destroyed by Israeli military action at Beirut Airport on 28 December 1968.

9G-ABO continued in service until December 1980, when the aircraft was flown to Prestwick and placed in open storage. Without a buyer, it was broken up in 1983.

Nigerian Airways

Nigerian Airways ordered two aircraft but cancelled before they were built. Instead, they entered into a number of lease agreements with BOAC and operated a variety of VC10s – including G-ARVI, -VA and -VC – between 1964 and 1969; some of these aircraft operated in BOAC colours with Nigerian Airways titles added. In 1966, G-ARVC was wet leased to the airline in full Nigerian Airways livery; however, it was returned to BOAC in 1967 at the end of the lease.

In June 1969, they purchased G-ARVA from BOAC and it was registered 5N-ABD.

ABOVE 9G-ABO was delivered to Ghana Airways in January 1965 and served with the airline until withdrawn from service in December 1980. At this point it was placed into storage at Prestwick, before being broken up in 1983. During its service life with Ghana Airways, it was a regular visitor to London Heathrow Airport, where this image was taken. *(Stefan Roehrich)*

BELOW G-ARVC was the third Type 1101 VC10 delivered to BOAC in December 1964. Nigerian Airways ordered two VC10s (Type 1104), but these were later cancelled and never built. Instead, Nigerian Airways wet leased two BOAC VC10s in basic BOAC livery – but with Nigerian Airways stickers applied – in 1964. These two aircraft (G-ARVA and G-ARVI) continued in service until 1966. Later in that year, G-ARVC was wet leased from BOAC and painted in full Nigerian Airways livery at Brooklands, where this photograph was taken ahead of delivery to the airline. The aircraft was returned to BOAC at the end of the lease in 1967. *(BAE SYSTEMS Image Ref MP24594)*

ABOVE **Although Middle East Airlines (MEA) had wanted to buy VC10s, they never did. Instead they leased two aircraft: the first was 9G-ABP from Ghana Airways and the second was G-ARTA, which was leased from Freddie Laker for 12 months as OD-AFA, before being returned. G-ARTA was photographed at Wisley in MEA colours ahead of the lease period.** *(BAE SYSTEMS Image Ref WCN2543)*

It was introduced on the London–Kano–Lagos–London route but was soon lost in a landing accident at Lagos on 20 November 1969 when all 87 passengers and crew aboard perished.

BELOW **VC10 aircraft of both East African Airways (EAA) and BUA had been regular visitors to Malawi when Air Malawi purchased the former British Caledonian VC10 Type 1103 G-ASIW in November 1974 and operated it as 7Q-YKH. It was painted in these bright red colours and was the flagship of the company for several years until, in 1979, it was deemed beyond economic use. It was placed into storage at Hurn, where this image was taken in August 1980. Eventually, it was flown home to Malawi where it was left to decay, eventually being scrapped in 1994.** *(Richard Vandervord)*

Middle East Airlines lease

In the mid-1960s, Middle East Airlines (MEA) was looking to re-equip its fleet. It entered protracted negotiation with Vickers but due to the political mess surrounding the aircraft then at its height in the UK, MEA were forced to walk away. In the end, MEA ordered the Boeing 707. However, the airline was still short of jet airliners and entered into two short-term lease arrangements involving standard VC10s.

When the second Ghana Airways VC10 – 9G-ABP – was delivered, it was soon realised that the airline was suffering from overcapacity. When the aircraft was put up for sale in 1967, MEA stepped in and negotiated a short-term lease. The aircraft was painted in full MEA colours but retained the Ghana Airways registration. The short-term lease proved even shorter than expected when the aircraft was destroyed by Israeli military action at Beirut in December 1968.

Meanwhile, Freddie Laker had leased the remanufactured, former prototype VC10 – G-ARTA – from BAC and immediately sub-leased it to MEA for a 12-month period, where it operated as OD-AFA. It was returned to Freddie Laker at the end of the lease and entered service with BUA as G-ARTA.

MEA were just about to take delivery of their Boeing 707s, so their relationship with VC10s drew to a close.

Air Malawi

Air Malawi code-shared a VC10 with BUA on services from Gatwick to Malawi, with the aircraft operating in BUA livery. From 1974 onwards, the aircraft was operated in BCAL livery.

Later, the Malawian government purchased BUA's first Type 1103 example – G-ASIW – from BCAL, along with a training and spares package. The aircraft was repainted in bright red Air Malawi livery and registered 7Q-YKH before commencing regular services to London, the Indian Ocean, South Africa and the Netherlands.

By the end of 1978, strong competition and rising fuel costs ended its economic life and 7Q-YKH was flown to Hurn for storage. Here it remained, incurring storage charges. Eventually, 7Q-YKH was made airworthy for one last flight back to Malawi, where it then sat for more than a decade, just rotting away. By 1994, the aircraft had been cut up for scrap.

Air Ceylon

Air Ceylon entered into a lease agreement with BOAC to operate a standard VC10 on the London to Colombo route, which were allocated on an availability basis. Aircraft operated (which included G-ARVG) carried standard BOAC livery with Air Ceylon titles on the nose and over the doors. Later, they took a 12-month lease on a Gulf Air VC10 (A4O-VL).

Gulf Air

In April 1974, the British Overseas Airways Corporation (BOAC) and British European Airways (BEA) merged to become British Airways (BA). During merger discussions a number of decisions were considered and one of these was the disposal of the remaining standard VC10s being operated by BOAC. Around this time, Gulf Air were rapidly expanding their routes and awaiting delivery of a number of new aircraft. In the short term, they leased five of BOAC's VC10s (G-ARVC, -G, -I, -K and -L), the first being delivered in February, while the last was at the end of 1974. All were painted in Gulf Air colours. While the aircraft were still being leased, Gulf Air purchased all five aircraft outright (between October 1974 and the end of 1975) and the aircraft were duly registered as A4O-VC, -VG, -VI, -VK and -VL respectively.

One of these aircraft (A4O-VL) was leased on to Air Ceylon for a 12-month period.

The VC10s allowed Gulf Air to develop its routes to Europe, India and the Far East. After a hectic three-year schedule, the Gulf Air VC10s were withdrawn from service by the end of 1977 and flown to the UK to be placed in storage at Filton. All were subsequently converted into VC10 K.2 three-point tankers for the RAF.

Super VC10 for BOAC

Long before the first flight of the prototype G-ARTA, Vickers and BOAC had discussions regarding a stretched version capable of accommodating sufficient additional seating to effectively reduce the overall seat-per-mile

ABOVE G-ARVG was the seventh VC10 Type 1101 delivered to BOAC in September 1964. Air Ceylon never owned a VC10 but leased aircraft from BOAC to operate the London to Colombo route, which were allocated on an availability basis. G-ARVG was photographed at Heathrow with Air Ceylon titles on the aircraft nose and doors. *(BAE SYSTEMS Image Ref MP27293)*

cost to a level suitable for the competitive transatlantic routes.

Vickers was always confident that the stretch required was relatively easy to achieve, and so it emerged. Initially, Vickers offered a 212-seat version but after some consideration, BOAC

BELOW G-ARVK was the tenth VC10 Type 1101 ordered by BOAC and delivered in March 1964. It was later leased to Gulf Air in 1975, where it operated in their colours while retaining its UK registration. It was finally acquired by Gulf Air in June 1975 and adopted the marks A4O-VK. This image was taken while still on lease to Gulf Air. The aircraft was on approach to Heathrow with full trailing-edge flaps and leading-edge slats deployed. *(Richard Vandervord)*

ABOVE BOAC's third Super VC10 – G-ASGC – is preserved with the Duxford Aviation Society's British Airliner Collection. G-ASGC entered service with BOAC on 1 January 1965 and was finally withdrawn in April 1980 when it was flown to Duxford for preservation. This image shows the first-class cabin of the aircraft preserved just as it was when it was withdrawn from regular airline use. The plastic covers seen on the headrests of the two rows adjacent to the aisles have been added to prevent damage by visitors to the aircraft at Duxford. *(Keith Wilson)*

ABOVE The forward galley on G-ASGC, the area that provided food and refreshments to passengers in the first-class cabin. The BOAC bag adds a nice touch! *(Keith Wilson)*

BELOW The starboard rear galley which provided the refreshments to the economy-class passengers. *(Keith Wilson)*

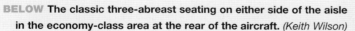

BELOW The classic three-abreast seating on either side of the aisle in the economy-class area at the rear of the aircraft. *(Keith Wilson)*

eventually opted for an aircraft that could accommodate 174 people (including cabin staff), or a typical figure of 163 economy-class passengers. Designated the Type 1151, it featured a fuselage lengthened by 17ft 8in by inserting a 71in parallel section plug between the flight deck and forward cabin section, with a similar 81in plug between the centre and rear sections. More powerful Rolls-Royce RCo.43 Conway engines, each producing 22,500lb of thrust were fitted. The range was increased with the addition of a 1,350-gallon fuel tank inside the tailfin.

In June 1960, BOAC had converted 20 options on the standard VC10 for 10 firm orders for the 212-seat version. In 1961, this number was increased to 20. This order was amended in January 1962 to just 30 Super VC10s – with 8 of them in a passenger/freight 'Combi' format – featuring a large forward fuselage freight door, along with a strengthened fuselage floor. However, the final order for Super VC10s was later reduced to just 17 with the 'Combi' version being entirely cancelled.

The first Super VC10 – registered G-ASGA – made its maiden flight from Brooklands on 7 May 1964, when it became the largest aircraft ever to lift off from the 4,200ft Brooklands runway. This aircraft performed a memorable display at the SBAC show at Farnborough in September 1964.

The first two Super VC10 deliveries to BOAC were G-ASGC and -E, which joined the airline at London Airport on 27 March 1965. They were shortly followed by three others, so, by the end of April 1965, five Super VC10s were already in BOAC service.

G-ASGG was retained by the manufacturer to conduct automatic landing trials and arrived with BOAC on 21 June 1967. The final (and 17th) Super VC10 – G-ASGR – made its first flight at Brooklands on 12 February 1969 and was delivered to BOAC on 31 May that year.

East African Airways

In March 1965, East African Airways (EAA) placed an order for three Type 1154 Super VC10s, each to be fitted with a large forward freight door and powered by the uprated Rolls-Royce RCo.43 Conway engines. The

ABOVE Another beautiful air-to-air study, this time of BOAC Super VC10 Type 1151 G-ASGD ahead of its delivery to the airline in April 1965. G-ASGD was withdrawn from service by British Airways in 1981 before being acquired by the RAF as ZD232. It was flown to Brize Norton and placed into storage before being broken up in 1982. *(BAE SYSTEMS)*

BELOW A typical Heathrow scene in the mid-1960s. Five BOAC VC10 aircraft (both standard and Super examples including G-ARVK and G-ASGF) are seen on the ramp with a Ghana Airways example – 9G-ABO – alongside a BOAC Boeing 707-436 (G-APFD) and an unidentified Middle East Airlines Comet 4C. *(BAE SYSTEMS Image Ref MP27292)*

RIGHT 5X-UVA was the first aircraft of five ordered by EAA towards the end of the VC10's relatively short production run. It was built as a Type 1154 and was delivered to EAA on 3 September 1966. It had a relatively short career, however, as it was destroyed in a take-off accident at Addis Ababa on 18 April 1972.
(BAE SYSTEMS Image Ref WCN2017)

aircraft were being funded by a lease/purchase agreement and the first – registered 5X-UVA – was handed over at Wisley on 30 September 1966. The second aircraft (5H-MMT) was delivered less than a month later and both were soon operating on EAA's routes. In May 1967, the third aircraft (5Y-ADA) was delivered and at the same time an order was placed for a fourth aircraft (5X-UVJ) with an option for a fifth (5H-MOG). These were delivered in April 1969 and February 1970 respectively. 5H-MOG was the very last VC10 to leave the production line at Weybridge, making its first flight on 16 February 1970.

All five aircraft served EAA well. However, following the 'Open Skies' agreement – an international policy concept that called for the liberalisation of the rules and regulations of the international aviation industry (especially commercial aviation) to create a free-market environment – things got much tougher for EAA and impacted upon their financial position.

Then disaster struck when 5X-UVA crashed while taking off from Addis Ababa on 18 April 1972, killing 43 of the 107 passengers on board.

Political troubles in the area added to EAA's woes and when the leaders of both Uganda and Tanzania were unable to fund their share of the airline, the end was in sight. On 28 January 1977, EAA ceased to operate and the aircraft were placed into storage at Nairobi. Eventually, the remaining four EAA Super VC10s were repossessed by BAC and flown to Filton, the last aircraft arriving on 3 August. The aircraft were stored in protective 'dri-clad' covers while a decision was made on their future. This wasn't long in coming – it was decided that all four would be converted to VC10 K.3 standards for the RAF.

VIP VC10s

Government of the United Arab Emirates

In 1974, G-ARVF was sold to the government of the United Arab Emirates. After conversion it

BELOW An EAA Super VC10 with the large main cargo door – a feature of all Type 1154 aircraft constructed for EAA – demonstrates the ease of loading and unloading cargo at Heathrow Airport.
(BAE SYSTEMS Image Ref MP26089)

was flown in a VVIP fit until being retired in 1981 and flown to Germany for preservation at the Flugausstellung Hermeskeil.

Omani Royal Flight

Between 1975 and 1981, G-ARVJ was operated by BA for the Emir of Qatar under a wet-lease arrangement. The aircraft was painted in a Gulf Air colour scheme and was sometimes used as a standby aircraft for them.

Sultanate of Oman

Originally built as a Type 1103 for BUA as G-ASIX, this aircraft featured the large main deck cargo door. The aircraft was acquired by the Sultan of Oman and converted into the VVIP

ABOVE G-ARVF was the sixth VC10 Type 1101 produced for BOAC and was delivered in September 1964. Following the merger of BOAC and BEA to form British Airways, G-ARVF was painted into the new airline's colours. It was sold to the United Arab Emirates in June 1974 and had the interior converted for a VVIP role. It was withdrawn from service and flown to Germany (where this image was taken) for preservation at the Flugausstellung Hermeskeil, in 1981. *(Stefan Roehrich)*

BELOW Another VVIP conversion was carried out to A4O-AB. The aircraft was initially built as a Type 1103 for BUA as G-ASIX and featured the large main deck cargo door. The aircraft was acquired by the Sultan of Oman and converted into the VVIP role in a style befitting the owner. The large main cargo door was not required in the new role and was sealed during the conversion process. The aircraft was a regular visitor to London Heathrow where this image was taken in October 1982. In 1987, the aircraft was withdrawn from service and flown to Brooklands for preservation, where it is displayed today. *(Richard Vandervord)*

LEFT The interior of A4O-AB preserved at the Brooklands Museum; a Type 1103 VC10 originally constructed for BUA as G-ASIX. Its conversion to a VVIP configuration makes an interesting comparison with the former BOAC Super VC10 G-ASGC preserved at Duxford (see page 58). This image shows the main cabin area, including the seat with the royal crest, usually occupied by the sultan. *(Keith Wilson)*

LEFT The main state room usually occupied by the sultan. *(Keith Wilson)*

BELOW LEFT At the rear of the aircraft the original six-abreast economy seating was replaced with velvet-covered first-class seating. *(Keith Wilson)*

BELOW The starboard rear galley. *(Keith Wilson)*

ABOVE The rear of the gold royal lavatory area. *(Keith Wilson)*

BELOW The front of the royal lavatory area provided an obviously high level of luxury for the occupant although perhaps a little surprisingly, the fittings were not gold! *(Keith Wilson)*

role in a style befitting its owner. The large main cargo door was not required in the new role and was sealed during the conversion process. The aircraft – now registered as A4O-AB – was a regular visitor to the UK. In 1987, it was withdrawn from service and flown to Brooklands for preservation at the Brooklands Museum, where it resides today.

Royal tours

A special VVIP cabin interior was developed by Vickers for BOAC use when the aircraft had members of the royal family, prime ministers or senior cabinet ministers on board. The VC10 was a particular favourite with the royal family and especially HM the Queen, who used the aircraft on a number of her Commonwealth tours.

In February and March 1966, she toured the Caribbean in a BOAC VC10. In March 1970 she visited Australia to participate in the

BELOW Her Majesty Queen Elizabeth II shakes hands with Keith Granville, BOAC's deputy chairman, on her arrival at London Airport. She had been on one of the airline's Super VC10 aircraft after her Caribbean tour in February and March 1966. *(Speedbird Heritage Collection/BOAC image 66792)*

James Cook bicentennial celebrations and was accompanied by the Prince of Wales and Princess Anne.

In January and February 1974, accompanied by HRH the Duke of Edinburgh, Princess Anne, Captain Mark Phillips and the Prince of Wales, the Queen attended the Commonwealth Games in Christchurch, New Zealand.

In May 1980, accompanied by HRH the Duke of Edinburgh, she made a short tour to open the new High Court of Australia building.

British Airways withdraw the standard VC10

When BOAC and BEA merged in April 1974 to form British Airways, the days of the VC10s – particularly the standard examples – were numbered. The arrival of the large fan-engined Boeing 747-100 and -200 signalled routes being lost by the VC10.

As part of the purchase agreement for new Boeing 747 aircraft, Boeing took three standard VC10s – G-ARVB, -E and -H – in part payment. Most had expected the aircraft

ABOVE Her Majesty Queen Elizabeth II, accompanied by HRH Prince Philip, receives a salute from the captain of the British Airways VC10 as they board at Heathrow Airport ahead of a visit to Australia in May 1980. *(Speedbird Heritage Collection/BOAC image 800963)*

BELOW A very famous air show image involved a British Airways VC10, G-ARVM, providing a low pass at White Waltham during the show in May 1977. One wonders just how low it actually was. *(Peter R. March)*

to be flown to an Arizona resting place but, in a move that shocked many, Boeing decided to break them up at Heathrow, right in front of the public and airline employees alike. Using mechanical diggers to smash them to pieces, it was an ignominious end to three aircraft that had served the airline well. More importantly, it was a clear statement of intent from Boeing that kept VC10 aircraft off the commercial market!

Five standard VC10s were leased to Gulf Air before being sold to the airline; G-ARVF had been sold to the government of the United Arab Emirates; G-ARVJ had been leased to the Qatar Amiri Flight from 1975 to 1981; while G-ARVM was kept in service in full BA livery as a back-up aircraft for the Super VC10 fleet until 1979, when it was donated to the RAF Museum at Cosford. The five remaining standard VC10s were sold to the RAF in 1977 for spares, although they were later converted to K.2 tankers in about 1982.

The final Super VC10 commercial flight

The BA fleet of Super VC10 aircraft lasted until 1980. Most airframes were removed from service and placed into storage at either Prestwick or Abingdon, to await their eventual fate. Their period of storage was much longer than many had expected and eventually, in 1987, the RAF purchased the entire fleet. A number were subsequently broken for spares; however, five were converted into two-point K.4 tankers and continued to serve with the RAF for many years. One aircraft – G-ASGC – was preserved. It was flown to Duxford in April 1980 where it remains today with the Duxford Aviation Society and is resplendent in a blue, white and gold BOAC Cunard livery.

The last commercial flight operated by a BA Super VC10 fell to G-ASGF, which flew from Dar es Salaam, via Larnaca into Heathrow on 29 March 1981. The flight marked the end of an era.

Following this, BA operated three commercial charters for enthusiasts using G-ASGL, with the last of these touching down at Heathrow on 30 March 1982. All that remained were the ferry flights to Abingdon and Prestwick.

CIVILIAN VC10 ACCIDENTS AND INCIDENTS

- 28 December 1968: Middle East Airlines 9G-ABP was destroyed at Beirut Airport in the 1968 Israeli raid on Lebanon.
- 20 November 1969: Nigerian Airways Flight 825 (5N-ABD) crashed on landing at Lagos, Nigeria, killing all 87 passengers and crew.
- 27 November 1969: BOAC G-ASGK had a major failure of No 3 engine, debris from that engine damaged No 4 engine and caused a fire. A safe overweight landing was made at Heathrow without any casualties.
- 9 September 1970: BOAC G-ASGN was hijacked, and on 12 September was blown up at Zerqu, Jordan, in the Dawson's Field hijackings.
- 28 January 1972: British Caledonian G-ARTA was damaged beyond economic repair in a landing accident at Gatwick.
- 18 April 1972: East African Airways Flight 720 5X-UVA crashed on take-off from Addis Ababa, Ethiopia, killing 43 of the 107 passengers and crew.
- 3 March 1974: BOAC G-ASGO was hijacked and landed at Schiphol, the Netherlands, where the aircraft was set on fire and damaged beyond economic repair.
- 21 November 1974: British Airways Flight 70 from Dubai to Heathrow, carrying 45 people, was hijacked in Dubai, landing at Tripoli for refuelling before flying on to Tunis. The three hijackers demanded the release of Palestinian prisoners, five in Egypt and two in the Netherlands. One hostage was murdered. The hijackers surrendered after 84 hours to Tunisian authorities on 25 November.
  Captain Jim Futcher was awarded the Queen's Gallantry Medal, the Guild of Air Pilots and Air Navigators Founder's Medal, the British Airline Pilots Association Gold Medal and a Certificate of Commendation from British Airways for his actions during the hijacking, returning to fly the aircraft knowing the hijackers were on board.

Chapter Four

Royal Air Force VC10s at peace

With the arrival of the VC10 C.1, a significant new addition was made to the strategic long-range force of RAF Transport Command and its airlift capacity. Until the advent of the Lockheed TriStar in 1983, it was the heaviest aircraft ever to enter service with the RAF and offered true global mobility. With its combination of speed and capacity, it offered a higher productive factor than ever previously attained by a Transport Command type.

OPPOSITE A beautiful air-to-air study of a 10 Squadron Vickers VC10 C.1, XR807, photographed 8 December 1971. The aircraft's graceful lines justify her nickname 'Queen of the Skies'.
(Crown Copyright/Air Historical Branch image TN-1-6481-125)

ABOVE An unidentified Royal Air Force VC10 C.1 on the production line at Brooklands in 1966. At the time of the image, the aircraft was without engines and still up on jacks. *(Crown Copyright/Air Historical Branch image T-6149)*

BELOW XR806 was the first VC10 C.1 for the RAF. It is seen here waiting outside the main production facility at Brooklands in February 1965 ahead of its first flight, which was made on the 26th. *(BAE SYSTEMS Image Ref MP24169)*

History

On 29 November 1955, the government cancelled the Vickers V.1000 project, which had primarily been developed for BOAC, although it also met an RAF requirement. Shortly afterwards, under Air Ministry pressure, the RAF were forced to make budget cuts; they too cancelled their order for six V.1000 aircraft, replacing them with Britannia aircraft assembled at the Shorts factory in Belfast, an area suffering high unemployment. Interestingly, Shorts was 69.5% owned by the government and the second Britannia production line situated there was in need of work, owing to a lack of orders.

Licking their wounds, Vickers went back to the drawing board, and continued to develop concepts and ideas, one of which was the four-engine VC10, designed to a very tight specification for BOAC to operate on their 'Empire' routes to Africa and the Far East. Interestingly, the RAF also served bases in the Far East, and therefore had an interest in this type of aircraft.

In 1958, BOAC placed an order with Vickers for 35 VC10 aircraft. The VC10 was first considered as a potential new aircraft for RAF Transport Command in discussions on future strategic long-range requirements during 1959. These discussions eventually led to an order for ten Shorts Britannics (later named Belfast) to handle outsize, bulky loads then being conveyed by the Blackburn Beverley.

In April 1960, the VC10 was selected along with the Comet 4 – five of each – to replace the Comet 2 fleet which was expected to reach the end of its fatigue life in 1963–64. The five Comets were quickly placed under contract and delivered into service in 1961–62. The military version of the VC10 was produced to RAF Specification C239 of 1960 and the order for the five VC10 C.1 aircraft was officially made public at the SBAC show at Farnborough in September 1961.

Initially, Vickers allocated Type 1105 for the version covering transport of passengers and

aeromedical evacuation. However, the Air Staff were reappraising the situation, planning to take advantage of the large forward fuselage freight door fitted to the BUA Type 1103.

In November 1962, Vickers issued a revised specification for what was effectively a 'hybrid' VC10. It featured an enhanced take-off weight of 323,000lb – a significant increase of 11,000lb over the Type 1105. The new variant combined the short fuselage of the standard VC10 with the Super's wings, tailplane, undercarriage and fuel capacity along with the higher-powered RCo.43 Conway Mk 550 engines – designated Mk 301 by the RAF – plus the large forward freight door along with a significant strengthened floor with cargo lashing points. Air Staff Requirement (ASR) 378 and Ministry of Aviation (MoA) Specification C239 were issued for the aircraft.

Type 1106 military specification changes

The basic design of the C.1 followed the commercial VC10 in meeting British Civil Airworthiness Requirements with the military changes made in accordance with MoA requirements covered in their AvP370 manual. The main elements of these changes were:

- A strengthened cabin freight floor with cargo lashing points on the floor, lower and upper cabin sidewalls. The floor was designed to accept the *Rolomat* side-guidance roller conveyor system for palletised loads (similar to that installed in the Argosy).
- Additional lighting at lower sidewall level to assist freight loading operations.
- An air-quartermaster (loadmaster) station at the rear of the passenger cabin.
- Additional military avionics and instruments including enhanced HF communications, multi-channel UHF, TACAN and IFF.

RIGHT A view of the forward freight area on the VC10 C.1, looking from the cockpit door towards the tail. This was a flexible installation and could be used for straight cargo, a troop transport or have rows of rearward-facing seats installed to fit the mission requirement. *(BAE SYSTEMS Image Ref MP26123)*

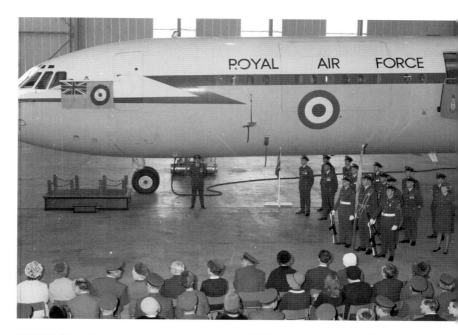

ABOVE The official delivery ceremony for the RAF's first VC10 C.1 – XR806 – was conducted at Wisley on 7 July 1966. At the same ceremony, the aircraft was formally named *George Thompson VC*, which it carried just behind the cockpit. *(Crown Copyright/Air Historical Branch image PRB-2-527-8)*

LEFT All RAF VC10 C.1s featured the forward freight door originally designed for the BUA Type 1103. *(BAE SYSTEMS Image Ref MP32574)*

LEFT The VC10 could be quickly converted for the casualty evacuation (Casevac) role. In this configuration, the VC10 was able to carry up to 78 stretchers on these special bunks, along with further seats for six medical attendants and two air-quartermasters. *(BAE SYSTEMS Image Ref MP26437)*

- A comprehensively equipped navigator's station to enable operations away from civil air routes and to remote bases worldwide.
- An air-to-air refuelling (AAR) receiving capability utilising a 9ft-long nose-mounted probe with two nose-mounted spotlights for night-time illumination.
- The design and future embodiment of AAR-dispensing capability via fuselage and wing-mounted hose/drogue refuelling pods.
- A liquid oxygen system similar to that developed for the BOAC standard VC10 but, like that variant, subsequently replaced by a conventional gaseous system.
- A Bristol Siddeley Artouste auxiliary power unit (APU) mounted in the fuselage tailcone to provide ground electrical power and compressed air for engine starting. This made the aircraft effectively self-supporting, especially at some of the remote bases it was expected to visit.

The remaining aspects of the aircraft – cabin trim, amenities, galleys – were largely unchanged from the civil airline variants.

Following the initial order for five aircraft, a further six were ordered in 1962 and a final three in July 1964, making a total order of fourteen. The last three aircraft had originally been Type 1152 Super VC10 aircraft destined for BOAC, but when the airline negotiated a reduction in their order, the aircraft were complete as Type 1106 aircraft for the RAF.

RIGHT The VC10 C.1 was designed with a provision of in-flight refuelling facility, although the removable 9ft-long probe was not fitted at the time of their delivery. Subsequently, most aircraft had this facility added during their service lives, which provided a genuine global range to the aircraft. *(BAE SYSTEMS Image Ref MP24885)*

LEFT One addition unique to the RAF VC10 C.1 aircraft was the installation of a Bristol Siddeley/Turboméca Artouste 520 auxiliary power unit (APU) in the tailcone. The APU provided compressed air for engine starting and could drive a 40KVa generator to operate essential electrical services on the ground. *(BAE SYSTEMS Image Ref WH17801)*

ABOVE **Shortly after delivery to 10 Squadron, then based at RAF Fairford, XR808 commenced crew standardisation trials before operating route-proving flights to Hong Kong, where it was photographed on 23 August 1966.** *(Crown Copyright/Air Historical Branch image T-6677)*

The MoA allocated serial numbers XR808–10, XV101–6 and XV107–9. The MoA also issued a further batch of five serials (XV110–14) covering a further five aircraft, but these were never ordered.

First flight

The first VC10 C.1 for the RAF (XR806) made its initial flight at Weybridge on 26 November 1965 and it was followed by XR807 on 25 March 1966. Both aircraft participated in company flight testing before being delivered to the A&AEE at Boscombe Down – arriving on 19 and 24 May 1966 respectively. These trials effectively covered the military elements of the Type 1106 and included a 15-hour air-to-air refuelling sortie with a Victor tanker.

First deliveries and proving trials

RAF Transport Command took delivery of its first VC10 (XR808) on 7 July 1966 during a formal ceremony at Wisley. Handing the aircraft over to Air Chief Marshal Sir Kenneth Cross, AOC Transport Command, was Lord Portal, chairman of the British Aircraft Corporation. The AOC professed himself very pleased that the aircraft had been 'delivered two months earlier than originally planned, British and best'.

The first overseas route proving flight (by XR808) took place to Hong Kong and left Lyneham on 22 August 1966. The captain,

Sqn Ldr B.E. Taylor, and co-pilot Sqn Ldr A.C. Musgrove, had been part of the Transport Command liaison team, working with Vickers and BAC for the previous three years.

BELOW **Leading the crew on the route-proving flights were Sqn Ldr B.E. Taylor (captain) and Sqn Ldr A.C. Musgrove (co-pilot). Both had been with the Transport Command liaison team working with BAC and Vickers on the VC10 project for the previous three years.** *(Crown Copyright/Air Historical Branch image T-6672)*

ABOVE Transport Command's fleet of long-range aircraft photographed at RAF Fairford in April 1967. Alongside VC10 C.1 XR807 (of 10 Squadron) are Comet C.4 XR396 (216 Squadron), Britannia C.1 XM520 (99/511 Squadron) and Belfast C.1 XR365 (53 Squadron). *(Crown Copyright/Air Historical Branch image T-7158)*

RIGHT No 10 Squadron started scheduled services from RAF Brize Norton to a number of British overseas bases including Belize, Cyprus and Gütersloh, along with destinations in the USA and Canada. C.1 XR808 was photographed outside the main terminal at Brize Norton awaiting its passengers in April 1990. *(Keith Wilson)*

BELOW An unusual air-to-air formation photograph of a 10 Squadron VC10 C.1, XV103, while flying in formation with Vulcan B.2, XL387, of 230 OCU. The photograph was taken from a Lindholme Hastings on 14 August 1972 in a photoshoot flown to show the importance of both aircraft types to the then new-look RAF Strike Command. *(Crown Copyright/Air Historical Branch image TN-1-6629-4)*

Into service with 10 Squadron

No 10 Squadron, initially based at RAF Fairford and later at RAF Brize Norton, operated the VC10 C.1 fleet. The first operational flight was to Changi, Singapore, on 20 January 1967. Regular scheduled flights commenced on 4 April 1967 with Hong Kong the destination. Eventually, VC10 C.1 aircraft operated 27 flights per month to the Far East via the Persian Gulf and, later, regular scheduled services were added to Washington/Dulles ('The Washington Trooper') and then on to Belize, as well as to Akrotiri, Cyprus. As the second largest operator of the VC10 to BOAC, 10 Squadron performed a true 'military airline' operation and were often nicknamed 'RAF Airlines'.

The VC10 C.1s of 10 Squadron, nicknamed 'Shiny Tens' because of the finish on the aircraft,

shared their Brize Norton base with the Belfast C.1s of 53 Squadron, and both types used the 'Autoland' blind-landing system installed at the base. At the time, this was the most advanced of its type anywhere in the world.

Transport Command was renamed Air Support Command (RAFASC) on 1 August 1967 and those VC10 aircraft flying with Transport Command titles on the fuselage were quickly replaced with the titles of their new owners. Air Support Command's VC10 service to Singapore took 19½ hours, including transit stops at Bahrain and Gan. This was 4½ hours faster than the Comet C.4 and 12 hours faster than the Britannia. Hong Kong could be reached by VC10 in 22 hours from the UK.

Royal and VIP flights

An early addition to the VC10 C.1's capability was the Royal Flight and VIP duties, conducted using aircraft 'Modification No. 21'. This introduced all of the necessary alterations to the cabin to accommodate an interior worthy of the VVIP passengers it was designed to carry. The first use as a royal aircraft was one arranged at very short notice, carrying the Prince of Wales, prime minister Harold Wilson and leader of the opposition Edward Heath to the memorial service for the late Harold Holt, the Australian prime minister who had tragically died in a swimming accident. XV105 departed Heathrow on 20 December 1967, flying to Melbourne in 21 hours and 46 minutes – an unofficial record – with stops at Muharraq and Gan for refuelling and crew changes.

The first dedicated royal flight took place in November 1968, when XV107 took HM the Queen from London to Recife on a state visit to Brazil and Chile. Royal and VVIP flights were to become a major feature of 10 Squadron's activities in the next 33 years.

The last occasion that a VC10 C.1 was used by HM the Queen was on a three-week visit to the Caribbean, with the aircraft (XV108) arriving at Heathrow on 10 March 1994. The last VC10 ministerial flight took place on 21 November 2001 when the then foreign secretary, Jack Straw, flew to Tehran, Islamabad and Bahrain in XV102.

Wallis, Duchess of Windsor

When Wallis, Duchess of Windsor, died in Paris on 24 April 1986, 10 Squadron were asked to return her body to the UK for burial, under Operation Haze. A VC10 C.1 was specially prepared for the flight and flown to Orly Airport the following day. On board was the Lord Chamberlain, the Earl of Airlie, along with the royal undertakers and embalmers, plus the movements team to load, secure and then unload the lead-lined coffin. The forward hold was fitted out with black curtains to ensure privacy.

The return flight to RAF Benson on 27 April was uneventful, as would have been expected of a royal duty; however, timing was of paramount importance. A vehicle was placed near the runway threshold, in radio contact

ABOVE The flight crew from 10 Squadron chosen to fly HM the Queen and HRH Prince Philip on state visits to Brazil (5–11 November 1968) and Chile (11–18 November 1968), gathered outside their VC10 at RAF Brize Norton ahead of the trip. *(Crown Copyright/ Air Historical Branch image T-9804)*

LEFT One of the cabin crew demonstrates the luxury of the special VIP interior fitted to the aircraft for the state visits to Brazil and Chile in 1968. *(Crown Copyright/Air Historical Branch image T-9806)*

with the aircraft to ensure its touchdown was accurate to the second.

Once parked on to the special stand, the coffin was released and carefully manoeuvred on ball rollers, feet first through the curtain, on to the shoulders of the waiting RAF Regiment pallbearers. The oak lid of the coffin had been polished before unloading, as one of the wreaths placed on the coffin had dampened it. Being lead-lined, the coffin weighed over 600lb and the bearers gave quite a gasp once they shouldered the full weight.

Her funeral was held at St George's Chapel, Windsor Castle, and she was buried next to Edward in the Royal Burial Ground near Windsor Castle, as 'Wallis, Duchess of Windsor'.

Engine test bed G-AXLR

10 Squadron reached full strength with the delivery of the 14th and final VC10 – XV109 – on 31 July 1968. However, this was to be short-lived as after less than nine months later the squadron strength was reduced when XR809 was leased to Rolls-Royce to be used as a flying test bed for the RB211 engine destined to power the Lockheed TriStar. XR809 was delivered to Hucknall on 17 April 1969 and after conversion flew in her new guise as G-AXLR on 6 March 1970. A single RB211 had replaced the pair of Conway engines on the port side of the aircraft.

At the conclusion of the programme, the aircraft was never returned to the RAF. In 1973,

BELOW Perhaps a little surprisingly, the RAF made XR809 available to Rolls-Royce as an engine test bed. A pair of Rolls-Royce Conway engines was retained on the starboard side of the engine mountings, while a single RB211 was fitted to the port side. The aircraft, registered G-AXLR, made its first flight in this configuration at Hucknall on 6 March 1970. The RB211 engine was being tested ahead of its use in the Lockheed TriStar. (BAE SYSTEMS)

a team was gathered together by BAC to consider the cost and engineering implications of returning the aircraft back to its Type 1106 specification but, in the end, the cost of restoration was just too high – especially when one considers the cuts to the defence spending programme at the time. The aircraft was flown to Kemble on 26 September 1975 where it was gradually stripped of spares before being used for SAS training exercises, during which time it was painted with 'Crab Air' (a common army nickname for the RAF) on the forward fuselage. In October 1982, it was finally scrapped.

Round-the-world trip

From 29 to 31 July 1969, a VC10 C.1 undertook a round-the-world flight from Brize Norton in just 45 hours and 15 minutes. The 20,960 miles were completed at an average 450mph. Two aircrews were involved, the purpose being to investigate fatigue effects on aircrews, with four doctors on board undertaking monitoring activities.

XX914

British Caledonian Airways (BCAL) had inherited three standard VC10 aircraft after their acquisition of British United Airways (BUA) in November 1970. The type did not fit into their planned fleet profile and by 1973 were looking to dispose of them. One was sold to Air Malawi, another to the Oman Royal Flight while the third – G-ATDJ – was acquired by MoD (PE) in March 1973 for use by the Royal Aircraft Establishment (RAE) at Thurleigh as XX914. The aircraft was painted

ROLLS-ROYCE RB 211 FLYING TEST BED

G-AXLR

in an attractive white, grey, red and yellow livery with 'Royal Aircraft Establishment' titles by BAC, Filton. It served with Aero Flight on flight testing duties, including airframe structural responses to turbulence, which involved the fitting of a large number of strain gauges to the aircraft.

The aircraft had a remarkably short operational career with the RAE and was grounded in 1975, partly owing to the high costs of operating such an aircraft. It never flew again and was scrapped in 1983. It did, however, 'donate' its tailfin to K.2 ZA141 after that aircraft had suffered severely wrinkled skin damage to its original tailfin while engaged in its post-conversion flight test programme during the infamous 'Flight 16' episode over Wales. Two sections of the fuselage from XX914 were later delivered to the Air Movements School at Brize Norton where they were once again joined together and operated as 8777M. Its shortened fuselage was used by the school until the VC10 was withdrawn from RAF service in 2013.

VC10 K.2 and K.3 conversions

An AAR tanker variant of the VC10 had long been sought by Air Staff as far back as the mid-1960s (see Chapter 8 for more details). BAC undertook a number of design studies which confirmed the viability of such a

ABOVE XX914, a Type 1102, had originally been ordered by Ghana Airways and the registration 9G-ABQ allocated. When the order was cancelled, it was acquired by BUA and delivered in July 1965 as G-ATDJ. After the aircraft was then withdrawn from service in March 1973, it was procured by the RAF as XX914 and delivered to the Royal Aircraft Establishment. Here it was used by Aero Flight at RAE Thurleigh on flight-testing duties, including airframe structural responses to turbulence, which involved the fitting of a large number of strain gauges to the aircraft. The nose probe is not for AAR; instead it houses special instrumentation and sensors associated with the trials. *(BAE SYSTEMS Image Ref A4113-A)*

requirement, including the conversion of former airline aircraft, whenever they might become available. In 1977, a number of aircraft *did* become available. Firstly, following the financial failure of the East African Airways Corporation (EAA), four of the original five Super VC10 aircraft in storage at Nairobi were repossessed on behalf of the lessor by BAC. They were flown back to the UK and placed

RIGHT A technical diagram produced by British Aerospace demonstrating the modifications required to convert the standard airline version of the VC10 into a three-point air-to-air refuelling tanker. *(BAE SYSTEMS via Bristol Aero Collection Trust)*

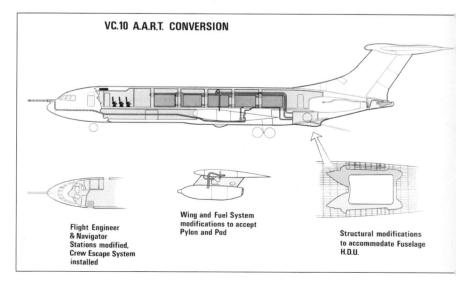

VC.10 A.A.R.T. CONVERSION

Flight Engineer & Navigator Stations modified, Crew Escape System installed

Wing and Fuel System modifications to accept Pylon and Pod

Structural modifications to accommodate Fuselage H.D.U.

LEFT **The scene at the British Aerospace Aircraft Group facility at Filton in the early 1980s. Three ex-EAA Super VC10s (including 5X-UVJ/ZA149) along with a pair of former Gulf Air standard VC10s (including A4O-VI/ZA142) are seen undergoing conversion to VC10 K.3 and K.2 tankers, respectively. The first K.2 conversion, ZA141, made its first post-conversion flight from Filton on 22 June 1982.** *(BAE SYSTEMS Image Ref A6072 via Bristol Aero Collection Trust)*

into storage at Filton. Shortly afterwards, in October and November 1977, five former BA and Gulf Air standard VC10s were being withdrawn from service and were therefore available. Initial informal discussions between British Aerospace and the RAF are said to have taken place after the annual cricket match between BAe and the Air Staff in the summer of 1977. Formal discussions continued between

Sir George Edwards and Air Marshal Sir Peter Terry and the feasibility of converting all nine aircraft into the military role was confirmed. The studies made more than a decade previously were dusted off and updated.

The first hurdle to overcome was one of ownership of the four former EAA Super VC10s. These had been leased to the airline utilising another government office in the form of the ECGD – the government's provider of export finance. Effectively, the ownership needed to be moved from one government office to another.

Correspondence made available during research for this book shows that in July 1977, British Aerospace were trying to broker an arrangement with ECGD on behalf of the RAF. The two oldest aircraft (5H-MMT and 5Y-ADA) were valued at £700,000 each, while the youngest pair (5X-UVJ and 5H-MOG) were valued at £750,000 each. With a spares

BELOW **Before being installed into the tanker aircraft, the fuselage auxiliary fuel cells underwent significant testing in the factory.** *(BAE SYSTEMS Image Ref WH12732)*

BELOW RIGHT **One of the VC10 K.2 conversions (probably ZA141) at Bristol with the auxiliary fuel cells having been installed into the fuselage.** *(BAE SYSTEMS Image Ref A6480 via Bristol Aero Collection Trust)*

package estimated at £1 million, the four aircraft were available for just £3.9 million – a bargain! Air Staff Requirement ASR406 was quickly issued for the purchase and conversion of all nine aircraft.

By November 1978, the aircraft were in storage at Filton, with BAe entering into a storage and maintenance agreement with MoD (PE) while awaiting the start of the conversion programme. This was confirmed in March 1978 with the British Aerospace Aircraft Group at Filton undertaking the work under the detailed design leadership of Weybridge – where many of the original team were still present.

Eventually, the aircraft moved into the Filton facility and work to convert them into three-point tankers commenced. The main features of the K.2 and K.3 conversion programme were:

- A centreline Mk. 17B hose drum unit (HDU) for refuelling large receiver aircraft.
- Two wing-mounted Flight Refuelling Mk. 32 AAR Pods (for the smaller receiving aircraft).
- Five fuel tanks installed in the former passenger cabin, mounted on a strengthened floor (a relatively easy task on the K.3 aircraft as they featured the large forward-fuselage freight door, but a significantly more complex one on the K.2 aircraft, which required sections of the fuselage to be removed in order to gain access).
- A permanently mounted 9ft-long nose-mounted AAR in-flight refuelling probe.
- A common engine – the Rolls-Royce RCo.43 Mk 301 Conway – was to be installed into both variants.

ABOVE LEFT Adding the auxiliary fuel cells to the fuselage of the former EAA VC10 K.3 conversions was relatively easy, as they could be added through the forward fuselage freight door and then moved into position. The process for the K.2 aircraft was far more complex and involved removing a number of the roof panels to gain access, as seen here. *(BAE SYSTEMS via Bristol Aero Collection Trust)*

ABOVE The installation of the fuselage centreline hose drum unit (HDU) involved significant engineering in the fuselage adjacent to what was previously the rear underfloor freight hold. Holes had to be cut into the pressurised structure and new pressure bulkheads rear and aft of the new structure added. The modifications enabled the installation of a Flight Refuelling Ltd Mk. 17B HDU, along with its associated equipment. *(BAE SYSTEMS Image Ref A6424 via Bristol Aero Collection Trust)*

LEFT Another change made to the K.2 and K.3 tanker conversions was the installation of a crew escape hatch on the port side of the fuselage, just behind the cockpit. This installation replaced the port forward entrance door; the only forward entrance then being possible was by using the starboard forward door. *(BAE SYSTEMS Image Ref A7106 via Bristol Aero Collection Trust)*

ABOVE **The first K.2 tanker conversion to fly was ZA141 and here we see it photographed at Filton on 22 June 1982, just ahead of that first flight. ZA141 was the only tanker conversion to fly in this grey/green camouflage and all of the remaining eight conversions were delivered in the then-standard 'hemp' colours. By early 1987, ZA141 was also operating in the 'hemp' colours.** *(BAE SYSTEMS Image Ref A6941 via Bristol Aero Collection Trust)*

- A Turboméca Artouste APU mounted in the fuselage tailcone (as fitted to the RAF C.1 variant).
- CCTV installed under the centre fuselage in a cupola to observe centreline HDU and wing pods.
- Military avionics.
- Flight engineer-operated AAR HDU and wing pod control panel and CCTV monitor.

The first conversion, K.2 ZA141, made its maiden flight at Filton on 22 June 1982, in a rather strange green/grey camouflage on the fuselage, tailplane and upper wing surfaces, earning itself the nickname 'The Lizard'. Development work continued and the aircraft was flown to Boscombe Down for testing. Later, after delivery to 101 Squadron, ZA141 was repainted in the standard all-over hemp colour scheme.

The first VC10 K.2 delivered into service was ZA140, which was flown from Filton to Brize Norton on 25 July 1983 to join the new Tanker Training Flight (TTF) officially formed on 1 August 1983 as part of 241 OCU.

No 101 Squadron was formed at Brize Norton on 1 May 1984 while deliveries continued and tasking commenced. The first K.3 – ZA150 – was delivered on 1 February 1985 with the last conversion – K.3 ZA148 – arriving at Brize Norton on 27 March 1986. It brought 101 Squadron up to its full strength of nine aircraft.

VC10 C.1K and K.4 conversions

The RAF had purchased the entire fleet of 14 remaining Super VC10 aircraft from British Airways on their retirement from service in 1981, together with a quantity of spares including a valuable pool of Conway engines – all at a

LEFT **Once accepted into service, the VC10 K.2 and K.3 tankers were called upon for testing a variety of receivers. Here, an unidentified Canberra from the Royal Aircraft Establishment was photographed while undergoing trials and is seen connected to the centreline HDU.** *(Crown Copyright/Air Historical Branch image AHB-101SQN-SLIDE-101-998)*

very 'economical' price. During April and May 1981, eleven aircraft were ferried to Abingdon for long-term storage, while the remaining three were ferried to Brize Norton for spares recovery and as ground instructional airframes. Serials in the range ZD230 to ZD243 were allocated, with some aircraft having this number applied just below the cockpit. In addition, the final former BA standard VC10, G-ARVJ, which had spent the latter part of its life operating in a VVIP configuration with the Emir of Qatar was also acquired by the RAF. It was ferried from Heathrow to Brize Norton in September 1982 with the serial ZD493 having been allocated.

The storage at Abingdon was to be a rather protracted affair. Sadly, funding for the conversion programme was difficult to achieve and the aircraft suffered badly from the elements during the delays. Eventually, five (ZD231 and 236–39) were broken up for spares between 1985 and 1987.

In 1989, the long-awaited approval for additional VC10 tanking capability in the form of the C.1K and K.4 was finally forthcoming. Staff Requirement (Air) (SR(A)) – formerly ASR – 415 covered the conversion of the five remaining former British Airways Super VC10s, then held in storage at Abingdon, into three-point tankers.

SR(A)-416 dealt with the conversion of eight of the remaining thirteen VC10 C.1 aircraft into two-point C.1K tankers that retained their air transport capability.

The conversion work was put out to tender by MoD (PE) and eventually won by BAe Manchester, with a contract being finally issued in January 1990. The five remaining former BA Super VC10s stored at Abingdon would each be made ready for a 'one-flight' only basis for transfer to Filton for conversion to K.4 configuration. Interestingly, these aircraft were flown by contractors under strict VFR day-only flight rules with the undercarriage remaining down throughout the short transit.

Meanwhile, on a subcontract basis to BAe, Flight Refuelling Aviation (FRA) at Bournemouth/

ABOVE During the acceptance trials at Boscombe Down, VC10 K.2 ZA141 underwent air-to-air refuelling trials with a Nimrod AEW.4 refuelling from the centreline HDU. This could dispense fuel at the rate of 500 gallons per minute. (BAE SYSTEMS Image Ref A6977 via Bristol Aero Collection Trust)

BELOW All of the remaining VC10 C.1 aircraft were converted to C.1K aircraft by Flight Refuelling, Hurn. XV101 was one of the first aircraft converted and returned to 10 Squadron in its 'shiny' colour scheme. It was photographed with both hoses trailing while on an air-to-air tow-line over the North Sea awaiting its next 'trade'. (Keith Wilson)

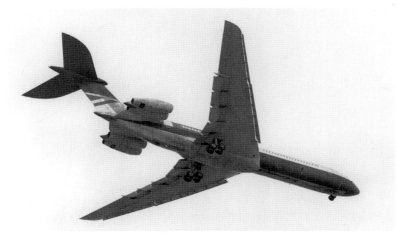

Hurn Airport would modify eight VC10 C.1 aircraft to C.1Ks, although this contract was later increased in 1992 to cover all 13 of the remaining VC10 C.1 fleet.

The first VC10 to undergo the K.4 programme (ZD242) was ferried to Filton on 27 July 1990, with the remaining four following within a year. A sixth (reserve) airframe was cut into sections and moved to Filton by road, being used for spares. The K.4 conversion was virtually identical to the K.3 programme, other than the addition of the five fuselage fuel tanks which were omitted for economic reasons. Instead, the passenger

compartment was retained, although rearward-facing seats were fitted.

The C.1K conversions were slower to get under way as FRA waited for a new purpose-built hangar to be completed. It came into use on 28 February 1991 when XV101 was flown into Hurn from Brize Norton. Once up and running, the hangar could accommodate two conversions, side by side. The first C.1K delivered back to 10 Squadron was XV103, which arrived back at Brize Norton. With the transition from 'air transport' to 'air transport and AAR', the squadron traded in their original blue uniforms for green flying suits as worn by the nearby 101 Squadron crews.

On 29 July 1993, the first flight by a K.4 was made at Filton by ZD242. After test flying by BAe, it was transferred to the A&AEE at Boscombe Down for flight trials. On 28 April 1994, it was the first aircraft delivered to 101 Squadron. The other four conversions followed in the next two years with ZD235 being the last to arrive at Brize Norton, when it landed on 8 March 1996.

The delivery of the last C.1K was made to 10 Squadron at Brize Norton when XR808 arrived on 7 February 1997. This now provided a total tanker force of 27 airframes, although this strength

did not last long as some of the K.2 airframes were already reaching the end of their design life.

Tow-lines and trails

No 101 Squadron earned a wonderful reputation for themselves and were regarded by many military operators as one of the very best air-to-air refuelling squadrons across the globe – aided greatly by the reliability of the VC10. Much of this was gained from their military exploits (covered in Chapter Five) although their peacetime operations are still highly regarded, especially by the 'trade' they refuelled on a daily basis.

Their bread-and-butter operations usually covered air-to-air refuelling of other RAF and occasionally Royal Navy assets, particularly fast jets. Most of these were conducted in special Air-to-Air Refuelling Areas (AARAs) around the UK, strategically located over the sea. Within these areas the VC10s would operate 'tow-lines', normally flown like a race track pattern, while providing air-to-air refuelling to the RAF's fast-jet assets, prolonging their sortie length and therefore maximising their training opportunities and effectiveness.

The VC10 aircraft were also popular when employed on 'trails', providing air-to-air refuelling capabilities for a group of fast-jet assets. This enabled the fast jets to transit to overseas destinations safely and then operate with other air forces or on training exercises. For example, exercise 'Maple Flag' is an advanced aerial combat training exercise hosted at the Canadian Forces Base at Cold Lake, Alberta. Established in 1978, 'Maple Flag' is one of the largest of such exercises in the world, as it makes use of the extensive

ABOVE VC10 K.4, ZD242/P, refuelling a 13 Squadron Tornado G.4A ZG713/F during an AAR tow-line over the North Sea. *(Crown Copyright/Air Historical Branch/Geoff Lee/Planefocus image GL-021123)*

BELOW With trials complete and deliveries to 101 Squadron progressing, the VC10 soon became a popular tanker aircraft with the fighter crews it was supporting. Here, XZ104/M, a 41 Squadron Jaguar GR.1A, is seen taking fuel from the starboard Mk. 32 pod of a K.3 while en route to Gander for a 'Maple Flag' exercise in 1992. *(Keith Wilson)*

BOTTOM VC10 K.2 ZA141/B of 101 Squadron in its then-standard 'hemp' colour scheme. It was photographed over the North Sea while refuelling a pair of 4 Squadron Harrier GR.7 aircraft – ZG856/CJ and ZG509/CH – in 1992. *(Keith Wilson)*

ABOVE Both the K.2 and K.3 variants of the VC10 had three-point tanking capabilities and the centreline HDU is seen here being put to good use. The view is over the captain's left shoulder as he moves the K.3 receiver aircraft on to the centreline basket of the K.2 tanker, high over the north-east coast of the UK, while the receiver was en route to Canada with a pair of Jaguar aircraft on their way to a 'Maple Flag' exercise. *(Keith Wilson)*

ABOVE RIGHT The K.3 is now plugged in and the green light on the K.2 HDU indicates that fuel is flowing. In a scenario such as this, where one tanker aircraft provides fuel to another, to ensure it is at its maximum capacity when setting off, was common with long-distance trails. The tanker aircraft in this situation is often referred to as the 'Whirler'. *(Keith Wilson)*

Cold Lake Air Weapons Range (CLAWR). The exercise itself currently occurs annually over a four-week period and provides realistic training for pilots from the Royal Canadian Air Force, as well as a number of allied air forces from around the world. The RAF has been regular participants at the event with Buccaneers, Harriers, Jaguars and Tornados participating over the years. The VC10 was usually the tanker of choice and would often act as the escort while providing up to eight air-to-air

refuelling brackets to each aircraft that it was escorting from its UK base to Cold Lake.

Similarly, the RAF has made regular use of Armament Practice Camps (APCs) – usually at Akrotiri in Cyprus. Once again, the VC10 was a popular tanker providing the AAR support to enable UK-based jets to get to Akrotiri in one hop.

The RAF's air-to-air refuelling assets were considered by senior officers as a 'Force Multiplier', meaning that with good AAR capabilities, their remaining fast-jet, transport and maritime reconnaissance assets could be effectively relocated to any theatre of conflict in a very short time. They could thereby become a rapid-reaction force, while effectively preventing the need to keep aircraft permanently stationed across the globe.

Farewell to No 10 Squadron

On 14 October 2005, No 10 Squadron was formally disbanded after 39 years' continuous service with the VC10. Ten of the original fourteen airframes originally delivered to the squadron were transferred to 101 Squadron, located on the opposite side of Brize Norton. The actual crews of both squadrons had been co-located since 2001 and qualified to operate all of the variants of the VC10.

LEFT All of the tanker conversions are equipped with a CCTV system, enabling the tanker's flight engineer to review proceedings from his position in the cockpit. The camera is mounted on the lower rear fuselage and is able to swivel between the two wing hose units, as well as viewing the centreline HDU on the K.2 and K.3 variants. Here, a Harrier GR.7 can be seen on the small screen. *(Keith Wilson)*

RIGHT No 101 Squadron sent VC10 K.2 ZA143/D to Miramar, California, in late 1995 as part of Exercise 'Scorpion Wind' to undertake a series of flights refuelling non-RAF aircraft. ZA143/D was photographed on 1 December 1995 refuelling a pair of EA-6B aircraft from MCAS Yuma, while three RAF Tornado GR.1s (one each from Nos 17, 617 and 9 Squadrons) await their turn. *(Crown Copyright/Air Historical Branch/AHB-MIS ScorpionWing-VC10-001)*

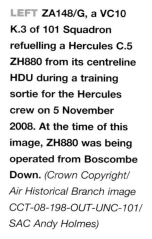

LEFT ZA148/G, a VC10 K.3 of 101 Squadron refuelling a Hercules C.5 ZH880 from its centreline HDU during a training sortie for the Hercules crew on 5 November 2008. At the time of this image, ZH880 was being operated from Boscombe Down. *(Crown Copyright/ Air Historical Branch image CCT-08-198-OUT-UNC-101/ SAC Andy Holmes)*

LEFT ZA149/H, a VC10 K3 of 101 Squadron, refuelling development Typhoon DA2 ZH588 fighter during AAR trials on 12 January 1998. ZH588 ceased flying in January 2007 and is now displayed at the RAF Museum, Hendon. *(Crown Copyright/Air Historical Branch image DPR-889-9)*

LEFT A 101 Squadron VC10 K.3, ZA149/H, refuels the prototype Airbus A400M (F-WWMT) during AAR trials in the autumn of 2010. F-WWMT was withdrawn from use in November 2013. *(PRM Aviation Collection)*

Special colours

The first special anniversary colour scheme added to a VC10 was probably unofficial when 101 Squadron hand-painted a cartoon on to the tail of VC10 K.3 ZA150/J in celebration of the 75th anniversary of the squadron in 1992.

The 40th anniversary of the VC10 was celebrated in July 2006 when XV104 was painted with a bright red fin, along with '40 Years of RAF Service' titles. It made regular appearances at shows up and down the country and was a popular performer that summer.

In the following year, XV105 was painted in special markings to celebrate the 90th anniversary of 101 Squadron. It featured an all-black tailfin with gold '101 Squadron' lettering, plus a large rendition of the squadron badge. Sadly, both of these schemes were only short-lived, each lasting around a year.

To commemorate the 50th anniversary of the VC10's first flight, XR808 – alias 'Bob' – was given special fin markings. The special markings also recognised the 95th anniversary of 101 Squadron.

The final flights

The long-established Brize Norton to Dulles Airport, Washington, VC10 schedule ceased in August 1995, being replaced by chartered seats on civil airline flights. However, 10 Squadron did continue the scheduled trips to Germany and Cyprus for a number of years, although all passenger services on VC10 C.1Ks were brought to an abrupt end on 15 January 2010 following an announcement concerning 'airworthiness issues'.

TOP No 10 Squadron VC10 C.1K, XV109, photographed refuelling ZD578/715, a Royal Navy Sea Harrier FA.2 from 899 Squadron. *(Crown Copyright/Air Historical Branch image DPR-750-8)*

ABOVE VC10 K.3, ZA148/G, accompanied by four Jaguar GR.3A aircraft (XX117/ES, XX723/EU, XZ109/EN and XZ399/EJ) from 6 Squadron at Coltishall, as they pass over Buckingham Palace on the occasion of HM the Queen's 80th birthday flypast, 17 June 2006. *(Crown Copyright/Air Historical Branch image VC10/SAC Ben Tritta)*

LEFT No 101 Squadron VC10 C.1K, XV107, was photographed with an Ilyushin IL-78 Mk. 1 – serial number RK-3452 – of the Indian Air Force (IAF) in the background, during Exercise 'Indra Dhanush' (ID) 06' in October 2006. The exercise aimed to further develop the good defence relationship between the IAF and the RAF. An 8 Squadron Sentry AEW.1 and the single VC10 were deployed to the IAF base at Agra, while six Tornado F.3 aircraft from 43 (F) Squadron were deployed to the IAF base at Gwalior. *(Crown Copyright/ Air Historical Branch image CCT-06-116-UNC-OUT-0088/Cpl Scott Robertson)*

RIGHT A 20 (R) Squadron Harrier T.10 along with two Harrier GR.9s fly in formation with a pair of Finnish Air Force F-18 Hornets while taking their turn to refuel from VC10 C.1K, XV108, over Finland during Exercise 'Lone Kestrel', 8 September 2001. *(Crown Copyright/Air Historical Branch image MNT01-119-OUT-UNC-008)*

RIGHT A 101 Squadron VC10 C.1K, XV108/Y, escorted four Typhoon aircraft from RAF Leuchars to the Royal Malaysian Air Force (RMAF) airbase at Butterworth, Malaysia, to take part in Exercise 'Bersama Lima' 11, marking the 40th anniversary of the Five Powers Defence Agreement (FPDA). The 7,000-mile trip from Leuchars to Butterworth took the pilots four days with stops in Jordan, Oman and Sri Lanka. Here, XV109 is seen with Typhoon FGR.4s ZK304/EB and ZK313/EN, accompanied by three Royal Australian Air Force (RAAF) F/A-18A aircraft during one of the exercise sorties. *(Geoff Lee/Planefocus image GLD-113139)*

RIGHT These special 'United States Air Force' colours were added to XR808 at Gatow in May 1990 for its part in the political thriller *The Package*. Set during the Cold War, the film starred Gene Hackman and Tommy Lee Jones. Many of the station airmen and their families were used as extras during the weekend's filming and were each paid £150 for two days' work. The RAF Benevolent Fund received a donation of £10,000. *(PRM Aviation Collection)*

BELOW No 101 Squadron hand-painted a cartoon on to the tail of VC10 K.3, ZA150/J, in celebration of the 75th anniversary of the squadron in 1992. *(Keith Wilson)*

LEFT VC10 C.1K, XV104, was painted in this special colour scheme to celebrate 40 years of service with the RAF for the VC10. The first aircraft – C.1 XR806 – entered service with 10 Squadron, then based at RAF Fairford, on 7 July 1966. *(PRM Aviation Collection)*

CENTRE VC10 C.1K, XV105, was painted into this special colour scheme to celebrate the 90th anniversary of 101 Squadron, which took place in July 2007. *(PRM Aviation Collection)*

BELOW To celebrate the passing from service of the VC10, the 50th anniversary of the first flight of the VC10 and the 95th anniversary of 101 Squadron, a special three-ship air-to-air formation sortie was planned. It had been hoped to fly one of each remaining variant of the VC10 (C.1K, K.3 and K.4) but, sadly, on the day the K.4 was replaced by the 'spare' aircraft, another C.1K. 'Lion Formation' was flown over AAR5 in the North Sea on 28 August 2013. It consisted of VC10 C.1K XR808 – nicknamed 'Bob' – nearest the camera in the special markings, K.3 (ZA147/F) and C.1K (XV108/Y). The formation was led by Sqn Ldr Tim Kemp of 101 Squadron.
(Geoff Lee/Planefocus image GHL-126036)

With the arrival of the C.1K and K.4 variants into the tanker fleet, it was time to say farewell to the five VC10 K.2 aircraft. These were the oldest aircraft in the fleet and had the highest number of airframe hours and cycles. ZA143 was the first to be withdrawn when it flew to St Athan on 21 August 1998 for a 'spares recovery programme' – a polite way of saying 'being broken up'! ZA142 was the last to leave; having made its final sortie on an AAR tow-line over the North Sea on 22 March 2001, it was flown to St Athan just five days later.

Some of the older C.1K aircraft were also involved in this programme. XV103 was flown to St Athan on 11 December 2001 to meet an ignominious end.

The final fleet drawdown commenced on 6 April 2010 when the first two (XR807 and XV109) of the 15 remaining VC10 aircraft in 101 Squadron service were flown to Bruntingthorpe for the dreaded 'spares recovery programme' – undertaken by GJD Services under contract from BAe Systems.

Three more C.1Ks were withdrawn in the lead-up to Christmas 2011 when XV102, XV107 and XV101 made their last flights into Bruntingthorpe.

Thankfully, while VC10s continued to make their last flight into Bruntingthorpe, it wasn't all bad news. ZA148 was ferried to Newquay for preservation, while ZA150 flew into Dunsfold for a fitting preservation with the Brooklands Museum.

The very last VC10 flight was made on 25 September 2013, when ZA147 was retired into Bruntingthorpe. It ended more than 47 years of VC10 operations with the RAF.

VC10s NAMED AFTER WINNERS OF THE VICTORIA CROSS

All VC10 C.1s were named after winners of the Victoria Cross. The full list is:

XR806	George Thompson VC
XR807	Donald Garland VC/Thomas Gray VC
XR808	Kenneth Campbell VC
XR809	Hugh Malcolm VC
XR810	David Lord VC
XV101	Lanoe Hawker VC
XV102	Guy Gibson VC
XV103	Edward Mannock VC
XV104	James McCudden VC
XV105	Albert Ball VC
XV106	Thomas Mottershead VC
XV107	James Nicolson VC
XV108	William Rhodes-Moorhouse VC
XV109	Arthur Scarf VC

VC10 LOSS IN RAF SERVICE

On 18 December 1997, RAF VC10 C.1K, XR806, was damaged in a ground defuelling accident at RAF Brize Norton. The aircraft had a problem with the fin tank indicator on the flight engineer's panel and it continually showed 'zero'. The engineer charged with defuelling the aircraft, an odious task, elected to perform this from the flight engineer's panel. He removed all the fuel from the wing tanks, but the fin tank showing 'empty' was ignored. XR806 had wing-mounted AAR refuelling pods fitted, which moved the centre of gravity rearward. With no counterweights placed in the aircraft cabin to oppose it, as a result of the incorrect sequence of defuelling actions, XR806 gently sat on to its tail, causing significant damage to the airframe including the rear fuselage pressure bulkhead. After a detailed investigation the damage was considered 'Cat 5' – damaged beyond economic repair – and the aircraft was later scrapped.

Withdrawal from service and replaced by Airbus A330MRTT

VC10 C.1K freight operations had been transferred to the C-17A fleet which entered service with 99 Squadron from May 2001, with the C-17A fleet increasing to eight aircraft by 2012.

On 8 July 1998, the Strategic Defence Review announced the end of VC10 and TriStar operations. They were to be replaced by a new, yet-to-be-identified type, chosen after a thorough review. On 26 January 2005, the Air Tanker Consortium was chosen as the Future Strategic Tanker Aircraft (FSTA) preferred bidder to replace all VC10 tanker/transport aircraft with the Airbus A330MRTT. Interestingly, the fleet would not be purchased outright; instead a private funding initiative (PFI) would fund the £13 billion deal over 27 years. The first aircraft were due to enter service in January 2008 but suffered significant delays to the programme. Consequently, the first 'Voyager' did not enter service until 2012.

Sadly, by September 2013, the VC10 was consigned to history.

ABOVE On 24 September 2013 another special air-to-air formation shoot was organised to celebrate the replacement in service of the VC10 with the Airbus A330MRTT Voyager KC.2 and KC.3. Once again, it was flown over the North Sea and featured a 10 Squadron Voyager KC.2, ZZ231, in formation with 101 Squadron VC10 K.3, ZA150/J. The sortie also marked the very last flight for ZA150, which was landed at Dunsfold at the end of the trip and handed over to the Brooklands Museum for preservation. (Geoff Lee/Planefocus image GHL-132321)

Chapter Five

VC10 operations in theatre

It may come as a surprise that an aircraft initially designed for use by the airlines as a long-range passenger jet, and by the RAF as a troop carrier and casualty evacuation platform, would later produce an air-to-air refuelling tanker of worldwide acclaim – and then go on to operate in so many theatres of conflict. One of the major lessons learned from the Falklands conflict was the essential role played by air-to-air (AAR) refuelling tankers.

OPPOSITE Although initially based at Muharraq, Bahrain, for Operation Granby, the entire 101 Squadron VC10 tanker force was moved to King Khalid International Airport, Riyadh. ZA144/E was photographed refuelling a pair of armed 6 Squadron Jaguar GR.1As. The Jaguars are in the special 'Gulf War' camouflage, while ZA144 carries the titles 'The Empire Strikes Back' on the forward fuselage. *(PRM Aviation)*

The following represents a good selection of the unclassified operations that VC10 aircraft were involved in. They include humanitarian airlifts, peacekeeping, casualty evacuations and trooping flights, as well as AAR missions in support of both RAF and NATO forces. They are presented here in chronological order.

Evacuation from Aden

Britain had been involved in the South Arabian Peninsula since 1839. Little attention was paid to the tribal wars while the Second World War was raging, but shortly afterwards the RAF returned to the area. Here they remained for the next 20 years, often in the company of the British Army and the Royal Navy, trying to quell the activities of a number of rebel armies. During this period, the base at Khormaksar became an important base for operations, as well as being a staging post for the RAF.

In July 1964, the British government announced its intention to grant Aden

independence by 1968, but with the intention of maintaining a military base. However, this news resulted in fighting in and around Aden. As the situation continued to deteriorate, Britain stated in February 1966 that it would not be keeping the military base, although this only served to increase the levels of violence. As British forces prepared to leave in 1967, unrest spread and the withdrawal was expedited.

From 1 November a carefully planned military evacuation was executed with Hercules and Britannia aircraft flying 5,800 personnel out from Khormaksar to Muharraq for their return to Lyneham. Most of these flights were conducted by 10 Squadron VC10 C.1s, along with VC10 aircraft chartered from BOAC.

Anguilla

With a population of around 6,000, Anguilla had been linked to St Kitts and Nevis since 1822. In June 1967, Britain entered into discussions with islanders after a local declaration of independence and on 11 March 1969, the parliamentary under-secretary responsible visited the island but was besieged and small arms were discharged.

The British government responded by sending a total of 315 men and 7 policemen to restore order. Five Hercules aircraft carried the equipment, while three VC10s of 10 Squadron flew in the main force. In reality, order had never been seriously threatened and the troops left in September.

Operation Burlap

In November 1970, a cyclone devastated the coastal area of East Pakistan (now Bangladesh). In Operation Burlap, VC10 C.1s of 10 Squadron flew medical and relief supplies to Dhaka, which was distributed by Hercules C.1 aircraft of 48 Squadron based at Changi, Singapore.

More flooding in East Pakistan

Further heavy rain brought more flooding to East Pakistan in 1971. Around 400,000lb of supplies were flown in by VC10 C.1s of 10 Squadron, along with Belfast and Hercules aircraft.

Evacuation of British servicemen from Malta

In January 1972, the Maltese government ordered the immediate removal of British troops from the island. During a two-month period, 8,000 servicemen and -women, along with their dependants, were airlifted to Cyprus, together with a large quantity of equipment. Once again, the VC10s of 10 Squadron were involved, along with Britannia, Belfast and Hercules aircraft.

Operation Bold Guard

With very little warning, there was a coup in Cyprus on 15 July 1974, when President Makarios was deposed by the Greek National Guard. Two days later, Nicos Sampson, a leading figure in EOKA-B, was declared president. The Turkish reaction was predictable, if leisurely.

On 20 July, the Turkish armed forces started military action on the island. The attacks caused great concern for the safety of foreign nationals caught up in the fighting. RAF Phantom FGR.2 aircraft were deployed to Akrotiri from Coningsby.

At Akrotiri, the RAF was busy evacuating families of servicemen to the UK in Operation Bold Guard, while bringing in supplies and troop reinforcements.

When the evacuation was completed by 8 August, 13,430 people had been returned in a well-organised operation. The airlift involved Hercules, Belfast and Britannia aircraft, along with VC10 C.1 aircraft from 10 Squadron.

Evacuation from Angola

Independence for Angola from Portugal had been set for 11 November 1975. Immediately ahead of this date around 300,000 Europeans departed ahead of the impending civil war. During October 1976, VC10s C.1 aircraft of 10 Squadron evacuated 5,700 people and 350,000lb of freight.

Humanitarian support in Zaire

In March 1978, Katangenese rebels crossed into Zaire from bases in Angola. They soon occupied Kolwezi where they held around 2,000 Europeans hostage. By May, the situation had become critical, and following a failed operation by Zaire's army troops, paratroops of the French Foreign Legion were dropped on 18 May. By 20 May they had occupied the town, but not before 130 hostages had been massacred.

The French were backed by Belgian paratroopers, while Italian Air Force and USAF

transport aircraft brought in supplies and equipment. The British contribution comprised a medical team and equipment brought into Lusaka by a VC10 of 10 Squadron, along with three Hercules aircraft from the Lyneham Transport Wing.

Evacuation from Iran

In 1978, there was a revolution in Iran. The ruling monarch, Shah Pahlavi, was overthrown following huge demonstrations in December. At the time, the USA had a large number of 'military advisers' in Iran and the US government arranged the evacuation of dependants from Tehran. They were flown out in C-5A Galaxy aircraft from the 436 MAW. British nationals were evacuated in January 1979 by VC10 C.1 aircraft from 10 Squadron, as well as Hercules aircraft from 24 Squadron.

Operation Agila

In 1965, Rhodesia had made a unilateral declaration of independence, to which the British government reacted with a blockade and sanctions. By late 1979, with the Rhodesians attacking guerrilla bases in Mozambique and Zambia, the white Rhodesian government was forced by international pressure to allow local elections, after which the white minority rule collapsed.

A ceasefire between Rhodesia and Zambia came into effect on 28 December 1979, by

ABOVE Following the coup in Cyprus on 15 July 1979, the RAF was busy evacuating families of servicemen to the UK in Operation Bold Guard. Here a 10 Squadron VC10 C.1 was photographed at Brize Norton after arriving with a full load of dependants. *(Crown Copyright/Air Historical Branch image PRB-2-3478-1)*

and the South Sandwich Islands. It began on Friday, 2 April 1982, when Argentina invaded and occupied the Falkland Islands (and, the following day, South Georgia and the South Sandwich Islands) in an attempt to establish the sovereignty it had claimed over them. On 5 April, the British government dispatched a naval task force to engage the Argentinian Navy and Air Force before making an amphibious assault on the islands. The conflict lasted 74 days and ended with the surrender of Argentinian forces on 14 June 1982, returning the islands to British control. In total, 649 Argentinian military personnel, 255 British military personnel and 3 Falkland Islanders died during the hostilities.

No 10 Squadron's VC10 C.1 aircraft were soon called into the conflict and their first visit to the South Atlantic was on 3 April 1982. XV106 was dispatched from Brize Norton to Montevideo (with a technical stop at Ascension Island) to collect the governor of the Falkland Islands, Rex Hunt, along with the small force of Royal Marines captured when the Argentinians first invaded.

As the build-up increased, 10 Squadron became more and more involved in Operation Corporate at the expense of some other commitments. Regular supply flights from Brize Norton to Ascension helped the build-up of troops and equipment.

While very busy with 'Corporate' operations, 10 Squadron were never in the limelight. They undertook numerous ambulance flights, monitored by the International Red Cross, and

which time a five-nation ceasefire-monitoring force was in place. The British contribution deployed in Operation Agila comprised Hercules aircraft operating from Salisbury, along with 33 Squadron Puma as well as army helicopters. All of these remained in place until early 1980. Much of the equipment was brought from the UK in USAF Galaxy aircraft, as well as VC10 C.1 aircraft of 10 Squadron.

Operation Corporate – the retaking of the Falkland Islands

The Falklands War was a ten-week conflict between Argentina and the United Kingdom over two British overseas territories in the South Atlantic: the Falkland Islands and South Georgia

each of the VC10s involved in these operations had the Red Cross markings added to the side of the fuselage if they visited Montevideo in neutral Uruguay.

Following the attack on HMS *Sheffield*, VC10s made a number of trips from Wideawake Airfield on Ascension to Brize Norton, returning the wounded. None of these flights, however, carried the Red Cross markings.

Numerous ambulance flights were made after the ceasefire, including ferrying the wounded from *Sir Tristram* and *Sir Galahad*. However, it soon became necessary to return the soldiers back to the UK and the number of trooping flights, supported by a number of chartered airline aircraft, increased significantly with flights to Brize Norton, Arbroath and Leuchars. Data recorded at the time shows that 10 Squadron flew a total of 28 trooping flights in May and 33 in June, most routing Brize Norton–Dakar–Ascension–Brize Norton.

By the end of July 1982, the tasking situation was showing signs of returning to normal, although with a considerable British presence at Wideawake Airport on Ascension Island, would continue to receive regular resupply flights for the foreseeable future.

Operation Granby – the First Gulf War

Operation Granby was the name given to the British military operations during the 1991 Gulf War. The build-up to the conflict had started earlier when the decision was taken to deploy British forces to the Gulf. In August 1990, No 5 Squadron Tornado F.3 aircraft were deployed to Dhahran and No 6 Squadron Jaguar GR.1A aircraft to Thumrait, all with the

ABOVE No 10 Squadron VC10 C.1s provided Casevac capabilities both during and after Operation Corporate. Some of the sorties were monitored by the International Red Cross and each of the VC10s involved in these operations had the Red Cross markings added to the sides of the fuselage, especially if they visited Montevideo in neutral Uruguay. *(Crown Copyright/Air Historical Branch image)*

BELOW A 101 Squadron VC10 K.2, ZA144/E, refuelling a group of Jaguar GR.1As including XZ356. This image was taken in November 1990, just before hostilities commenced. At the time, the VC10 K.2 was based at Muharraq, Bahrain, and the Jaguars at Thumrait, Oman. *(PRM Aviation)*

ABOVE No 101 Squadron VC10 K.3 ZA146/G providing AAR to three Tornado GR.1s of 20 Squadron. All three Tornados are equipped with the JP233 runway denial weapon. Each JP233 as fitted to the Tornado was divided into a rear section with 30 SG-357 runway shattering bomblets, while the front section carried 215 anti-personnel mines. Both types of munitions were retarded by small parachutes. *(PRM Aviation)*

CENTRE No 10 Squadron VC10 K.2, ZA142/C, refuelling a pair of 20 Squadron Tornado GR.1s. *(PRM Aviation)*

RIGHT Another view of ZA142/C in action, refuelling an unidentified 20 Squadron Tornado GR.1 in Gulf War colours. *(PRM Aviation)*

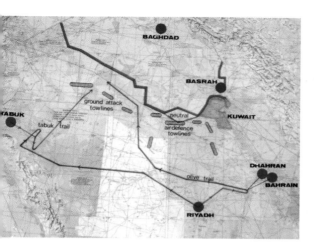

ABOVE A wall chart displayed in the 101 Squadron operations room showed the AAR routes used during Operation Granby including the 'Tabuk' Trail and the 'Olive' Trail; along with the locations of the ground attack and air defence tow-lines. *(Keith Wilson)*

ABOVE No 101 Squadron VC10 K.2, ZA140/A, refuelling an 11 Squadron Tornado F.3, ZE962/DI, over the desert during Operation Granby. *(Crown Copyright/Air Historical Branch image)*

LEFT At the conclusion of the First Gulf War, a number of 101 Squadron VC10s had special artwork applied. Here, VC10 K.3, ZA140/B, was photographed at a Brize Norton photo day with the BP logo and the titles 'The Empire Strikes Back' applied. Each of the black aircraft symbols represents an air-to-air tanking sortie conducted during the conflict, indicating that ZA140/B participated in 43 such sorties. *(Keith Wilson)*

support from 101 Squadron's VC10 tankers. Later, VC10s were co-located at Thumrait to support the Jaguars; however, the base proved unsuitable for VC10 operations and they were moved to Seeb.

The first part of the Gulf War air campaign was directed against the Iraqi Air Force. Careful planning ahead of the campaign instigated a precise rendezvous point with the formations of Tornado aircraft, at night and in radio silence. The formation would then fly a pre-planned route that would involve VC10s providing pre-strike AAR to them before releasing them at the cast-off point within seconds of the briefed timing. The Tornados would then attack their targets before returning for a post-strike refuelling and recovery to their base. These trails were given the names 'Olive' and 'Tabuk' (see the photograph above).

Early on 17 January, the RAF's Tornado GR.1s flew into Iraq, with tanker support. The first targets were Iraqi airbases, which housed a variety of defence systems and aircraft. These attacks were coordinated in Riyadh by the Joint Allied Headquarters; aircraft from a variety of air arms were almost totally integrated into a single coalition force. Support aircraft in raids, therefore, could be from any coalition power.

Within 24 hours of the outbreak of the offensive, a hundred sorties had been flown. After just seven days, the RAF's focus, like the rest of the coalition air forces, was moved to targets related to the support of Iraqi forces in Kuwait. These included an oil refinery and strategic bridges over the River Euphrates.

During the conflict, all nine VC10 K.2s and K.3s of 101 Squadron were deployed to bases in Bahrain, Saudi Arabia and Oman as part of Operation Granby. The contribution made by the RAF was a total of 5,000 flight hours across 381 sorties in theatre, flying both aerial refuelling and logistical missions in support of coalition forces in combat, with the occupying Iraqi forces in Kuwait. The VC10 force proved highly reliable and during the seven-month period 101 Squadron was deployed, they achieved a sortie success rate of over 99%. They flew 981 sorties involving 3,650 hours, while offloading 22,800 tonnes of fuel.

Following the ceasefire, VC10 aircraft

LEFT ZA460/AJ-A, a Tornado GR.1B of 617 Squadron, receiving fuel from the port wing hose of a VC10 K.3 during 'Storm Trail N21'; a flight down to Riyadh in 1992 for a 'frame change' – exchanging an airframe into and out of theatre. After topping-off the Tornado during its last scheduled refuelling bracket to the north of Egypt, the VC10 K.3 tanker flew to Akrotiri, Cyprus, for an overnight stop. *(Keith Wilson)*

ABOVE The K.3 returned to the UK the following day, escorting another 617 Squadron Tornado GR.1B, ZA374/AJ-L, which it 'collected' just to the north of Egypt. ZA374 was returning to the UK for maintenance after a period in theatre during Operation Granby. *(Keith Wilson)*

OPERATION ALLIED FORCE
LEFT No 10 Squadron VC10 C.1K, XV105, photographed at Split while operating an IFOR trooping flight on 1 February 1996. Interestingly, while the underwing racks are still in place, the VC10 had the air-to-air refuelling pods removed for this sortie. *(Peter R. Foster)*

LEFT A VC10 C.1K aircraft photographed just after touching down at Vilnius International Airport on 9 October 2004 to launch the British contribution to NATO's Air Policing Mission for the Baltic nations. About 80 RAF personnel were on board. These would run the three-month detachment at Siauliai Air Base. NATO's Air Policing Mission began in April 2004 when F-16s of the Belgian Air Force started patrolling the Baltic skies for a three-month commitment. They were then replaced by more F-16s from Denmark for a further three months. *(Crown Copyright/ Air Historical Branch image MNT-04-0130-OUT-UNC-001/Cpl Paul Saxby)*

RIGHT A 101 Squadron VC10 refuels an unidentified US Navy F-18 from VFA-97 Squadron on 15 December 2001. At the time of the image VFA-97 was operating from the aircraft carrier USS *Nimitz*. *(Crown Copyright/Air Historical Branch image VC10 Tanking US F18)*

RIGHT Three Tornado GR.1As of II (AC) Squadron take on fuel from a 101 Squadron VC10. The nearest Tornado has an asymmetric centreline load of a 2,250-litre tank (known as 'Hindenburgers') along with 1,000lb bombs, while the other two just have 1,000lb bombs attached. *(Crown Copyright/Air Historical Branch image)*

remained stationed in the region throughout the 1990s, supporting allied aircraft enforcing no-fly zones over parts of Iraq, and later during the 1998 airstrikes on Iraq.

Operation Allied Force

The NATO bombing of Yugoslavia was NATO's military operation against the Serbian people during the Kosovo War. According to NATO, the operation sought to stop human rights abuses in Kosovo and it was the first time that NATO used military force without the approval of the UN Security Council. The air strikes lasted from 24 March to 10 June 1999. The official NATO operation code name was Operation Allied Force, while the United States called it Operation Noble Anvil. The bombings led to the eventual withdrawal of Yugoslav forces from Kosovo and the establishment of the UN Mission in Kosovo (UNMIK).

During the 1999 NATO bombing of Yugoslavia, VC10 tankers were stationed at bases in southern Italy to refuel NATO aircraft in theatre, as part of Operation Allied Force. The VC10 tanker aircraft allowed Tornado GR.1 fighter-bombers stationed at RAF Bruggen in Germany to conduct long-range strike missions against targets inside Serbia.

Operation Veritas

Operation Veritas was the code name used for British military operations against the Taliban in Afghanistan in 2001. British forces played a supporting role to the US Operation Enduring Freedom, but it was an important contribution to

ABOVE VC10 C.1K XR807 at work over the Mediterranean on 7 May 2003. The four Harrier GR.9 aircraft were ZG857/89, ZD437/49, ZG505/78 and ZG510/81. They used the callsigns 'Ascot 9665–9668'. *(Peter R. Foster)*

BELOW No 101 Squadron VC10 K.3, ZA150/J, landing at the Royal Air Force of Oman (RAFO) Base at Musannah on 10 March 2010. At the time, a number of VC10s were detached here as part of the 902 Expeditionary Air Wing (EAW). *(Crown Copyright/Air Historical Branch image AUAB-10-061-0143/Corporal Dave Blackburn)*

ABOVE A VC10 C.1K, XV109, on the ramp at 'a Middle-Eastern' base on 5 January 2009. The aircraft was operating in support of RAF and US forces in the region during operations over Afghanistan. The ramp at the top of this image shows some interesting US assets also operating from this location. *(Crown Copyright/ Air Historical Branch image AUAB-09-004-022/ Sergeant Laura Bibby)*

the overall forces deployed. Oman-based VC10s were used in some of the first missions of the war in Afghanistan, refuelling US carrier-based aircraft carrying out strikes on Afghan targets. The VC10s also provided air transport missions in support of British and allied forces stationed in Afghanistan and fighting against the Taliban.

A large number of British forces were on exercise 'Saif Sareea II' in Oman when the 9/11 attacks commenced. This permitted the swift deployment of some forces to Afghanistan for operations against the Taliban.

Operation Veritas also incorporated Operation Oracle (the UK component of coalition operations against Al Qaeda and Taliban forces

LEFT VC10 C.1K, XV108/Y, on the ramp at RAFO Musannah on 14 October 2010. This photograph was taken while the aircraft was operating as part of the 902 EAW along with RAF Sentinel and Nimrod aircraft. *(Crown Copyright/Air Historical Branch image AUAB-10-255-OUT-UNC-030/ Sergeant Corrine Buxton)*

RIGHT **A 101 Squadron VC10 K.3 refuelling a pair of Tornado F.3s during Operation Telic in April 2003.** *(Crown Copyright/Air Historical Branch image MNT-03-003-OUT-UNC-0995/SAC Sarah Burrows)*

with Afghanistan) and Operation Fingal (the UK contribution to the International Security Assistance Force established in January 2002), the latter of which was succeeded by Operation Herrick from 2002 onwards.

VC10s remained on long-term deployment to the Middle East for 12 years, ending just before the type's retirement.

Operation Telic

Operation Telic (Op TELIC) was the code name given to the UK's military operations in Iraq during the US-led coalition, which was conducted between the start of the invasion on 19 March 2003 and the withdrawal of the last remaining British forces on 22 May 2011. The bulk of the mission ended on 30 April 2009 but around 150 troops, mainly from the Royal Navy, remained in Iraq until 22 May 2011 as part of the Iraqi Training and Advisory Mission.

Operation Telic was one of the largest deployments of British forces since the Second World War. Interestingly, around 9,500 of the British servicemen and -women deployed on Operation Telic were reservists, the vast majority of them from the Territorial Army.

A VC10 wing was stationed at Prince Sultan Air Base in Saudi Arabia with a mixed fleet of seven VC10s from both 10 and 101 Squadrons, where they supported Tornado GR.4, Harrier, Nimrod and Hercules operations. In addition, one VC10 C.1K from 10 Squadron was maintained at RAF Akrotiri for aeromedical evacuation and more than 1,000 casualties from the conflict were evacuated to Cyprus.

In the aftermath of the invasion, a number of VC10s were commonly stationed in Iraq. In June 2009, the remaining VC10s were withdrawn from Iraq, along with most other British military assets.

Operation Sharpener

Following North Korea's claim that they had tested a nuclear device on 9 October 2006, a rapid deployment was made of two VC10

BELOW **A 101 Squadron VC10 tanker, callsign 'Esso 01', prepares to depart Al Udeid Air Base, Qatar, during Operation Telic on 27 February 2007. In the left seat is Flt Lt McConnell with Flg Off Chambers in the right.** *(Crown Copyright/Air Historical Branch image DPR-07-006-RAW-9/Sgt Graham Spark)*

BOTTOM **Meanwhile, the navigator, Sqn Ldr John Dyson, calls out the checklist.** *(Crown Copyright/Air Historical Branch image DPR-07-006-RAW-11/ Sgt Graham Spark)*

OPERATION HERRICK

LEFT No 1 Squadron, with their Harrier GR.9 aircraft, were deployed to Afghanistan under Operation Herrick between April and June 2009. Here, two of their aircraft were photographed while refuelling from a VC10 C.1K, XV102/T, during their stay in theatre. *(Crown Copyright/Air Historical Branch image F540-0609-WIT-1SQN-040)*

OPERATION ELLAMY

ABOVE Three 101 Squadron VC10 C.1Ks (XR808/R, XV102/T and XV106/W) at Brize Norton on the afternoon of 19 March 2011, ahead of the planned air-to-air refuelling operations in support of the enforcement of the no-fly zone over Libya. *(Crown Copyright/Air Historical Branch image MNT-11-050-OUT-UNC-0111/SAC Neil Chapman)*

LEFT VC10 C.1K, XV106/W, on the runway at Brize Norton on 19 March 2011 just before its departure. RAF VC10 tankers accompanied Tornado GR.4s from RAF Marham that struck Libyan air defences in the longest strike mission flown since the 'Black Buck' operations during the Falklands conflict. *(Crown Copyright/ Air Historical Branch image 45152514/SAC Neil Chapman)*

LEFT No 101 Squadron VC10 K.3, ZA148, photographed while on station at 23,000ft awaiting its 'trade' during Operation Ellamy on 7 July 2011. *(Crown Copyright/Air Historical Branch image Ellamy-906-110707-0275-OUT-UNC-0126/ SAC Sally Raimondo)*

aircraft to Kadena AFB in Japan. (For more information on this, see the 'VC10's Secondary Role' on p. 104.)

Operation Ellamy

Operation Ellamy was the code name for the UK's participation in the military intervention in Libya in 2011. The operation was part of an international coalition aimed at enforcing a Libyan no-fly zone in accordance with the United Nations Security Council Resolution (UNSCR) 1973, which stipulated that 'all necessary measures' shall be taken to protect civilians.

The no-fly zone was proposed during the Libyan Civil War to prevent government forces loyal to Colonel Muammar Gaddafi from carrying out air attacks on anti-Gaddafi forces. Several countries prepared to take immediate military action at a conference in Paris on 19 March 2011.

The UNSCR 1973 was passed on the evening of 17 March 2011 and gave a mandate to countries wishing to enforce a no-fly zone over Libya. A conference involving international leaders took place in Paris on the afternoon of 19 March 2011. International military action commenced after the conference finished, with French military fighter jets being the first to participate in the operation when, only a few hours after the conference finished in Paris, the first shots were fired at 16.45pm GMT against a Libyan tank.

During Operation Ellamy, a small number of VC10s were dispatched to bases in the Mediterranean and were used to refuel NATO strike aircraft being used in theatre. Initially, the RAF Tornados were flown into theatre direct from Marham with support from VC10 tankers, but later these and a group of Typhoons were deployed to Giola Dell Colle AFB as the 906 Expeditionary Air Wing (EAW).

On 24 October 2011 the people of Libya celebrated their 'Liberation Day'. The National Transitional Council's (NTC) historic announcement brought to an end the bitter and savage civil war that had been raging throughout the country for eight months and signalled the cessation of offensive operations over Libya.

ABOVE The 101 Squadron VC10s were supporting a number of different air arms participating in Operation Ellamy, including the Canadian Armed Forces (CAF). Here, a CAF CF-18A, 188746, was photographed while refuelling from the VC10 starboard wing pod on 7 July 2011. *(Crown Copyright/Air Historical Branch image Ellamy-906-110707-0275-OUT-UNC-0208/SAC Sally Raimondo)*

BELOW Further trade on 7 July 2011 came in the form of two Italian Navy AV-8Bs operating from the Italian aircraft carrier *Giuseppe Garibaldi*. These aircraft worked alongside Italian Air Force aircraft during Operation Unified Protector, as part of the 2011 military intervention in Libya. They conducted air strikes as well as intelligence and reconnaissance sorties over Libya, using the **LITENING** targeting pods while armed with **AIM-120 AMRAAMs** and **AIM-9 Sidewinders**. *(Crown Copyright/Air Historical Branch image Ellamy-906-110707-0275-OUT-UNC-0235)*

Andy Townshend recalls Mission 1671 during Operation Engadine . . . proof, if ever it were needed, of the great tanking catchphrase:

NO ONE KICKS ASS WITHOUT TANKER GAS!

We train like we fight. Every sortie was operated as though it were an operational mission, be it a practice scramble in the middle of the night getting airborne from fast asleep in just 25 minutes, to complicated multi-tanker/multi-receiver trails around the world. This type of training helped make the operational sorties feel 'normal', not routine, as there was no such thing as 'normal'.

Tanking is a customer-based business and we like to be prepared for anything. Any sortie had the potential to be an adventure and we all have sorties that stick in our minds; be they interesting air transport sorties to unusual destinations, Casevac or compassionate flights, busy AAR . . . the list goes on. This is just one of mine.

Mission 1671 during Operation Engadine started much like all the other missions 101 Squadron had flown from RAF Bruggen. While this was only my second mission of the campaign, the squadron had flown many over the previous days and weeks. The previous night I had flown as captain of the number 'two' VC10, but tonight it was my lead. We met as two crews on the evening of 25 May 1999 in our temporary squadron planning room around two and a half hours before take-off. As I mentioned earlier,

planning these kinds of sorties was quite normal for us, even though this was an operational sortie rather than training. On paper the plan looked relatively simple: six Tornado GR.1s and two VC10s to depart from Bruggen and route to Croatia, refuelling on the way. The Tornados would be cast off at some point to route to their individual targets and do their thing, while we held close by. Once complete, the Tornados would route back to us and we would bring them home, topping them up with fuel as required.

We liaised with the Tornado crews and then briefed and walked for the jets, leaving plenty of time to get the aircraft ready and to squeeze in as much fuel as possible for the mission. My crew had been allocated ZD230 or 'Kilo' as she was usually known; all the 101 Squadron tankers had tail letters; A–E were the K.2s, F, G, H and J were the K.3s and K, L, M, N and P were the K.4s and that is how we identified them. 'Kilo' was a K.4 and had once been a Super VC10 operating with BOAC and then BA as G-ASGA.

Unlike the K.2 and K.3 variants, the K.4s did not have the extra fuel tanks in the fuselage, so we were limited to a maximum fuel load of 70 tonnes. However, due to a snag we were limited to 68 that night, 2 tonnes less than normal and much less than a K.3's 80 tonnes. We were going to need all of it!

For a sortie like this the lead VC10 crew would take care of all the flight plans, liaison with air traffic control and once everyone was on frequency we would do all the talking for the whole formation. At the pre-briefed time we checked everyone in on the 'back box' – the second radio that was used for formation chat – and confirmed that all the jets were serviceable. We then called for start clearance for the whole formation on the 'front box' with Bruggen ATC.

The two VC10s had the call signs 'Buck 31' and 'Buck 32'. In formation with me would be three of the Tornados, call signs 'Pacer 41', '42' and '43'; and with Nick in 'Buck 32' would be Tornados 'Nova 31', '32' and '33'. With everyone running and serviceable, we called for departure and got clearance for take-off of all eight aircraft. This was always an interesting sight to watch from the ground. The VC10 would line up and depart followed immediately by the first three Tornados; 2 minutes later the

BELOW VC10 K.4, ZD230/K, at Brize Norton in January 2001. This is the aircraft flown by Andy Townshend on Mission 1671 during Operation Engadine. *(PRM Aviation)*

second VC10 would roll, again followed in quick succession by their 'chicks'.

The next task was for everyone to join up and this had become a very slick operation now that the German and French air traffic controllers had got used to what we were doing. In fairly short order we were all together at 20,000ft, 'Buck 31' with 'Pacer 41' and '42' on the left and '43' on the right. Behind us was 'Buck 32' in what we called 'Cell', 1 nautical mile behind and 1,000ft above, with 'Nova 31–33' in a similar formation around him.

For the majority of the route out we followed the standard airway structure and spoke to various air traffic centres; however, as we approached Croatia we were handed over to our tactical military controller:

'Buck 31 flight, clear switch tactical . . . good luck.'

As we topped up our three chicks so that they had plenty of fuel, we arranged the formation split with the E.3 that was looking after us. Our six Tornados dropped away, lights off and into the dark. Nick in 'Buck 32' and myself slowed down to save fuel while we sat and waited in our hold for the Tornados to return.

The previous night's sortie had been somewhat uneventful and we had flown around our hold with little, if anything, to see out of the window. The target areas were visible over the border, but not surprisingly there were no lights in any of the towns or villages; all was pitch black. From what I had gathered this had been much the same over the past few days.

However, tonight was different. We had a good idea of the target times and with a few minutes to go the sky in the area erupted. There was tracer fire everywhere and it was clear that there was a concerted attempt to bring down one of our 'chicks'. We could see huge amounts of AAA and a few missile plumes and all went quiet on the flight deck. We knew that our 'chicks' would not be away from us for long. We got an early call from 'Pacer 41' informing us they were on their way back. There was, however, a change of RV if we were able. Of course we said, 'yes, no problem', and noted the lat and long. The nav plotted the point and passed the chart forward; the new position was over the border … there was no discussion, we were here to help. Tanking is all about the customer!

With all our lights off we headed in to pick the 'chicks' up. We had been told that all but 'Pacer 43' had dropped their external fuel tanks for extra manoeuvrability and thus they would need extra top-ups on the way home. We arrived at the RV exactly on time and the silhouettes of three Tornados appeared on our wing; the same with Nick behind me.

We turned round and headed home. As we crossed back over the border, we turned our lights back on and cleared our receivers astern to take some fuel. The relief in their voices was obvious and we as a crew were very happy to have the six Tornados back with us.

We could not talk much over the radio, but it was obvious that the mission had been a very tough one, but also very successful. For us, though, we still had some work to do. We now had to give away more fuel than we had planned for and the limitation of the K.4 tanker's lighter fuel capacity was now causing us some issues. Our priority was to get the Tornados back to Bruggen, so we gave them the fuel they asked for. Once they had enough to get home we sent them ahead and we slowed down and climbed to save gas. We had a few more tricks up our sleeve, and eventually made it back to Bruggen with nothing to spare; probably the lowest fuel level I had ever landed with. The figures for the night were 68 tonnes loaded and 22.4 tonnes given to the three Tornadoes.

The crews had an extensive debrief, but, in the very early hours of 26 May, we all met in the mess for a well-earned beer. The chat was animated and excitable with a tinge of relief … it had been an 'interesting' sortie and one of those I look back on with pride.

Andy Townshend

Andy Townshend joined the RAF in 1987 and on gaining his wings flew the Nimrod MR2. In January 1995 he joined 101 Squadron as a co-pilot and then as captain. After a tour as a QFI, he went back to the VC10 in October 2003, initially on 10 and then 101 Squadron as a captain, and then training captain, before moving to Boscombe Down and flying both the VC10 and the A330.

His first VC10 flight was on 27 March 1995 in K.3 ZA147/F and his last was returning from Toulouse after the A400M AAR Trials on 18 May

103

VC10 OPERATIONS IN THEATRE

ABOVE In addition to having flown more than 3,500 hours in the RAF VC10 fleet and having completed 206 AAR contacts as the receiver in the process, Andy Townshend also 'flew' more than 850 hours in Brize Norton's VC10 simulator. *(Crown Copyright/Air Historical Branch/JS-93-13-1)*

2012, also in ZA147. During that time he flew more than 3,500 hours on the VC10 – 2,500 of them as captain. In addition, he completed more than 850 hours in the flight simulator and did 206 AAR contacts as a receiver pilot: 'By far the most exciting and satisfying thing you can do in a large aircraft!'

Andy recalls one trip to the Falklands when his VC10 took 21.5 tonnes of fuel from a TriStar tanker in one 'prod':

We had no diplomatic clearance to go via Brazil, so we had to fly direct to Mount Pleasant and thus required the extra gas to get there. I was in XV101 and had to do it from the right-hand seat, which was not my normal seat for receiving; consequently, my hands were the other way round to normal which made it harder. As the VC10 fills up, the rate of onload reduces and you are also required to trim the aircraft as the fuel goes in. With one hand on the control wheel and one on the throttles, the aircraft does become heavier, especially if you are slow to trim out the forces. A nice hot cuppa is always welcome after a long onload!

Andy is a huge VC10 fan and can regularly be found at Bruntingthorpe helping to maintain ZD241 where his love affair with the old girl continues. 'I really enjoy being part of the team that gets to show her off at the Cold War Jet days . . . she still looks and sounds great!'

Secondary role – air sampling

While the air transport (AT), trooping, casualty evacuation (Casevac) and air-to-air (AAR) tanking roles are widely recognised as the major attributes of the VC10, what is perhaps not so well known is that the aircraft had a secondary role during its service life – that of air sampling: collecting debris samples from nuclear weapons tests.

This air sampling role was inherited from the earlier Vulcan B2MRR aircraft of which nine were operated by 27 Squadron. This involved flying through plumes of airborne contamination and using onboard equipment to collect fallout released from both above-ground and underground nuclear tests for later analysis at the Atomic Weapons Research Establishment (AWRE) at Aldermaston. Five of the nine 27 Squadron Vulcan B2MRR aircraft had small pylons fitted to the redundant Skybolt hard points, which could be used to carry sampling pods modified from drop tanks. These pods would collect the needed samples on a filter, while an additional smaller 'localiser' pod was fitted to the port wing, inboard of the main pylons.

It is believed that three VC10 K.3 aircraft operated by 101 Squadron had the capabilities to conduct this role, with the Mk. 32 air-to-air refuelling pods being removed and replaced with a pair of similar-looking sampling pods, as well as a small pod just under the nose of the aircraft. The role is often referred to at squadron level as '2R' or 'sniffing'.

ZA147/F was photographed in February 1990 while operating in the air sampling role, equipped with two underwing sampling pods, as well as the small, third pod located under the nose of the aircraft. At the time, it seems it was working with our US colleagues.

The most recent reported use of the aircraft in this role occurred in October 2006, when North Korea detonated its first nuclear device. A pair of VC10s was immediately dispatched to Kadena AFB on the island of Okinawa, Japan, shortly after the first test, under the code name Operation Sharpener. It was reported that K.3 ZA150/J was equipped for air sampling, while the second (C.1K

XR808) was carrying support equipment for the deployment.

The two aircraft arrived at Yokota, Japan, on 11 October 2006, just two days after North Korea announced that it had carried out a successful nuclear test. They then flew on to Kadena AFB, where the USAF had deployed its 'Constant Phoenix' WC-135W (61-2667) for atomic sampling duties. This aircraft is operated by the 45th Reconnaissance Squadron, part of the 55th Wing at Offutt AFB, Nebraska.

A press attaché at the British Embassy in Tokyo confirmed that the UK was 'assisting in international operations in respect of verifying the Democratic People's Republic of Korea's (DPRK) nuclear tests'.

A spokesman for RAF Strike Command confirmed that 'logistics support had been received at Kadena, Japan, from where the aircraft were operated, under the terms of the Status of Forces agreement between Japan and the UN'. He also noted that 'the RAF have previously deployed to Kadena in 1995, 2003 and February 2006'.

On 3 October 2006, North Korea had announced its intention to conduct a nuclear test; in doing so it became the first nation to give warning of such action. The blast is estimated to have had an explosive force of less than 1 kiloton, and some radioactive output was detected. US officials suggested that the device may have been a nuclear explosive that misfired.

An anonymous official at the North Korean Embassy in Beijing told a South Korean newspaper that the explosive output was smaller than expected. Because of the secretive nature of North Korea and the small yield of the test, there remains some question as to whether it was a successful test of an unusually small device (which would have required sophisticated technology), or a partially failed 'fizzle' or dud. A scientific paper later estimated the yield as 0.48 kilotons.

On 16 October 2006, US satellites detected vehicles and people near the site of North Korea's initial nuclear test site. US officials said they could not be certain of what the North Koreans were doing in the area, but the activity could be preparations for a second nuclear blast. On 18 October 2006, US officials said North Korea's military had informed the

People's Republic of China that it intended to carry out a series of underground nuclear tests. The Associated Press, citing CNN Television, reported that the North Koreans informed the People's Republic of China that they were prepared to make 'as many as three additional tests'. No further tests occurred in 2006, but a second test was conducted in 2009.

Sampling operations conducted by the VC10 and WC-135W in October 2006, collecting airborne radioactive contaminants, helped the analysts in determining whether or not a nuclear blast had occurred. It also provided some indication of its size and strength.

ABOVE The air sampling pod seen in place on the port wing of VC10 K.3, ZA150/J, at Brize Norton on 3 October 2006, just ahead of its departure to Kadena AFB, Japan, to participate in Operation Sharpener. *(Peter R. Foster)*

BELOW A beautiful air-to-air study of ZA147/F in February 1990. At the time of the image, the aircraft carried both air sampling underwing pods in place of the Mk. 32 AAR pods. This was in addition to the small sampling sensor located on the nose of the aircraft. *(J.T. Hieminga Collection via David Hedge)*

Chapter Six

Flying and operating the VC10

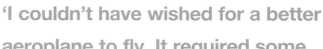

'I couldn't have wished for a better aeroplane to fly. It required some pure handling skills that other types didn't; and with at least four crew members on every sortie, it needed a high degree of Crew Resource Management to operate well. Job variation was good too: you might be on detachment in the Middle East one month and then off to the USA or Canada on a trooping or freight sortie the next, interspersed with a UK AAR sortie or two.'

Flt Lt Chris Haywood, RAF

OPPOSITE Famed and adored by so many enthusiasts for making lots of smoke and noise, VC10 K.4, ZD241, accelerates down the runway at Bruntingthorpe on 13 March 2016, during one of its regular public runs. *(Gary Spoors)*

LEFT The cockpit of VC10 K.4, ZD241, shortly after its 'live' run along the Bruntingthorpe runway on 13 March 2016. *(Keith Wilson)*

1 Weather radar indicator and controller
2 Airspeed indicator
3 Horizon director indicator (HDI)
4 Encoding altimeter
5 Standby, No 1 and No 2 yaw indicators
6 Machmeter
7 VOR RMI
8 Horizon situation indicator (HSI)
9 VSI/TCAS display unit
10 Time of flight clock
11 ADF/TACAN RMI
12 Normal wheelbrake pressure applied gauge
13 Standby wheelbrake pressure applied gauge
14 Alert warning light and cancel
15 Fire bell isolation switch and warning light
16 Fire control handle, No 1 engine
17 Fire control handle, No 2 engine
18 Fire control handle, No 3 engine
19 Fire control handle, No 4 engine
20 Fire warning system test switch
21 Alert warning light, cancel and isolate
22 HP rpm indicator, No 1 engine
23 HP rpm indicator, No 2 engine
24 HP rpm indicator, No 3 engine
25 HP rpm indicator, No 4 engine
26 Landing gear position indicator
27 Standby gyro horizon
28 Slat position indicator, left side
29 Flap position indicator, left side
30 Flap position indicator, right side
31 Slat position indicator, right side
32 Landing gear selector
33 Altimeter
34 Tailplane trim indicator
35 Aileron trim indicator
36 Outside air temperature (OAT) gauge
37 Flight director controller
38 Remote display unit
39 Flight director controller
40 No 1 autopilot 3-axis trim indicator
41 Accelerometer indicator
42 HSI true/magnetic changeover switch
43 No 1 TACAN distance indicator
44 No 2 autopilot 3-axis trim indicator
45 Airspeed indicator
46 Horizon director indicator (HDI)
47 Encoding altimeter
48 Machmeter
49 VOR RMI
50 Horizon situation indicator (HSI)
51 ADF/TACAN RMI
52 Turn-and-slip indicator
53 Vertical speed indicator
54 Cabin altimeter
55 LOC/VOR changeover selector switch
56 Tailplane trim levers, System B
57 Tailplane trim levers, System A
58 Aileron/spoiler disconnect lever
59 Speedbrake control lever
60 Thrust reverser control, No 1 engine
61 Thrust reverser control, No 2 engine
62 Flaps control lever
63 Slats control lever
64 Tailplane trim levers, System A
65 Station box
66 Station box
67 Autopilot turn control
68 Rudder trimmer control
69 No 1 VOR/ILS controller
70 No 1 VHF controller
71 No 1 UHF controller
72 No 1 HF controller
73 No 2 VOR/ILS controller
74 No 2 VHF controller
75 No 2 UHF controller
76 No 2 HF controller
77 ELRAT selector lever
78 HP cock levers for engine Nos 1, 2, 3 and 4
79 Stall protection system dump lever

LEFT The pilot's station forward roof panel on K.4, ZD241. Clockwise, from left to right, are: the supernumerary (jump seat) crew station box (top left), the supernumerary crew microphone selector box (top right), the SELCAL control panel, electronic switch panel, windscreen control panel (bottom right), control surface position indicator (middle), lamp switch panel (bottom left) and cabin control switches. The two 'holes' are where the No 1 and No 2 SIFF controllers were located before being removed immediately after the aircraft arrived at Bruntingthorpe. *(Keith Wilson)*

BELOW A close-up view of the control surface position indicator on ZD241. The position of the tailplane and rudder trimmers, spoilers, flaps and slats can all be seen with a glance upward by either pilot. *(Keith Wilson)*

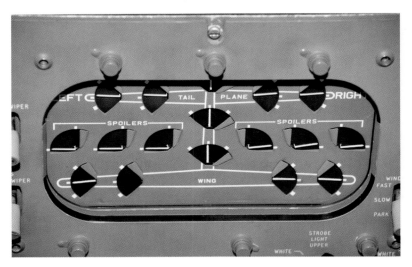

BELOW LEFT At the base of the centre console, closest to and accessible by the flight engineer, are (left to right), the ELRAT selector lever, four HP cock levers along with the stall protection system dump valve. On ZD241 shown here, the ELRAT selector lever has been wire-locked to prevent the inadvertent deployment while on the ground, where it might strike someone working underneath the fuselage at Bruntingthorpe. *(Keith Wilson)*

BELOW The nosewheel steering handle, often called the 'tiller'. The steering is relatively light as long as the aircraft has forward momentum. Tighter turns at slow speed are another matter and a fair amount of pressure is required to turn the nosewheel through its full 70° range of movement, the scale for which can be seen on the screen behind the tiller. *(Keith Wilson)*

Flying the VC10 with 101 Squadron

Chris Haywood first got into aviation as a three-year-old with a trip in a Dragon Rapide and later spent his summers at the Shuttleworth Collection's airshows. The first cockpit he ever sat in was that of the Collection's Gloster Gladiator – aged eight or nine – courtesy of a kindly engineer. He later joined the ATC in the mid-1990s and gained an RAF Sixth Form Scholarship and Flying Scholarship; the latter he completed with TG Aviation at Manston on their Cessna 152s, going solo on his 18th birthday. During the formal interview for the Sixth Form Scholarship he was asked by one of the two officers on the opposite side of the desk what he'd like to fly. He replied 'the VC10', but was told that they'd prefer a more ambitious fast-jet answer – so he decided on the Jaguar!

After school he went to university and joined the University of London Air Squadron, completing his second first solo on the Grob Tutor at RAF Wyton. Upon graduating, he joined the RAF in early 2004. After Initial Officer Training (IOT) at Cranwell, Chris held at Boscombe Down, where he was lucky enough to fly in aircraft ranging from the Alpha Jet and Harvard to the Andover and Hercules. He then went to Linton-on-Ouse and completed Basic Fast-Jet Training on the Tucano and was restreamed on to Multi-Engine Training. He then went to Cranwell to complete the 'Short Course' on the King Air with 45 Squadron. He recalls: 'On arrival I'd decided I'd like to go to the C-17. During the five months I was there somehow my mind

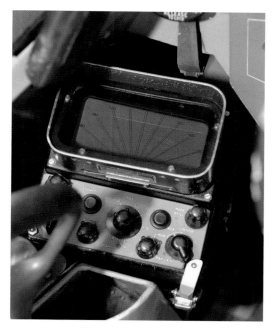

LEFT The weather radar indicator and controller. Each pilot has a set adjacent to his seat. The first pilot's is by his left knee while the co-pilot has it by his right knee. The navigator also has one on his panel. *(Keith Wilson)*

CENTRE The classic yoke on the VC10, seen here on ZD241 with the Vickers-Armstrong badge in the centre. These badges have become collectors' items, so most VC10 aircraft that remain with preservation groups no longer have them fitted. The switch on the top left is the intercom and transmit switch, operated by the left thumb. *(Keith Wilson)*

RIGHT Man-size rudder pedals seen here on the co-pilot's side on K.4 ZD241. The toe brakes are activated by pressing on the top of the pedals, with each brake working independently. *(Keith Wilson)*

was changed, and at the role disposal I was lucky enough to find I'd got my first choice and was sent off to the VC10. I arrived at the VC10 OCU in September 2007.'

The VC10 OCU

Chris Haywood continues his own story:

On my OCU course we had three aircrew: a captain (who had previously been a co-pilot, then had a tour as a Tutor QFI), a flight engineer (who had previously been on the C-130K) and myself. After the SERE (survival) course at RAF St Mawgan, the first element was three weeks of groundschool, culminating in the inevitable battery of exams at the end. Then it was on to the aircraft conversion, starting in the simulator and then a series of flights in the aircraft itself, including the first Instrument Rating (subsequent annual IRTs were flown on the simulator – and were far more difficult due to the fidelity of the simulator, particularly in the pitch channel!).

Once this was complete it was on to the Air Transport (AT) phase. Again, numerous simulator sorties were flown before flying proper routes with an OCU captain. I was lucky, as alongside the standard 'Akrotiri Schedule', I was also able to complete a trooping sortie to Evenes in Norway and another to Upington and Johannesburg in South Africa, stopping both ways on Ascension Island. This culminated in an AT route check.

The final phase of the OCU was the air-to-air refuelling (AAR). Again, it started with a series of simulator events – a golden opportunity to learn and practise the procedures and different radio calls required for AAR sorties. After that it was

a week or so of North Sea tow-lines picking up as much trade as possible! This was followed by a role check and, having passed that, a final chat with OC Training Flight before an arrival interview with OC 101 Squadron as a 'Limited Combat-Ready Co-pilot'.

After that I spent three years flying operationally, participating in Operation Telic – where I was privileged to fly the last RAF AAR sortie – Operation Herrick and latterly during Operation Ellamy.

On completion of my tour I was posted to CFS to complete the QFI course on the Tutor and since then I have instructed on East Midlands Universities Air Squadron and with 16 (R) Squadron at Wittering.

Chris Haywood takes us aboard a VC10 C.1K 'Tartan 22' on an AAR sortie on to one of the tow-lines located around the UK:

Planning for almost all sorties begins around 90 minutes before take-off. For an AT sortie the 'Jetplan' would be studied and checked before a final fuel load was decided. For an AAR sortie the tasking would be received and a fuel load would be calculated from the sum of the fuel used transiting to and from the area, the fuel used while on task and the planned fuel offload to the receiver aircraft. Once the fuel requirement was confirmed, the flight engineer would head out to the aircraft to complete his checks (on an AT sortie the cabin crew would also get to the aircraft at about the same time). A little later the rest of the flight deck crew would join him. The co-pilot had a reasonably long pre-flight/start checklist once on the flight deck and the navigator had all of his equipment to bring on line. The captain could arrive on the flight deck reasonably late as his individual checklist was somewhat shorter.

Engine start

Once the paperwork was signed and the admin completed, the call would be made for the steps to be removed and the doors shut. The 'plaque' is passed forwards, and hooked or balanced on the centre panel. This little laminated piece of paper, secured with a treasury tag is colour coordinated; if it's yellow, we are in a C.1K, if it's green, we should be

BELOW Flt Lt Chris Haywood 'at work' in the right-hand seat of C.1K, XV109, photographed 2 over the south-west approaches on 21 February 2008 during the formation flying phase of his OCU training. The other VC10 is another C.1K, XV101.
(Andy Townshend)

sitting in a K.3 or K.4. This 'plaque' contains vital information, written by the navigator and flight engineer: weight, take-off speeds (V_1, V_r, V_2) and speeds for the flap retract, both for the normal case (min flap retract and flap-up safety speed) and for the case of a double engine failure, where flaps and slats are retracted separately. Finally the calculated required engine pressure (P7), V_{AT} (landing speed for the weight) and POB would complete the plaque.

This is the cue for the take-off brief, delivered by whichever pilot was to fly the departure. With the brief complete the pre-start checks would be done, including the setting of the take-off speeds on the ASI – four plastic bugs – one set on each of V_1, V_R, V_2 and V_2+20 – at this weight 130kts, 151kts, 161kts and 181kts .

CHECKLISTS

For all checks: P = captain, C = co-pilot, N = navigator, E = flight engineer, LM = loadmaster, CS = cabin supervisor

All are based on C.1K checklists.

For simplicity and brevity only 'all-crew' checklists have been included as alongside these, particularly for the engineer, there are extensive crew position-exclusive checks. Some of these are referred to in the checklists included, such as the 'Engineer's taxi checks' in the Take-off checks.

Next, the pre-start checks are completed:

PRE-START CHECKS

Pre-flight checks	All	Complete
	E	All locks, covers, plugs removed
Documentation	P, C	Checked
Take-off briefing	P/C	Stated
Take-off information	P, C	Speeds bugged left, right
	E, N	Checked right, left
Fuel state	E	State fuel load
AAR lights	E	OFF
Pressurisation	E	As required
Oxygen	All	On, checked, 100%
	E	System checked
DV windows	P, C	Closed and locked left, right
Parking brake	P	On, STANDBY, pressure checked
	E	Pressure checked
APU	E	As required
Batteries	E	POWER ON
Booster pumps	E	On, pressure checked
Throttles	E	Closed
Cabin report (off i/c)	LM*, CS*, E	Ready for starting, POB

* There may not be an LM or CS on board, but they are listed as options.

With the pre-start checks completed, we commence the engine start using the starting checks:

STARTING CHECKS

Start/push clearance	N	Obtained
INU 2	N	NAV
Beacons and strobes	C	ON and DIM RED
Fridge master switches	E	ISOLATE
Groundcrew clearance	P, C, E	Obtained
Air supply	E	On, LP START selected
Engines	E	Starting
'Push-back as required'		
'Engines running'		
HP cocks	E	RUN
Start master switch	E	ALL OFF
Engine anti-icing	E	Checked, as required
Controls and speedbrakes	P	Checked
Radar	P, N	On and STANDBY – front, rear
Feel units	E	Both NORMAL, lights out
Door warning lights	E	Tested, out
Dump valve	E	Shut
Groundcrew and ground equipment	P, C	Clear and secure left, clear right
Taxi clearance	P/C	Obtained
Turn-off lights	P	ON

The navigator has obtained start clearance. The co-pilot switches the beacons and strobes to 'ON' and 'DIM RED'.

'Ground, are we clear to start?' checks the engineer.

'Clear start', is the confirmation from outside.

'Starting 3,' calls the engineer.

If the ground engineer outside wasn't plugged in, the co-pilot would hold up three fingers and with the other hand rotate his finger for the standard 'engine start' hand signal.

'Rotation,' comes from the fifth voice outside, accompanied by the rotation of a finger in the air.

With No 3 engine started and idling, engine 4 follows and then reaches idle rpm.

'B System Hydraulics checked,' calls the engineer.

The captain reaches for the TPI levers, which trim the aircraft using the all-flying tailplane perching on top of the fin. There are six levers in total, four on the captain's side, and two on the co-pilot's. Mounted in three pairs, a single lever moving independently would have no effect, but, moved with its adjacent lever, causes the whole tail to move. The captain first moves the taller trim levers one by one – the smaller set on his side are repeaters of the co-pilot's. Initially, there is no movement. However, when moved together they function, all the way forwards, testing the nose down trim. Outside the tailplane's nose edges skywards. It reaches the stop at –3°. The captain pulls them back and leaves the TPI at 0°. The start sequence continues as engines 2 and 1 are started. Engine 1 reaches idle rpm.

'Engines running . . . "A System" Hydraulics checked', from the engineer.

The co-pilot tests his TPI levers and then moves the tailplane through its full positive range. From the outside, at full deflection the whole upper surface of the tailplane can be seen. The captain tests the controls and speedbrakes by moving the heavy control column and the speed brake lever, which sits just left of the throttles.

The co-pilot clears the groundcrew: 'OK ground, thanks for the start. You're cleared to disconnect the intercom, close the hatch and come to the left where the captain can see you. We'll be taxiing out to the left for Runway 26.'

'Roger, have a good trip,' he replies before he unplugs.

The navigator finishes the checklist and confirms: 'Starting checks complete.'

Taxiing

The parking brake is released. It's a strange-looking vertical lever by the captain's right thigh, topped by a small forward-pointing handle that could have come from a 1950s car handbrake. The captain lowers the lever to disengage the brakes.

'Eng, power to move,' calls the pilot flying (PF) – today, that's the co-pilot. The PF will be in control for the majority of the sortie while the other pilot will act as pilot non-flying (PNF). As if by magic, the four throttle levers in the centre console move forward and the aircraft gently rolls forward as the idle whine of the four Rolls-Royce Conway engines increases in volume.

'My throttles,' calls the PF.

With the aircraft moving, the PF regains control of the engines for the taxi. The airframe lurches forwards as the brakes are tested on the 'Standby' system by the PF. The brakes are operated in the same fashion as any other aircraft, being applied by gently pressing against the top portion of the rudder pedals with the ball of the foot. The captain then sets the brakes to normal with a lever forward of the parking brake and the brakes are checked again, this time on the 'Normal' system. Once out of dispersal and turning on to the taxiway, the tiller is now used to steer. Shaped like the handle of a garden spade, this control is used to steer the aircraft on the ground below 80kts. Normal taxiing is quite easy; the aircraft moves easily under its own power and the steering is relatively light as long as the aircraft has forward momentum. Tighter turns at slow speed are another matter. A fair amount of pressure is required to turn the nosewheel through its full 70° range of movement – something we have to use to the full at Bruntingthorpe when turning around on the runway with ZD241.

Once clear of all obstacles the flaps are selected to 'TAKE-OFF'. The taxi checks are completed. The checks are conducted in a 'challenge and response' format, with the navigator reading the checklist to invite responses from the other crew members.

Now the taxi checks are complete.

The PNF then calls ATC for clearance for the initial routing and the squawk . . . 'Brize Ground, Tartan 22, request clearance.'

'Tartan 22, Clear OSGOD SID, climbing FL120, squawk 4762,' replies the Brize Norton ground controller.

The PNF reads back the clearance, sets the altitude alerter to 12,000ft (it makes no differential between altitude and flight level, as this is captured by having the correct altimeter pressure setting). The PF continues to taxi towards the hold, bringing the aircraft gently to a halt before the line on the taxiway.

TAXI CHECKS

Brakes	P	Checked, NORMAL
	E	Pressures checked
Speedbrake	P/C	Zero, baulk out
Rudder and aileron trims	P/C	Set for take-off
	TPIP/C	Checked, set at .° (dependent on fuel/weight load)
Yaw dampers	P/C	1 and 2 on
Reverse thrust	P/C	Checked
	E	Lights out
Flaps and slats	P/C	TAKE-OFF and OUT
	E	Confirmed
Aileron upset	P/C	A/B to ARM (odd days A, even days B)
TOCW	P/C	Checked
Generators	E	Paired, SSB MANUAL SPLIT
Flight instruments	P/C	Checked
Navaids	P/C, N	As briefed front, rear
RAD/NAV select	P, C	As required left, right
Radar	P, N	Checked front, rear
Seats and harnesses	All	Secure
Cabin checks	LM/CS/E	Complete, anti-g locks checked

TAKE-OFF CONFIGURATION WARNING (TOCW)

Horn sounds, when throttle open on the ground, if one or more of the following conditions do **not** apply:

■ Slats out

■ Speedbrake lever in

■ Tailplane trim within take-off range

■ One aileron upset switch at ARM

■ Ailerons normal (nil upset applied)

■ All PFCUs functioning

■ Both feel units functioning

Take-off

The PNF transmits: 'Brize Tower, Tartan 22, ready for departure.'

'Tartan 22, clear for take-off, surface wind 220, 12 knots,' comes the reply from ATC.

'Clear take-off Tartan 22,' responds the PNF.

TAKE-OFF CHECKS

Controls	P/C	Checked
	E	Lights out
Pitot and screen heat	P/C	ON and HIGH
	E	Probes checked
Strobes	P/C	As required
SIFF/TCAS	P/C	Set as required
Alert warning	P/C	Isolate
Landing lamps	P	EXTEND and LAND
Altimeters	P/C	Checked, QNH/QFE set
TCAS	P/C	Checked
HP stop valves	E	SHUT
Engineer's taxi checks	E	Complete
Igniters	E	As required

The take-off checks are completed and the aircrafts rolls towards the centreline of the runway, guided by the PF.

'Take-off checks complete.'

'Eng, your throttles,' calls the PF.

'My throttles,' comes the reply.

As previously mentioned, the co-pilot is PF today. His left hand is on the yoke – holding a little into wind aileron and a slight push nose down – and his right hand is on the tiller. The captain, as PNF, has checked the co-pilot's application of aileron and is now monitoring the centre console, ready to call an abort if required, his right hand on the throttles.

'Set factored power.'

The VC10 had three power settings for take-off. Full power would often be used when heavy and in hot conditions. Factored power would be more commonly known today as a 'de-rated' take-off power where 96% or 93% HP rpm (equivalent to N2 on a modern engine) would be used, depending on circumstances and take-off calculations.

The idle whine is now consigned to history as suddenly an almighty roar can be heard through the airframe. Those used to the buzzing drone of modern high-bypass turbofans may be forgiven for thinking they are now seated in a very large fighter jet. The PNF completes a gross error check of the HP rpm, the flight engineer confirms take-off power has been set.

'Power checked,' the captain calls.

The acceleration seems quick for such a large aircraft as the speed increases.

'80kts,' he calls.

The PF's right hand moves from the tiller and joins his other hand on the yoke; from now on directional control is coming from his feet on the pedals via the three rudder sections attached to the fin.

'V_1,' calls the PNF at 130kts – the point of no return. Up to now the call of 'ABORT, ABORT' could have brought the aircraft to a shuddering halt on what remained of Brize Norton's 9,000ft runway. The PF removes the forward pressure on the control column. The captain's right hand moves off the throttles. Committed to flight, the aircraft continues its thunderous acceleration.

'Rotate.' At 151kts it now wants to fly. With both hands on the yoke, the PF gently raises the nosewheel off the tarmac. The control column feels surprisingly firm and requires a fair amount of pressure to move it rearwards. Finally, a few seconds later, the mainwheels leave the ground.

Climb out

'Gear up,' calls the PF. Suddenly the volume in the cockpit increases as the nosewheel doors open and air rushes into the wheel well. As the wheels move into the bay their rotation is stopped by an abrasive strip which sends a judder through the flight deck.

'V_2,' as the aircraft continues its acceleration. The PF is able to pitch up a little further and by using the TPI levers trims out any forces he is holding to maintain V_2+20kts – a prolonged period out of trim would tire the arms quickly and still both hands are required on the control column. At 800ft the PF gets to feel the ailerons for the first time, again needing to use both hands to roll to about 20° angle of bank to turn on to a heading of 313°. The TACAN is set to receive Brize Norton's beacon, and the

PF is now looking to intercept the 283° radial outbound.

'Throttle,' calls the PNF as the aircraft reaches 1,500ft. This signals the start of the noise abatement procedure – a period of reduced power to lessen the aircraft's noise signature while on departure. At civil airfields this is key; set off the noise alarms and a fine would follow. However, in the desert at heavy AUW [all-up weight] the noise abatement would be dispensed with. In this case, on reaching 1,500ft the aircraft would be accelerated and the flaps and slats brought straight in, with ATC on occasion querying the apparent lack of climb progress. Today, though, we have the luxury of our cooler British climate, and the aircraft's performance is more than adequate.

'89%,' replies the flight engineer.

'After take-off checks,' requests the PF.

AFTER TAKE-OFF CHECKS

Landing gear	P/C	UP, lights out
Alert warning	P/C	Reset
Aileron upset	P/C	As required
Landing lamps	P	RETRACT and OFF
Igniters	E	OFF

'After take-off checks complete.'

Again, the throttles on the centre console move backwards, seemingly automatically. The noise abatement power has been calculated pre take-off and is scribbled on the same laminated 'plaque' as the weight and speeds. The aircraft's rate of climb slows dramatically; although the change in percentage of HP rpm from 93% to 89% is relatively small, the change in power is much greater. Meanwhile, the PF has brought us around to the left and is holding the 283° radial nicely. We're now heading for OSGOD, the final point on the Standard Instrument Departure. The noise abatement continues up to 3,300ft.

'Noise abatement complete,' calls the PNF.

'Climb power,' requests the PF. The throttles advance to set 93% HP rpm and the PF coordinates and trims to lower the nose to accelerate to the minimum flap retract speed (MFR). Today the AUW is just over 140 tonnes, so the MFR is 200kts.

The PF calls, 'Flaps up.'

'Speed checked, selected, looking for 234,' confirms the PNF.

'Running,' confirms the flight engineer.

In reality, the flap lever operates both the flap and slat levers, being connected by a retractable pin. In the event of a failure of one or other, the lever can be split. More importantly, they can also be split to allow independent retraction of each in the event of a double engine failure, where the flaps will be brought in first, and then the slats.

The flaps and slats start to move. The coordination skills of the PF are tested again. The PNF commentates on the flap and slat positions, and the speed to go until the 'flap-up safety speed' (FUSS) is reached.

'Through 14½ [degrees], 26kts to find,' advises the PNF. The PF is active on the TPI, trimming to adjust to the trim changes with the flaps and slats moving up and in.

'Half to go, 15kts,' the commentary continues.

'Quarter to go, 7kts.' Looking up at the control position indicator we see the ailerons moving upwards; having 'armed' the aileron upset in the taxi checks, as the flaps retract, this is coming on, causing a downward aerodynamic force on the outer wings and reducing the stress on the wing structure. Finally the PF confirms, 'Flaps and slats up and in.'

'Confirmed,' says the eng, 'FL100 buffet* 245.' The pilots respond by putting two of the ASI bugs to represent 245kts and the other pair on V_{NO}, 310kts (IAS).

Now, with the aircraft clean, the PF has some light relief as we can finally engage the autopilot. He selects 'Autopilot 2' using the switch on his left on the centre console. 'Heading' (HDG) mode is selected using the rotary knob on the far left of the autopilot control panel and the autopilot follows the heading 'bug' on the co-pilot's HSI (with 'Autopilot 1' selected it

---

*:The 'buffet speed' is the speed at which the aircraft will encounter the onset of buffet provided that excess 'G' is applied at a particular weight and altitude. The C.1/C.1K used the 1.35G buffet (or if that was limiting, the 1.2G buffet); the K.3 and K.4 the 1.35G buffet (and 1.25G buffet). It was updated as the aircraft climbed and later as weight decreased.

would follow the captain's HSI 'bug'). At the moment pitch is being controlled by a pair of wheels either side of the manual turn control on the autopilot console. The PF controls the aircraft's attitude using these and steadies us at 290kts. Once steady, he pushes forward the white 'IAS' switch. Now the autopilot is controlling both our heading and attitude. The feel of the autopilot and its switches will be second nature to both pilots; should the aircraft suffer an incident with smoke in the cockpit they'll be able to operate the autopilot blindly, and they practise this at least once every six months in the simulator.

CLIMB CHECKS

Aileron upset	P/C	As required
Flaps and slats	P/C	UP and IN
	E	Confirmed
Speedbrakes	P/C	Baulk in
Altimeters	P/C	As required
Engineer's climb checks	E	Complete

CLIMB CHECKS: Engineer
(After flap retract)

Flap isolation switches	ISOLATE
Galley load	ON (as role permits)
SSB	Auto
Fuel transfer	As required
Spill valves	NORM
Pressurisation	Check
Flight deck flow	As required
AAR lights	As required

'Climb checks complete.'

The climb continues at 93% HP rpm – with this set we are getting just over 1,400fpm rate of climb. If we wanted to climb faster we could ask the flight engineer to set 'Ops Essential Power' – either 96% HP rpm or the highest power below this with the engines remaining within their operating limit. The PNF is talking to ATC, and we are handed over from Brize Departures to a Swanwick ATCC military controller as we climb towards the Lichfield Radar Corridor's western end.

Cleared to FL140, the PNF sets this in the 'Altitude Alerter' on the top left corner of the centre panel.

'2,000 to level,' states the PNF as we pass FL120. This is the first warning of the impending level-off.

1,000ft later as we pass FL130, the 'Altitude Alerter' emits an audible 'bong' over the intercom and illuminates an orange light. The PF braces the control column, deselects the IAS hold and transfers his left hand back to the trim wheels. He carefully coordinates the aircraft's pitch attitude and power to reduce the rate of climb, which at this stage is still fairly rapid. If we were levelling higher on a passenger or transport sortie, the rate of climb may be far lower, around the 500fpm minimum required. He calls power settings to the flight engineer, as we level off at FL140. Finally we are steady and level at 300kts, and he pushes forward the 'ALT' switch on the autopilot to engage the altitude hold.

Into the cruise
'Eng, yours for 300kts,' he calls. The flight engineer will now adjust the engines to maintain this speed.

300kts, our Indicated Air Speed (IAS), is used at all levels for cruising at or below FL320 (FL310 in the K.3/4). Above FL330 Mach 0.84 is used for the C.1K (FL320 and Mach 0.82 for the K.3/4). Flying at height is more economical – any sector greater than 250 miles is best flown at FL330 or above.

TOP-OF-CLIMB CHECKS

Turn off lights	P	OFF
TCAS	P/C	As required
Selcal	P/C	ON
Seatbelt signs	P/C	As required
Standby altimeter	P/C	As required
RVSM check	P/C	As required

'Top-of-climb checks complete.'

Passing through the Lichfield Corridor there is now a little time to relax. The fuel graph is passed around the cockpit as the routine checks are completed.

Exiting the Lichfield Corridor we turn north-east and climb to FL190 to pass through the Gamston Radar Corridor. This is our last controlled airspace to negotiate before we can head out to the Air-to-Air Refuelling Area (AARA) over the North Sea.

VC10 tanking

'The first receivers are inbound,' the navigator advises. The 'boom frequency' is used for communication between the tanker and its receiver aircraft, allowing them to communicate without taking airtime on an ATC frequency. On a quiet day, however, if the ATC controller doesn't have much traffic, they may be happy to vector the fighters to you and you talk to them on their frequency.

'Tartan 22 this is Marham 41 Flight,' crackles over the airwaves. A pair of Tornado GR.4s are inbound.

'Marham 41 Flight, Tartan 22, this is for RV Alpha, my flight level 1-8-0, your flight level 1-7-0 set TACAN 38,' responds the co-pilot, still acting as PF.

The fighters have been vectored towards us, ideally to a position about 1nm behind and 1,000ft below, although the crew, if possible, will try to manoeuvre to make the geometry as simple and efficient as possible. The fighter sets its TACAN to the briefed frequency. The navigator has set 101, a 63 channel split, on our TACAN and the display flickers to show the Tornados at 15.4nm. As we head to the eastern end of the AARA, we know they are behind us having heard them talking to 'Swanwick Mil'. The PF enters a left-hand turn. You notice he's now using the large rotary knob, about 5cm across, in the centre of the autopilot console, to manually control the aircraft's angle of bank. He's smoothly rotated it about to the left; as a consequence, the aircraft has adopted about 20° of bank. This is the second mode of automatic directional control and it allows the pilot fine control over the angle of bank they select – meaning turns – particularly with receivers in contact, it can be smoother and more predictable. The rotary switch he used earlier to select 'HDG' mode is now back in the twelve o'clock position.

'Pre-tanking checks please,' he requests.

PRE-TANKING CHECKS		
Turn-off lights	P	On
TCAS	P/C	TA
Beacons	P/C	OFF
Strobes	P/C	As required
Seatbelt signs	P/C	ON
HF	P/C	Deselected
Galley load	E	No 3 + 4 OFF
Limiting speeds	E	Stated
AAR lights	E	On
Autopilot	P/C	Checked and MAN
Hoses	P/C, E	Trail (when required)

The navigator reads through the check list. The captain makes a couple of switch selections to the boxes above. The transponder is switched to 'TA Only' and the strobes are now set to red, not white; the former will stop us having to respond to a full TCAS 'RA', mandating a climb or descent, while the latter will avoid the fighters being distracted by the glare of the strobes.

'Pre-tanking checks complete.'

The PF rolls the wings back to the level attitude, and then states, 'Eng, clear to trail.'

'Trailing . . .' replies the flight engineer as the hoses begin to travel.

This is the cue for the flight engineer to trail the two wing hoses. Should we be refuelling another large aircraft in a K.3 or K.4, we could use the centreline hose. Today, though, in a C.1K, we only have the Mk. 32 wing pods. The flight engineer turns to the refuelling panel to his right where the shape of the pod on the left wing can just about be seen on the rather fuzzy CCTV monitor.

The TACAN display counts down as the fighters close in. At 2.0nm the 'trade' can be seen by looking outside the left window, behind the captain's seat, in the eight o'clock position.

'Full trail, red on left and right,' the flight engineer confirms as the hoses reach their full extent. The Mk. 32 AAR pod is equipped with a series of lights – two green, two amber and two red. These will be used not only during normal refuelling, but also allow AAR in complete radio

silence. On this occasion, the red indicates to a receiver not to make contact.

'Marham 41 Flight visual,' comes over the radio.

'Marham 41 Flight, Clear Join Observation Left,' replies the co-pilot, still acting as PF.

'Join Observation Left, Marham 41 Flight,' the fighters acknowledge. Observation left is, to those familiar with formation flying, more commonly known as echelon left. In tanking parlance 'Observation' is used to describe the joining area on the left, while 'Reform' is used to describe the echelon right position the aircraft will move to once tanking is complete. Aircraft will, or should, never join directly astern.

'Marham 41 Flight, State Requirements?' asks the PF.

'Fill to full Marham 41, approximately 1.5 tons.'

'Fill to full Marham 42, approximately 2 tons.'

'Roger,' the co-pilot acknowledges.

The Tornados bring themselves into the Observation position as the PF rolls the wings level again. We'll maintain this heading for the next 50 miles or so.

'Moving in nicely,' observes our captain as he peers over his left shoulder. 'Moving forward and up.'

'Marham 41 Flight, Observation Left,' the lead Tornado informs us.

'Yep, they're there,' confirms the captain.

It is time to get the receivers behind the two hoses trailing from each wing. They have both deployed their AAR probes, each protruding out to the right-hand side of the cockpit.

'Marham 41 Clear Astern Right, Marham 42 Clear Astern Left,' calls the PF.

'Clear Astern Right, Marham 41,' comes the first reply.

'Clear Astern Left, Marham 42,' replies his wingman.

As the formation move on to their own hoses, communication now becomes individual between the tanker and each receiver. The captain watches as the leader moves down and back while the flight engineer picks them up on the camera. He provides a commentary as each aircraft moves behind either hose.

'Marham 41 appears to be astern the right,' he concludes. The PF lets the Tornado call in to confirm.

'Marham 41, Astern Right,' the Tornado calls.

'Marham 41 Clear Contact Right,' replies the PF

'Clear Contact Right, Marham 41.'

'Red out right,' states the flight engineer. The amber light on the pod illuminates.

The flight engineer continues his commentary: 'Moving forward. . . . moving forward . . . approaching the basket . . . Missed . . . dropping back . . . steady . . . moving forward . . . approaching the basket . . . contact . . . pushing in . . . fuel flows . . . green on . . . steady.' The green light indicates fuel is flowing.

He slews the camera left: 'Marham 42's astern the left.' The wingman has been sitting silently astern the left. He knows that he'll only be cleared to make contact once his leader is in, so hasn't cluttered the radio.

'Marham 42 Clear Contact Left,' confirms the PF.

The process repeats as 'Marham 42' makes contact. The Tornados remain in contact for a few minutes. The tanker holds steady on its course, the autopilot keeping it straight and level, although the PF's hand stays on the yoke. He's holding it both to ensure he can regain control immediately if the autopilot 'drops out' and it also ensures his thumb is close to the intercom/transmit switch on the top outer portion of the yoke. He adjusts the heading, again using the manual turnwheel to introduce a small angle of bank and induce a slight heading change.

Eventually the fuel flow begins to drop off, meaning both are close to full.

'Marham 41 complete,' states the first Tornado.

'Marham 41, Disconnect,' the PF orders.

The Tornado pulls the hose out slightly as he moves back. There is a slight jerk as he pulls his probe out of the basket.

'Red on.' The flight engineer confirms that he is disconnected and steady astern the hose.

'Marham 41, Go Reform Right,' calls the PF, also passing the fuel transfer.

'Reform Right, Marham 41.'

The Tornado moves across, forward and up into the Reform position. Marham 42 also completes and moves to join his leader. With the pair steady in Reform Right, the PF clears them to leave.

'Marham 41 Flight, Clear to leave,' calls the PF.

'Clear to leave Marham 41 Flight. Thanks very much,' replies the lead Tornado.

This carefully choreographed process is repeated with other trade during the day until it is finally time to head home. The navigator has already set up the FMS (flight management system), and after final confirmation that we are no longer required on station, the PF engages 'INS' mode on the autopilot. This is the third and final mode of heading control, and the aircraft will now follow the route in the FMS. The PNF requests a climb to FL210 – our most efficient cruising altitude – to get home via the Pole Hill and Shawbury VORs. The plaque is passed back from the PF to the eng and nav for the landing details to be inserted – V_{AT}, landing weight, landing runway and minima and diversion. Today the diversion is Lyneham with 5.7t being the diversion fuel.

POST-TANKING CHECKS

Hoses	E	Stowed
AAR lights	E	As required
Buffet speed	E	Stated
Galley load	E	As required
Seatbelt signs	P/C	As required
TCAS	P/C	As required
Beacons	P/C	ON
Strobes	P/C	As required
Turn off lights	P	As required

'Post-tanking checks complete.'

AIR-TO-AIR REFUELLING SIGNAL LIGHT INDICATIONS

SIGNAL INDICATION	MEANING
Steady **RED**	Do not make contact
Steady AMBER	Tanker ready for contact
Steady **GREEN**	Fuel flows
Flashing AMBER	Planned off-load complete, no more fuel available, receiver to disconnect
Flashing **GREEN**	Planned off-load complete, more fuel available, receiver may remain in contact or disconnect as required
Flashing **GREEN** (within one minute of contact)	Soft contact. Receiver to disconnect
RED while in contact	Breakaway
All lights out	Equipment malfunction. Disconnect and do not make contact

Notes:

The HDU fuel valve is selected to AUTO for dry contacts by large aircraft. Therefore, the AMBER light will be replaced by the **GREEN** light when the receiver has pushed in for both wet and dry contacts.

For dry contacts with fast-jet aircraft, the HDU fuel valve is selected SHUT; the AMBER light will remain on during contact. This maintains standardised signals, for fast-jet aircraft, using wing pods and HDU.

Descending

The plaque returns to the front of the flight deck. 'BZN TACAN' is now tuned and we are just over 80 miles out from the beacon. The captain will act as PF for the approach and landing. The crew check in for the approach brief.

The captain conducts the brief, confirming the ATIS (airfield traffic information service), type of descent, the radio and nav aids set up, the approach procedure and whether idle or full reverse will be used on touchdown; for noise abatement purposes the former is preferred. If the weather was very poor, he could brief a 'monitored approach'. In this eventuality the co-pilot would fly the approach leaving the captain to monitor and also devote attention to gaining the visual references required for landing. If they are not seen the co-pilot continues to fly the missed approach procedure.

With the brief concluded the descent checks are completed and now approaching 50 miles to run to the beacon, the captain

RIGHT After conversion from civilian airliners, all of the K.2 and K.3 tankers featured a small number of rearward-facing seats. These were located just behind the cockpit and ahead of the bulkhead into the main fuselage and the five extra fuel tanks. These seats were often used when the aircraft travelled away from its Brize Norton base and was able to carry its own team of engineers. Seen here are the starboard-side seats in K.3 ZA150/J at Dunsfold. *(Keith Wilson)*

starts a standard descent. This is flown at idle power with speedbrakes in, giving a rate of descent (RoD) of about 2,000fpm at 290kts IAS. If required, the RoD can be increased by deploying the spoilers – this would give a rate of descent of up to 3,500fpm. In an emergency the RoD can be increased further by descending at V_{NO} or M_{NO}. Using fairly low power settings the RoD is decreased as we approach Brize Norton overhead. The approach checks are completed as the aim is to start our procedural approach at 4,000ft.

DESCENT CHECKS

PA announcement	P/C	As required
Briefing	P/C	Stated
Standby altimeter	P/C	As required
TCAS	P/C	BELOW
Selcal	P/C	OFF
Seat belt signs	P/C	ON
Turn off lights	P	ON
Fin fuel	E	Checked
Thrust augmenters	E	SHUT
Pressurisation	E	QNH/QFE set

'Descent checks complete,' is confirmed.

APPROACH CHECKS

Seats and harnesses	All	Secure
RAD/NAV select	P, C	As required left, right
Engineer's approach checks	E	Complete

'Approach checks complete.'

Approach and landing

Once cleared for the procedure, we depart overhead the 'BZN TACAN' at 4,000ft QFE. The captain, who is now the PF, is using the needle on the TACAN RMI on the panel in front of his right knee. He keeps the 'tail' of the needle pointing towards the 101° bearing; the range on the 'TACAN 1' indicator in the centre panel is counting upwards through 1nm as you glance at it. The navigator is commentating on the drift that the INS is calculating. The PF steadies the aircraft at 210kts, having levelled at 2,500ft, steadying at a power setting around 80% HP rpm. He also arms the autothrottles for all four engines. This panel sits just ahead of the main autopilot control. He sets a speed of 175kts using a small rotary knob ready to engage in a few moments' time.

As the TACAN range reaches seven miles the PF calls for flaps to take-off.

'Speed checked', the co-pilot glances at ASIs to confirm that we are below the flap limiting speed.

'Selected', he moves the conjoined flap/slat lever to the take-off position.

'Running,' confirms the flight engineer.

The aircraft continues on its path. As the extra drag of the flaps bite, the speed decreases more rapidly. It approaches 180kts.

'Eng, my throttles,' calls the PF.

'Your throttles,' is the response.

'Autothrottle.' The captain flicks a small switch to the left, engaging the autothrottle with 'Autopilot 1'.

The throttles appear to move of their own accord, setting the appropriate power to maintain somewhere around 175kts.

At 9nm on the TACAN, we enter the left base turn. Just before we do . . .

'Gear Down, Landing Checks,' the PF calls.

'Speed checked.' This time the landing gear limiting speed, which we should be well below.

'Selected,' replies the PNF.

The navigator reads the checks, with the PNF and flight engineer replying as and when required.

LANDING CHECKS

Landing brief	P/C	Stated
Altimeters	P/C	Checked, QNH/QFE . . . set
Speedbrake	P/C	Zero, baulk out
Flaps and slats	P/C	As required
	E	Confirmed
Threshold speed	P, C	Bugged left, right
	E, N	Checked right, left
Landing gear	P/C	DOWN, three greens, brake lights out
Steering	P/C	Central
Landing lamps	P	EXTEND and LAND
Prior to final landing:		
Cabin landing checks	LM/CS/E	Complete

'Landing checks complete.'

The aircraft is now in a steady turn to the left and descending to 2,000ft. On the pilots' approach plates it is drawn as a continuous teardrop turn; in reality the PF will be completing the majority of the turn sooner, as to give a 'cut' on to the ILS, by approaching our final approach track at a 30–40° angle. He's using the 'HDG' mode again. As we pass though about 185kts there is a small 'kick' of yaw; this is the rudder channel changing sensitivity to increase the control effectiveness at lower speed. Levelling off the power is again increased.

'ILS checks complete,' calls the co-pilot.

As the PF he engages the 'ALT' lock, once more the engines spool up to about 85%. The PNF says goodbye to the approach controller and contacts the talkdown controller.

'Brize Talkdown, Tartan 22, 1012 set,' transmits the co-pilot.

'Tartan 22, Brize Talkdown, QFE read back correct, report glidepath descending, gear down,' crackles the reply.

The ILS checks are completed and the 'flags' on the HSI localiser and glideslope indications have gone. The autopilot directional control is now set one click to the right on 'LOC/VOR'; the autopilot will now automatically place itself on the ILS localiser. Almost immediately he selects another click to the right, 'GS Auto'; the autopilot should now also descend the aircraft with the ILS glideslope.

The vertical white line on the HSI gradually moves in from the right and the aircraft banks left to intercept the centreline. Minor power adjustments keep us safely above our minimum speed, which with take-off flap deployed is $V_{AT}+30$. The glideslope indicator is also now live, a horizontal white bar coming down from the top of the instrument – we have to intercept the ILS from below. The HSI has four white dots, aligned vertically and spaced equally above and below the centre of the instrument. As the glideslope bar hits the second dot from the top it is time to configure for the approach:

'Flaps approach,' calls the captain.

'Speed checked, selected,' replies the co-pilot, moving the flap lever as he speaks.

'Running,' calls the flight engineer.

The glideslope indicator is almost in the centre of the instrument. There is a loud click as the 'ALT' lock disengages, indicating that the autopilot has captured the glideslope. The autothrottles now bring the power back. The captain adjusts them, now aiming for a speed of $V_{AT}+20$.

Approaching 1,500ft, the captain calls 'Flaps land.'

'Speed checked, selected,' replies the co-pilot as he moves the lever.

The aircraft is now configured for landing. 'Runway in sight,' calls the co-pilot. ATC passes clearance to land.

'Noted, continuing on instruments,' states the captain. Although the weather is good, the training value of the approach is not to be wasted. The minimum speed is now $V_{AT}+10$ until the final stages of the approach.

'1,000ft,' the captain states. The co-pilot

confirms the altimeter setting. The flight engineer has just completed his final checks.

The captain continues to fettle the autothrottle position, settling just above 130kts – our landing weight is a shade under 85 tonnes, giving a V_{AT} of 118kts. The descent continues. We approach the decision height (DH) of 200ft.

'200 to decision,' states the co-pilot as we pass 400ft.

'100 to decision', as we pass 300ft.

'Decide,' he states at 200ft.

'Decision Land,' confirms the captain. He presses the instinctive cut-out switch on the top outer horn of his control column, immediately disconnecting both the autopilot and autothrottles.

'83%', the flight engineer passes the current power setting – he is now back in control of the throttles.

'79 . . .' calls the captain. '81. . . .' We approach the flare.

'79 . . . 77. . . .' The captain begins to raise the nose and enter the flare. With a crosswind from the left, he uses the rudder to bring the nose of the aircraft on to the centreline – a 'wing down' crosswind technique cannot be used due to the proximity of the pods to the ground. As he applies the rudder he also applies left aileron to keep the wings level; if the crosswind was close to or at the limit – 28kts across – almost full aileron would be applied.

'75. . . .' We are now a couple of feet above the runway.

'Idle power,' calls the captain. There is a thud as the mainwheel bogies contact the runway.

'Spoilers,' calls the captain. The co-pilot reaches across and pulls the speedbrake lever fully back. He then operates the reverse thrust, which is only on the outer engines, Nos 1 and 4.

'Idle reverse,' he responds. The captain lowers the nosewheel on to the tarmac.

'Full reverse,' calls the captain. The co-pilot pulls the reverse thrust lever fully rear to selects full reverse thrust.

The speed approaches 80kts. 'Reverse idle,' requests the captain. The co-pilot pushes the reverse levers forward to idle reverse.

'60kts,' calls the co-pilot.

'Cancel reverse,' the captain responds.

The aircraft decelerates to taxiing speed – the reassuring idle whine of the four Conways is heard once again. The co-pilot is 'cleared to clean up', bringing in the flaps, slats and spoilers, and holding the control column central to ensure the control surfaces are in a central position while the flight engineer isolates their PFCUs (powered flight-control units).

AFTER-LANDING CHECKS		
Igniters	E	OFF
Airframe anti-icing	E	SHUT
Speedbrakes	P/C	Zero
Pitot and screen heat	P/C	OFF and LOW
Strobes	P/C	DIM RED
SIFF/TCAS	P/C	OFF
Autothrottles	P/C	OFF
Land/taxi lamps	P	OFF
Radar	P, N	STANDBY front, rear
Spill valve	E	As required
Dump valve	E	As required
Flaps and slats	P/C	As required
	E	Confirmed
TPI	P/C	Zero
Yaw dampers	E	ISOLATE
Flight engineer's after-landing checks	E	Complete

We taxi into dispersal, the flight engineer starting the APU as we do. Under the guidance of the marshaller the captain manoeuvres on to the stand. We stop, and the parking brake is applied. There is an electrical blip as the electrics are transferred from the engine-driven generators to that of the APU. Finally the flight engineer shuts all four HP cocks to shut down the engines. Relative quiet descends on to the flight deck.

'After-landing checks complete.'

SHUTDOWN CHECKS

Parking brake	P	On
External power/APU	E	Established
Engines	E	Shutdown
Beacons and strobes	C	OFF
Taxi and turn off lights	P	RETRACT and OFF
Engine anti-icing	E	OFF
Fridge master switches	E	ISOLATE
Pod isol. valves	E	SHUT
Radar	P, N	OFF front, rear
ADR	N	OFF
TACANs	N	OFF
Brakes	P	Off (when chocks in)
Ground/flight	E	GROUND
Seatbelt signs	C	Off
Autopilot master switches	C	OFF
Navaids and radar altimeter	P, C, N	Off
Engineer's shutdown checks	E	Complete
Red dome light	P	Off
When passengers are deplaned:		
Station boxes	All	OFF
Radio	C	OFF
Radio and gyro supplies	N	OFF

'Shutdown checks complete.'

'Mayday' from the flight deck

Chris Haywood recalls an inflight emergency on a VC10 flight:

Having a good team in the cockpit is crucial. The VC10 was a very 'manual' aircraft, so relied on each crew member being able to do their job reliably. Any breakdown in the crew environment

could be critical. Detachments were a good opportunity to get to know people – sometimes you might not see another squadron member for several weeks – but on detachment you operated as a crew together for a number of missions. The rapport you developed generally made the environment very effective. Everyone in the cockpit brought something different. The co-pilots were almost invariably first tourists, but the captains, navigators and flight engineers were more of a mix. Some were very experienced but exclusively on the VC10, while others – particularly the navigators and flight engineers – had more of a depth of experience on other types.

A good example of VC10 teamwork was an emergency we suffered in April 2011 while over the Mediterranean. We were cruising at FL350 having completed our refuelling serial. I remember it vividly. I was facing over my left shoulder talking to the nav', Flt Lt Paul Morris, when suddenly there was a large bang, which actually sounded like the eng, MEng Derek Kyle, slamming the document 'bin' underneath his station. As I sat there, the sight of the nav donning his oxygen mask quickly gave me the impression that my initial diagnosis may have been incorrect. He pointed towards the front; the captain's windscreen had (quite comprehensively) delaminated.

ABOVE The delaminated windscreen on the VC10 C.1K that occurred while cruising at FL350 over the Mediterranean in April 2011.
(Chris Haywood)

The captain, Flt Lt Ian McNicholas, was flying at the time. Almost without thought we knew what to do. The captain started an emergency descent, and simultaneously I was transmitting the 'Mayday' call to Malta ATC. The nav was already working on both contingencies of a diversion to Malta and whether we could make it back to our base at Trapani. The eng's input was invaluable. During training, an 'emergency descent' is always that, a fast descent down to a level where the aircraft can be safely operated in an unpressurised state. However, we weren't yet depressurised and with the windscreen in the state it was, we actually needed to be flying as slowly as possible. Throughout the descent he kept up an effective supply of information to the captain. There was also a short debate as to where the captain should sit. Should he remain in his seat behind the damaged screen, or move into the jump seat? Either way, memories of Michael Buerk narrating the story of Captain Tim Lancaster on the television programme *999* (when he was almost sucked out of his BAC 1-11) came edging into the back of the mind! Whatever happened, our captain wouldn't be able to fly the approach.

In the end, it was decided he would remain in his seat as it was the best place to complete his drills as PNF. He'd still be able to monitor the approach and was afforded some visibility through the centre windscreen and the DV window to his left. Once we had descended to 8,000ft the nav, having been able to establish the cruise speed we could attain, was able to confirm the fuel would be sufficient to return to base. After that, other than the limited visibility, the approach and landing were uneventful.

Teamwork is imperative

As you've read in the sortie description above, it really is a closely controlled team effort focused around high-quality training along with a good understanding and use of Standard Operation Procedures (SOPs). Everyone knew exactly what they should be doing and when they should be doing it – and if they didn't, it would have been fixed with remedial training in the simulator. The simulator provided a good baseline of training, be it for a captain having to handle a double engine failure out of Nairobi or the co-pilot having to fly the relatively difficult IF scan; that is, having to fly using his own pressure instruments but also the small standby attitude indicator and altimeter just to the right of the captain on the centre panel, should the aircraft suffer an electrical failure and fly with the ELRAT extended to generate electrical power!

Everyone in the cockpit has an essential role, with the two pilots dividing the flying tasks, both as the pilot flying and that of pilot non-flying. Ultimately other than flying from the 'other' seat, in normal operations, the job is broadly the same – although the captain does have the extra responsibility of decision making and overall control of how we conduct the mission or task. That said, there were some areas of flight only the captains were permitted to fly – such as flapless or slatless approaches and AAR receiving.

The navigator's role was very much that of pure navigation, consisting of the flight planning, route navigation and fuel planning, particularly on Trail and AAR sorties.

The flight engineer was very much the systems expert, and the size of his panel detailed the depth of his task. Fuel, electrics, hydraulics and AAR were all very much his domain, and with few automatic systems it was a challenging task.

Into theatre

In an area of conflict very little changed. Operational AAR sorties were flown in just the same way as training sorties. We would always operate with the aim of giving as much of our fuel as we usefully could to receiver aircraft; possibly on operations we worked out the maths a little more precisely to ensure we could give every last permissible drop; and if necessary we'd try to position ourselves to be geographically of the most use. Other than that, very little changed.

The mechanics of flying an operational sortie weren't very different to a normal training North Sea 'tow-line'. Granted there were extra considerations, but the sorties were flown much in the same way. Depending upon the particular theatre, once in the operating area you may well have found yourself controlled by a ground-based controller or by an AWACS.

The main difference while working

operationally was in the mentality; maybe a greater urgency to help the receivers and give as much fuel away as you usefully could – landing with 9 tonnes of fuel on board when your diversion fuel is just 6 tonnes means you could have given a receiver another few minutes of time in theatre. In the latter years, the majority of operations were in support of RAF Typhoon and Tornado aircraft, alongside US Navy and Marine Corps jets, but there was also some refuelling of French Air Force and Navy aircraft, as well as Italian AV-8Bs and AMX.

A personal pleasure

I couldn't have wished for a better aeroplane to fly. It required some pure handling skills that other types didn't; and with at least four crew members on every sortie, it needed a high degree of Crew Resource Management (CRM) to operate well. Job variation was good, too. You might be on detachment in the Middle East one month, where you develop quite a close bond with your crew mates; and then off to the USA or Canada on a freight or trooping sortie the next, interspersed with a UK AAR sortie or two.

The other wonderful thing that we were not able to do, post-9/11, was to permit people to visit the flightdeck. It was something I'd been able to do as a child but, sadly, such an opportunity was no longer available on civilian flights. To see the smile on a youngster's face as they sat on the jump seat and took in the panoramic view was absolutely priceless.

Overall, it was a privilege to have had the opportunity to fly and operate the VC10. Generally the only bits that weren't fun involved the simulators!

Flight engineer with the airlines

John B. Williamson initially started his aviation career without any pre-conceived desires – save for the fact that his brother-in-law was a Second World War Hurricane pilot. 'I thought that I wanted to be a draughtsman or designer!' The de Havilland Aircraft Co. at Hatfield, some 6 miles from his home, was the largest engineering company locally and offered

ABOVE The navigator's station on K.4 ZD241 at Bruntingthorpe. *(Keith Wilson)*

1 Cartridge stowage
2 Data receptacle
3 VG and comparison monitor supplies switch No 1
4 Compass supplies switch No 1
5 VG and comparison monitor supplies switch No 2
6 Compass supplies switch No 2
7 Radio supplies AC/DC supplies switch No 1 main
8 Radio supplies AC/DC supplies switch No 1 emergency
9 Intercom supplies switch
10 Radio supplies AC/DC supplies switch No 2 main
11 No 1 TACAN controller
12 No 2 TACAN controller
13 No 1 compass latitude controller
14 No 2 compass latitude controller
15 Oxygen regulator Mk. 17F
16 ADF control unit
17 Station box
18 Oxygen mask stowage
19 Airborne radio relay control unit
20 Microphone selector panel
21 Joint tactical information distribution system (JTIDS)
22 Radio altimeter (RAD ALT) indicator
23 Altimeter
24 Airspeed indicator
25 Outside air temperature (OAT) indicator
26 TAS (true air speed) probe heater ammeter
27 VOR RMI
28 No 2 TACAN distance indicator
29 ADF/TACAN RMI
30 UHF/DF indicator
31 FMS control and display panel
32 INS control panel
33 INU No 2 control display unit
34 No 1 TACAN distance indicator
35 Weather radar indicator/ controller No 2
36 Compass true/magnetic switch unit
37 No 2 compass controller
38 No 1 compass controller
39 Intercom off/RT switch

RIGHT Close-up view of the navigator's main panel on ZD241. *(Keith Wilson)*

ABOVE Tucked away in its own drawer to the bottom left of the navigator's station is the joint tactical information distribution system (JTIDS). It provided secure support data communications capabilities, principally within the air and missile defence community. It was installed in preparation for Operation Enduring Freedom (Afghanistan) and Operation Iraqi Freedom. *(Keith Wilson)*

LEFT By way of a comparison with the navigator's station on ZD241 (see page 127), towards the end of its life, Super VC10 G-ASGC had been converted to a three-crew operation with the navigational responsibilities transferred to the two pilots. Consequently, the navigator's position was no longer required. *(Keith Wilson)*

a five-year apprenticeship. Little did he realise, at the time, it was the best he could have chosen.

In August 1955 he began the first year spent at Astwick Manor, the de Havilland Apprentice School, learning the basic skills of sheet metal work, machining and woodworking; all while attending technical college on day release, studying towards his Ordinary and Higher National qualifications.

Later, when he joined the factory 'environment', he spent time in the Comet 4 Fuselage Shop, before progressing through the Plastics Shop, Coppersmiths, Foundry, Assembly Shop and, finally, the Inspection Department.

John takes up the story:

My last two years were spent in the Flight Test Department. This is when I realised that my future desire was to become an accomplished aircraft maintenance engineer, or, better still, a flight engineer. The then de Havilland flight engineer on the Comet and later the Trident was one Brackston-Brown, who guided me to apply to one of the airlines. Sadly he was later killed in a Trident crash when the aircraft suffered a deep stall in East Anglia.

On completion of my apprenticeship in 1960, I tried unsuccessfully to join BOAC, so settled upon my next option and joined BEA. I studied for my Ground Engineering Licences, eventually holding Viscount 700/800 & RR Dart, HS Trident/RR Spey, Comet IV/RR Avon and Vanguard/RR Tyne, along with the Argosy/RR Dart certification approvals. At that time I was fortunate to work on the Handley Page Herald that the Duke of Edinburgh used on a South American trip.

I spent seven very happy and informative years as an Outstation Engineer, working at Berlin/Tempelhof, Amsterdam/Schiphol, Rome/Fiumicino International Airport and at Shannon crew training, to name but a few.

In 1967 the opportunity again presented itself to join BOAC, as a cadet flight engineer on either the VC10 or the Boeing 707; I chose the VC10 and commenced the 'Chalk & Talk' groundschool at Cranebank, near Heathrow. An anxious CAA type exam of around two hours followed. The pilots and flight engineer trainees

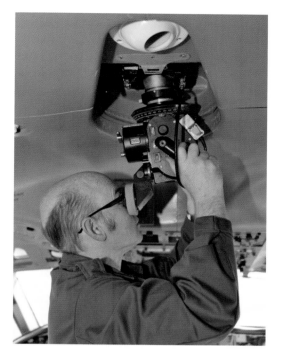

were the very first ones to sit the 'new' exam – 250 questions based on the Super VC10 speeds and weights. Shortly after the paper was delivered to us, a brave soul spoke out to say: 'We don't recognise the figures!' Amazingly, we had been given the wrong papers! A week

BELOW At the age of 77, John B. Williamson is still involved in aviation, albeit as a 'volunteer' – providing technical guidance and conducting a 'look-see' visit around the Cornwall Aviation Heritage Centre's VC10 exhibit, ZA148 – which he flew back in 1971 when seconded to East African Airways. *(Andrew Long)*

or so later we all took and successfully passed the 'Type Written Examination'.

Some 40 hours of simulator training followed – all normal and emergency drills – before we moved to a 'real' aircraft for base training at Shannon, together with cadet pilots.

Base training included undercarriage emergency lowering, ELRAT operation, smoke drills, Dutch Rolling, flapless and slatless landings – all things that could not be demonstrated in the basic flight simulators available at the time.

Again, luck was with me; normally we shared the training on a 4-hour flight with another trainee flight engineer. However, the chap I was paired with suffered from air sickness, so on several occasions I was allowed the entire 4-hour details to myself. Consequently, I completed my base training in very quick time.

Approximately 200 hours of 'line flying under supervision' followed, then a final base-training flight, this time 'circuits' at Stansted involving sixteen touch-and-goes plus one full-stop landing.

Fully-fledged flight engineer

In May 1969 I was a fully-fledged flight engineer on BOAC VC10s. In the early days, the flight engineer was strictly 'sideways-looking' – thereby expected to monitor the aircraft systems and not be fully integrated

with the remaining crew. This soon changed, and following training in flight path monitoring, the 'normal' checklist was amended and the flight engineers instructed on a basic '5 × 5' safety scan, to be completed at the end of each checklist. This included altitude, speed, heading, configuration, engine power (where the flight engineer would scan the engine instruments), fuel configuration, hydraulics, electrics and pressurisation.

The crew normally consisted of the captain, a flight engineer and two first officer pilots – one or both being qualified navigators who would role-swap, as required.

The cadet pilots also went through a lengthy and protracted route training with a 'landing card' which initially only allowed down-route landings with a training captain, in daylight and with limited crosswind restrictions. With long-haul flying it could take months to achieve an unrestricted landing card. A visit under supervision was also necessary for captains landing at Hong Kong's Kai Tak Airport, which featured a unique 'chequerboard' approach.

BOAC operated a 30-day roster (prior to any 'Bid-Line' system), but in order to ensure some stability they offered a 'PLATROS' (Planned Stand-Off Roster) system, with a guaranteed seven days off planned for six months in advance. The airline would even fly a delayed crew member home as a passenger to honour this. Many crews opted for a less restrictive roster and accepted whatever came.

Unusual routes and interesting accommodation

The VC10 had been designed to operate at hot and high airfields and possessed an excellent performance. Consequently, I regularly visited many African destinations including Nairobi, Entebbe, Johannesburg, the Seychelles, Blantyre and Dar-es-Salaam. A seniority rostering system was eventually introduced and worked well, as people's preferences differed; the golfers enjoyed Africa, while the 'Atlantic Barons' preferred the USA and Caribbean. A particular favourite route of mine was to Australia via the Pacific, which involved a 17-day trip with the same flight and cabin crew. The routing was London (Heathrow)–New York–Los Angeles–Honolulu–

BELOW John Williamson seen while working with BOAC in the early days. There was a problem with one of the Godfrey cabin air compressors during a transit stop at Geneva. He climbed using the ladder shown, which was much quicker than trying to 'borrow' a cherry picker from Swissair. Not sure what the health and safety brigade would make of it these days! *(via John Williamson)*

Fiji–Sydney–Melbourne, before returning via the same destinations.

When routing east, many of the crew hotels were fairly basic. The favourite night stops for all were the BOAC Rest Houses, Bahrain and Karachi both having happy memories of food being available 24 hours a day, including a full English breakfast anytime. Interestingly, the Qantas and RAF crews also stayed there, providing a great opportunity to swap stories.

On the technical side, in 1969 I did one flight to New York in a Super VC10 carrying a fifth engine in the spare pod.

Operating changes

Graduated power take-offs were introduced to extend the life of each engine. 'Autoland' was introduced, although it was not terribly successful, for a combination of reasons; mostly because the ground-based ILS systems were unreliable. Several aircraft were fitted with a 'Teleprinter' machine located below the navigator's table and, when in radio range, it was programmed to receive 'Met' (weather information) on a paper print-out; although once again, it was never a great success.

In the early days, the single inertial navigation system known as 'Carousel' was not fitted to the VC10s. Consequently, navigating over the North Atlantic involved the pilot-navigator shooting the Astro Sextant for star shots while also using both 'Loran' and 'Consul' long-range radio navigation systems.

Ocean station vessels were also stationed at sea and when requested on VHF, gave a radar bearing and range to aircraft in the vicinity. Having been at sea for a month, the ships' crews often passed personal messages, which we would then forward on by postcard.

When flying over the Christmas period, one pilot-navigator added a reindeer, sleigh and Father Christmas to his navigation plotting chart, all on track. This was not discovered for several months until there was a quality audit at head office; he was requested to 'turn up in uniform for an explanation'.

East African Airways

Together with another four BOAC flight engineers, I was seconded to East African Airways from 6 January until 13 April 1971.

I accrued some 245 flying hours with them. The operating procedures were very similar, but they employed straight navigators.

One I flew with from Nairobi to London was a 'radio ham' and having given us a heading shortly after take-off, which we maintained religiously, then spent the remainder of the time calling up his many contacts on HF. After several hours over Africa, we eventually picked up the VOR beacon at Caraffa in southern Italy and got us back on track!

BOAC Standard Operating Procedures (SOPs)

A normal day's work would start with your introduction to the other members of the flight crew; perhaps it may have been the first time you had been rostered together. Next, it was the briefing: covering the passenger and freight planned load; departure airport and en-route weather; weather at the destination; the choice of alternates and finally the SID (standard instrument departure), along with any aircraft defects. The captain would then have the final say on the required fuel load, plus any safety excess he wished to carry.

Then it was off to the aircraft where the flight engineer would liaise with the ground engineer, confirm the fuel required and complete his external walk-round inspections. These included removing and stowing the undercarriage ground lock safety pins; ensuring that all other blanks and covers were removed; checking for damage from baggage vehicles; ensuring the airframe was clear of snow and ice; or arranging for the aircraft to be de-iced, if required. Finally, a check would be made of the state of the baggage loading and if any live animals were to be carried in the hold. Once all this had been completed, it was off to the flight deck.

It always started with a safety check, followed by a scan check of all flight engineer systems and circuit-breaker check (usually conducted from memory). Meanwhile, the pilots would carry out their own scan checks before the non-handling pilot would first read the before-start checklist followed by the start checklist. The flight engineer would communicate with the ground (to enable the external air start to be powered up) before operating the start controls from his position. This was conducted with the pilot operating the HP

RIGHT The flight engineer's panel on K.4, ZD241. The size of the task undertaken by the flight engineer is clearly demonstrated here by the vast and complex array of systems he had to manage. *(Keith Wilson)*

1 Fuel system panel
2 Flying controls panel
3 Electrical power panel
4 Air conditioning panel
5 Oxygen and miscellaneous services panel
6 Fuselage and wing pod control, lighting and communications panel
7 Fuel dispensing control, CCTV and lighting panel
8 Airframe and engine anti-icing, hydraulic, pressurisation and flight instruments panel
9 Engine panel
10 Throttle quadrant
11 Engine start and door warning panel
12 Workstation with electrical storage compartment underneath
13 Oxygen regulator Mk. 17F
14 DC circuit-breakers and fuse panel

LEFT A close-up view of the engine panel on ZD241. To the bottom left are the four engine throttles with the Perspex-covered engine start and door warning panel (bottom-middle). *(Keith Wilson)*

BELOW The airframe and engine anti-icing, hydraulic, pressurisation and flight instruments panels at the flight engineer's station on ZD241. *(Keith Wilson)*

fuel cocks, the flight engineer monitoring the rpm rise, the EGT and oil pressure.

No 3 engine was normally always started first as it provided both electrical and hydraulic power. Once No 3 was running, the remaining engines were brought to life in the order 4, 1 and finally 2. Ground electrical power was not essential; an internal battery start gave the minimum (but adequate) instrument indications, until the first engine was started and its generator brought 'on-line'.

With all four engines running at idle and once the after-start checklist had been read and completed, the flight engineer would take over and control all the remaining normal and emergency checklists while the aircraft was moving off the stand.

The captain would handle the throttles for taxiing and to set take-off power, while the flight engineer would adjust or trim the engine throttles on take-off and then set climb power and control speed throughout cruise – usually at Mach 0.84. The RR Conways on the Super VC10 were very sensitive to 'surging' during the climb and needed close monitoring.

Within BOAC, the landing pilot would then handle their own throttles during the latter part of the approach and landing. However, when flying with Gulf Air, the former RAF 10 Squadron pilots would call out the power setting they wanted and the flight engineer would set it, right down to the touchdown with idle power called!

As well as monitoring and controlling speed during cruise, the flight engineer would be balancing fuel tanks, ensuring the fin tank was moved first on the Super VC10.

He would also monitor VHF and HF radios and collect weather broadcasts if required; all while maintaining a 'how goes it' fuel-burn log. Every hour a set of instrument readings was taken, which would show any fluid loss from the hydraulic or engine oil systems and any change to engine exhaust gas temperature (EGT) readings (usually the first indication of a problem).

Occasional cabin rectification was sometimes necessary, too – such as seat recline mechanism to be repaired, isolating water leaks in the toilets, replacing filaments in the overhead reading lights.

The BOAC flight engineers also had the

FAR LEFT Located on the top left of the flight engineer's station is the fuel control panel. Each of the eight fuel tanks – numbered 1, 2, 3, 4, 1A, centre, 4A and fin – all have their own gauges. It was imperative that the fuel content was carefully managed between tanks to ensure the correct centre of gravity on the aircraft. *(Keith Wilson)*

LEFT Located to the top right of the flight engineer's station are the panels for electrical power (left) and air conditioning (right). *(Keith Wilson)*

RIGHT Located in the top right-hand corner is the oxygen and miscellaneous services panel. *(Keith Wilson)*

FAR RIGHT The HDU and Mk. 32 Pod control panel on K.3, ZA150/J, at Dunsfold. To the middle right is the CCTV monitor with the fuel controls located just underneath it. *(Keith Wilson)*

BELOW The flight engineer's throttle quadrant. Cleverly located underneath the clear Perspex cover are the engine start controls and door warning lights. The red lights indicated which doors and panel were open (i.e. red light on means door open). The four switches (numbered 1–4) are the engine start and ignition switches (push forward for starting the engine and pull backwards to operate the ignitors only). The large black rotary switch is known as the start master. In military use it had two positions – 'Ignitors Off Motoring' and 'LP Start'. 'Ignitors Off Motoring' was used just for testing (when you didn't actually want the engine to start). 'LP Start' was for starting the engine. The orange square light was split in two halves – labelled '1' and '2'. These would light up when engine start was selected, to tell you the two ignition systems on the engine were on. The round orange light indicted that the start valve was open. *(Keith Wilson)*

BELOW With the Perspex lid raised, access is gained to the engine start switches. Before the Perspex cover can be properly closed, the engine start master selector switch must be in the correct position. A simple but clever Perspex shape under the shelf prevents closure unless the switch is in the correct position. *(Keith Wilson)*

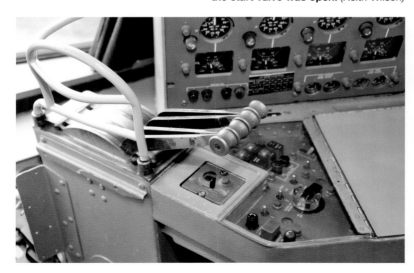

engineering authority to replace/rectify many aircraft components, including to interchange black boxes, replace air starter motors or replace a weather radar scanner. It was a long list and many of these interventions kept the aircraft flying down-route and must have saved the company a fortune – in both overnight hotel costs and upset passengers!

Gulf Air

Having operated with East African Airways, I was seconded to Gulf Air in November 1974 and then again from April to December 1976 where I completed 507 flying hours.

Ups and downs!

I clearly remember being rostered for a three-day trip to Dubai, but, due to the Indo-Pakistan War, I actually arrived home 15 days later after an around-the-world easterly trip via Colombo, Hong Kong, Sydney, Fiji, Los Angeles and New York. Although delayed, it was most enjoyable!

On one of my Pacific trips while staying in Honolulu, our VC10 and crew were put on standby, just in case HM the Queen and her royal flight heading for Australia had a problem. All went well and we were not required.

Fuel price hike

Following a significant hike in the price of aviation fuel, BOAC management brought in fuel-saving measures. As a consequence, captains had to justify any excess carried over and above what the computerised flight planning and fuel management system showed. This amount became known as 'SWORD' fuel. One captain in particular was always being reprimanded by the flight manager for taking excess fuel without justification.

One Sunday morning, the flight manager received a telephone call at his home, from the 'errant' captain: 'I've complied with your request, to only carry "SWORD" fuel.'

'Well done,' said the manager, 'but why the telephone call?'

'I'm phoning you from Manchester, where we had to divert. The aircraft and passengers will not be at Heathrow until tomorrow.'

Another flight engineer earned a £250 bonus for a fuel-saving idea: when there are no livestock being carried in rear bulk hold, then

switch off the cargo heat system, saving fuel. Sometime later, a flight from Caracas which was carrying fresh flowers in the hold had to divert into the Azores with a full emergency evacuation, due to a 'cargo fire' warning light. Thankfully, it was a false alarm. The faulty indication was put down to the cargo of fresh flowers sweating in the cold hold and, had the cargo heat been switched on, then it would have avoided the false alarm!

Instructing

Later in my career I became an instructor and CAA examiner and it afforded many opportunities. These included crewing G-ARVJ on lease to the Emir of Qatar (Sheik Al Thani) and transporting him and his family on hunting trips to Rawalpindi, with live falcons on board.

Instructing also meant many, many hours spent in G-ARVM – the aircraft BOAC kept for crew and command training – doing 'circuits' at Shannon and Prestwick.

Together with training manager Captain Tony Smith, we had the unique opportunity of flying a three-engine ferry flight from Heathrow to Bahrain in G-ARVM. This was due to an engineering strike at Heathrow, although the aircraft was being leased to Gulf Air for crew training. The ground ops people at Heathrow

TOP Lifting the flight engineer's workstation lid, a neat electrical storage area with an excellent selection of fuses, bulbs and tools is exposed. *(Keith Wilson)*

ABOVE A close-up of the fire extinguisher control panel on ZD241, located in the roof of the cockpit, near the entrance door. *(Keith Wilson)*

did a sterling job, in providing a cross-sectional plan of our route with all the two-engine drift-down heights – it wasn't needed, but was comforting. The spare RR Conway was being shipped out the same day and time on a TMA (Trans Mediterranean Airways) Boeing 707. Later, as I was monitoring his progress on VHF, Tony made the call to say that he had a technical problem, and was diverting to Beirut.

On our arrival at Bahrain there was no crew hotel accommodation available, but following a strong intervention by myself, explaining that Tony was a 'very senior manager', a luxurious suite in the Hilton became available.

What should have been a quick, simple engine-change, took some four or more days before we took the aircraft back to Heathrow and then on to Shannon, with around 20 or more Gulf Air pilots – anxious to complete their conversion training – relaxing down the back during the overnight trip.

Being an instructor, I was also cleared for Certificate of Airworthiness renewal flight tests. These usually lasted about 4½ hours and were usually carried out by CAA test pilots. They included three-engine climb performance, two-engine climb performance, relighting (starting) engines while in the air, emergency oxygen passenger release, pressurisation cabin leak rate check and the stall buffet. It certainly was a busy flight.

Royal Navy pilots

On one Prestwick training flight, we carried two Royal Navy Fleet Air Arm aircrew as passengers. Having finished our training, the captain asked one of them if he would like to sit in the right-hand seat as we flew around the island of Ailsa Craig. He coped very well with steep turns, keeping his height and speed.

The second RN passenger was then offered the chance to fly from the right-hand seat. We

SMOKE AND NOISE! – HIGH-SPEED TAXI RUNS AT BRUNTINGTHORPE

LEFT The flight crew for the high-speed taxi run on 13 March 2016. In the left-hand seat is Andy 'Tonks' Townshend, while Chris Haywood occupies the right-hand seat. Both are experienced RAF VC10 pilots. *(Keith Wilson)*

ABOVE The flight engineer for the run was Ollie Pallett. Once cleared, Ollie soon had all four engines running smoothly at idle – around 60% on the gauges. Before the run commenced, the flaps were set to 'take-off' and the slats were fully out. *(Keith Wilson)*

then experienced several minutes of flight, from 20° to 60° of bank, all with the height going up and down like the proverbial yo-yo!

'What do you fly?' asked the training captain.

'Oh, I'm not a pilot, I'm a winchman,' was his reply!

Goodbye VC10

In April 1980, towards the end of VC10 flying, I ferried both G-ASGD and G-ASGH to Prestwick for 'long-term storage'. My final flight on VC10s was in December 1980, just before I converted on to the Lockheed L-1011 TriStar. Subsequently, I went on to instruct on the Boeing 747 Classic 100 and 200 fleet before finally retiring from BOAC in August 1993.

It wasn't the end of my flying career, however, as a further very enjoyable period with Sir Richard Branson followed at Virgin Atlantic, as an instructor on Boeing 747s. My career finally came to a close with the events of 9/11. I was stuck in Las Vegas for five days before returning to Gatwick to be told: 'That's the end for the Classic.' It was also the end for me!

Still involved in aviation

At the age of 77 at the time of writing, John B. Williamson is still involved in aviation, albeit as a 'volunteer' – providing technical guidance and conducting 'look-see' visits around the Cornwall Aviation Heritage Centre's VC10 exhibit, ZA148 – which he flew back in 1971 when seconded to East African Airways. He also volunteers at Bruntingthorpe with restoration work on the Comet 4, XS235, as well as VC10 K.4, ZD241. He continues to hold a current BCAR Group A, B, C, D, X Maintenance Licence, an EASA Part 66 Licence and LAA and BGA Inspectors' privileges, with which he assists owners and companies, in certification- and airworthiness-related matters.

ABOVE The best view in the house – inside VC10 K.4, ZD241, during a high-speed taxi run! All four Conway engines roar as Andy Townshend opens the throttles to 98% on the engines and then, just after the brakes are released, the amazing acceleration kicks in. The ASI quickly reaches 68kts, while Chris Haywood in the right-hand seat covers the controls. *(Keith Wilson)*

ABOVE RIGHT Sadly, even with almost 9,000ft of runway available at Bruntingthorpe, the power remains on for just a few seconds before engines 2 and 3 are returned to idle, while reverse thrust is selected on Nos 1 and 4 at 90%. All too soon the aircraft is back to idle power! *(Keith Wilson)*

ABOVE With the outboard engines providing reverse thrust, along with the spoilers fully deployed, ZD241 slows down at the end of its run. *(Gary Spoors)*

Chapter Seven

Maintaining the 'Queen of the Skies'

'The VC10 is a magnificent piece of British engineering at its very best. Born out of 1950s technology, she is a good old-fashioned mechanical beast that, with the right team, could be tamed and operated to provide a very capable platform. For 50 years the VC10 was maintained by dedicated men and women in both civilian and military roles; I doubt you will find many who have a bad word to say about her.'

Ollie Pallett, RAF

OPPOSITE RAF maintenance technicians deployed from the joint 10/101 Squadron at Brize Norton prepare a replacement engine to be refitted into an RAF VC10 during a sandstorm at Prince Sultan Air Base, Saudi Arabia, on 26 March 2003. The aircraft was deployed here during Operation Telic. *(Crown Copyright/Air Historical Branch image 030326-F-9528H-001/Staff Sgt Matthew Hannen)*

LEFT Some fuel tank sealant repairs were being carried out to both the 1A and 1 tanks on this VC10 in Base Hangar, as it leaked from the upper surface at fuel loads where the 1A tank was full. The old sealant was scraped out and new sealant reapplied to the inner joints between the 1A and 1 adjoining wall and the inside of the upper skin, as well as the sealant on the upper surface. A vacuum bag was used to draw the sealant through any gaps in the joints to promote a good seal. Upon close inspection you can see that the front access panels were also removed from the tanks, an uncommon occurrence as the leading-edge slats had to be removed to gain access to them. Most work on the tanks could usually be completed through the tank 'lids'. One member of the team was working deep inside the tank as his legs are sticking out through the top! *(Cpl Adam 'Tommy' Cooper)*

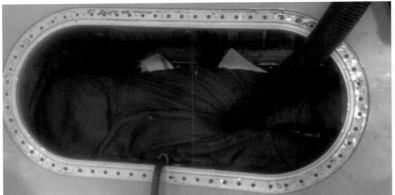

LEFT Another view of sealant work being undertaken in the No 1 fuel tank in a VC10. The black pipe is from a vacuum cleaner used to remove the old sealant. Here, Ollie Pallett can be seen with his head and shoulders inside an adjacent section of the tank. It certainly was a task that demanded physical dexterity! *(via Ollie Pallett)*

Servicing and support

All servicing of the RAF fleet of VC10s was undertaken at RAF Brize Norton in a purpose-built hangar, known as 'Base Hangar'. When it was constructed in 1969 it was the largest cantilever-roofed structure in Europe. It was 1,320ft long, with no internal supports. There was capacity for six VC10s inside, with plenty of space to allow for working around each one.

In the late 1980s, plans were drawn up to move major servicing to RAF Abingdon near Brize Norton. Abingdon, however, was closed and a new facility was built at RAF St Athan in

LEFT Another view in Base Hangar in 1991 with 10 Squadron C.1, XV105, undergoing a deep service. The wheels and undercarriages are up on jacks and the leading-edge slats and trailing-edge flaps have been removed, as have all four engines. *(Patrick Bunce)*

South Wales – No 1 Air Maintenance Squadron (1 AMS). January 1993 saw the first aircraft to undergo major servicing at the facility.

Following the closure of the British Aerospace sites at Brooklands/Weybridge and Hatfield, the responsibility for design and all commercial activities were transferred to BAe at the Manchester/Woodford and Chadderton sites. During the mid-1990s, when the design of detailed components was subcontracted, the design team transferred from Woodford to Chadderton. In 2003, responsibility for the commercial procurement of all spares items was undertaken by BAe Systems at Samlesbury in Lancashire. Meanwhile, the Chadderton site took responsibility for MoD contracts for project managing modifications, while major repairs and maintenance were carried out at RAF St Athan.

Ollie Pallett

Ollie Pallett is a current serving member of the RAF and also runs the ZD241 Bruntingthorpe Preservation Group that maintains VC10 K.4, ZD241, in a 'live' condition at Bruntingthorpe.

Ollie joined the RAF in November 1998 and after the standard square-bashing stint at Recruit Training School, RAF Halton, he was posted to No 1 School of Technical Training (1 SOTT) at RAF Cosford to undertake the basic aircraft propulsion (AP) course. After completion, he was posted to RAF Lyneham in September 1999 to work on the new Lockheed C-130J, where he spent much time assisting the team that was bringing the new type into service.

In June 2001 Ollie was sent back to Cosford to complete the fitters' course. A year later, in May 2002, he was posted to Brize Norton and joined the combined No 10/101 Engineering Squadron as a junior technician. He spent five-and-a-half happy (well mostly!) years on the line shift and a further two-plus years on the Heavy Rectification Flight, where he was promoted to corporal before being posted back to Lyneham in December 2009 on to the C-130J Primary Team.

In June 2012 he was selected and posted on to the RAF's new AAR/AT fleet, on the Airbus Voyager K.2 and K.3 at Brize Norton. He was promoted to sergeant during this tour and this is his current posting.

Keeping the VC10 flying

So, what was it like to work on the VC10? I asked Ollie Pallett and he takes up the story:

That's a very loaded question, I suppose, but easily the finest aircraft I've ever worked on. All those who have worked on her have nothing but praise – however, she could be difficult, temperamental and a downright pain!

Four main trades looked after the VC10. You had propulsion 'sumpies' who sorted the engines, APU, fuel systems, cabin compressors, CSDUs, air-to-air refuelling systems and fire suppression systems; airframe 'riggers' whose tasks included airframe, hydraulics, undercarriage,

BELOW Sgt Dave Ireland (left) and Jnr Tech Gareth Davies refitting the cabin compressor to a replacement engine on 26 March 2013. The engine had been replaced because it suffered with very high oil consumption and had to be shut down in flight due to low oil pressure. *(Crown Copyright/Air Historical Branch image 030326-F-9528H-003/Staff Sgt Matthew Hannen)*

tyres, galleys, cabin interior, airframe anti-icing and flying controls to name but a few; the avionics 'fairies' who fixed the navigational and autopilot systems; and, lastly, the electrical 'leckies' whose tasks included AC and DC generation systems, electrical distribution systems – they linked up with all the other trades' systems which had electrical components. Of these trades, those who worked on the line were commonly referred to as 'lineys'.

Back in 2002, I was a young junior technician posted to RAF Brize Norton to work on the combined No 10/101 Engineering Squadron, which was the centralised unit that maintained all the various VC10s (C.1K, K.2, K.3 and K.4) for the two squadrons flying the aircraft – Nos 10 and 101 Squadrons. Prior to this arrangement, both squadrons had their own set of engineers.

My first impression of the VC10 was of an aircraft that looked 'right' but was also old and tired. Over the next eight years I would spend

maintaining her as a 'liney', I would come to realise that no matter how old she looked, with the right care she could always do the job asked of her. Later, when 10 Squadron was disbanded in October 2005, the combined 10/101 Engineering Squadron was incorporated back into 101 Squadron.

When I joined the combined 10/101 squadron, it consisted of around 350 personnel across four line shifts, two Heavy Rectification ('Heavy Rects') flights and support personnel. By the time I left the squadron, the personnel had been halved.

The line shifts looked after the general servicing, dispatching and rectification of the aircraft while 'Heavy Rects' looked after primary servicing (a bit like a 10,000-mile check on your car) and other heavier tasks that the shift couldn't do, due to lack of manpower or time constraints.

The regular servicing on the VC10 was broken down into types known as 'Primaries', 'Minors' and 'Majors'. As already stated, the more basic primary was carried out by Heavy Rects. Within Base Hangar at Brize, there were two RAF teams that carried out the more in-depth 'Minor' servicing. This, however, was moved to St Athan and was also transferred to a civilian contract. Lastly, the deep strip 'Major' servicing was carried out by a team of civilians at RAF St Athan in Wales. This is where the aircraft were stripped down to nuts-and-bolts form and inspected before being rebuilt. This process could take upwards of six to eight weeks.

The VC10 was a time-consuming aircraft to work on; even the most basic of tasks – such as an after-flight service – would take four people and a couple of hours, depending on what lubricants and gases would need topping up. You would have to get up to all four of the engines and fill them with oil and inspect the compressor and turbine sections for damage (or fronts and backs as it was known). You would also have to walk around the aircraft and inspect the airframe, tyres and undercarriages before cleaning the cabin. All of this was completed outside – come rain or shine – and at times, your patience could be severely tested!

All of this could be relatively easy on the ramp at Brize Norton, but when operating the VC10 around the world it could be somewhat

BELOW A BUA engineer completing a Cat. 3 check on G-ASIX at Gatwick in 1965. *(Speedbird Heritage Collection/ British United Airways 306-1)*

challenging. You may know of the little luggage belt loaders you use at many airports? Well, many a VC10 technician has used them to conduct maintenance. VC10 technicians working away from home developed a sixth sense for what available equipment could be adapted for their use – all of which was needed before you could even think about fixing the snags the aircraft had!

Topping up

Every time the aircraft landed, every engine would need to be topped up with oil, with each engine having three different components to inspect and top up – the engine itself, the constant speed drive unit (CSDU) and the cabin compressor. Thankfully, each of them used the same oil, known as 'OX7'. The engine sump was easy to top up and was accessed via a panel in the engine door. It had a simple sight glass with a scale on it, measured in pints. The maximum level was 16 pints and after each flight you would need to top it back up to the 16-pint mark, then record how much you had added. This would enable you to calculate how much oil the aircraft had used per flight hour. The Conway normally used 0.3–0.5 pints per flight hour and the maximum acceptable consumption was 0.9 pints per flight hour (although this was changed to 1 pint per flight hour later in service life).

The CSDU had its own oil tank which again was accessed though a panel on the engine door. It was marked in pints and held 12 pints. It was checked every time, but rarely needed to be topped up.

Lastly was the cabin compressor. This unit was bolted to the top of the engine and had its own integrated oil sump. The problem with this was that in order to see the sight glass on it you had to shine your torch in just the right place while twisting your neck and squinting with one eye to see it through the access panel. The unit was a fill-to-spill tank, so you would pump the oil in using a handpump known as a 'Risbridger' and fill it to above the green band. You would then have to remove the 'Risbridger' connection and catch the extra oil from the pipe which ran up the side of the engine to the cabin compressor. Normally, this involved using a sick bag to catch the oil, while trying to avoid getting hot oil on your hands.

Changing a Rolls-Royce Conway

As a 'sumpie' the Conway 301 – which was fitted to all marks of VC10 operated by the RAF – was my bread and butter. The Conway is a low bypass twin-spool turbojet which produced 22,500lb of thrust, but most of all was extremely loud – a loudness the residents of the nearby village at Carterton would no doubt vouch for! Like the VC10 it powers, the Conway is strictly 1950s technology and is an engine with little electronic control, instead relying on complex fluid and air systems to regulate it. While a reliable engine in its day, the Conway required as much looking after as the VC10 itself and engine changes were a frequent thing.

Changing the Conway was fun, yet precarious, to say the least. Normally a team of six people would be involved in changing an engine. It would only take a couple to prepare the engine to be lowered, but more were needed when removing it completely. You would need people to operate the two winches when lowering an engine, but when raising an engine into place you would normally have four people on the winches so guys could swap over: a supervisor to oversee the task, someone upstairs watching the engine during lowering and raising, someone ready to attach cables and someone downstairs just running around helping when and where required completed the team.

Preparing an engine to be dropped was a relatively easy task. We would start by removing the fixed engine panels and opening the hinged

ABOVE Ollie Pallett checks the pressures on all four tyres on the starboard main undercarriage leg. Nitrogen gas is used to repressure them, each tyre requiring 150psi when fully laden, or around 120psi when lightly loaded; as was the case with ZD241 ahead of its high-speed taxi run. *(Keith Wilson)*

RIGHT A careful inspection of the undercarriage legs for faults – leaks, cracks, corrosion, tyre condition, etc. – are essential before any movement of the aircraft. *(Keith Wilson)*

BELOW Although not normally seen in the 'down' position, the main undercarriage doors were lowered to allow the team to carry out inspections inside the undercarriage bay for faults – leaks and corrosion – and were subsequently raised by applying hydraulic pressure after first resetting the freefall handles in the radio racks bays. *(Keith Wilson)*

BELOW Ollie Pallett inspects the upper surfaces of the starboard engines on ZD241 ahead of its engine runs. The upper forward engine access panel is being opened to enable a routine 'once over'. The specialised lifting equipment is essential to many aspects of maintenance on the VC10 and cannot be safely conducted without it. *(Keith Wilson)*

ABOVE Phil Juffs is one of the small but dedicated team of volunteers who maintain ZD241 in 'live' working order. Here he is working on another lifting frame undertaking pre-run maintenance checks on one of the engines. Phil is a former RAF engineer who worked on the VC10 for many years but now plies his trade with Rolls-Royce. *(Keith Wilson)*

BELOW Another member of the team of volunteers at Bruntingthorpe is William Rowe. He was photographed high up on the gantry at Bruntingthorpe inspecting the oil metering pump of No 4 engine after a small oil leak was detected. *(Keith Wilson)*

doors. Underneath them, we would disconnect the hydraulic and fuel connections, unplug the electrical connections (which included disconnecting and removing the generator), remove the pipe that connects the engine bleed air system to the airframe, unclamp the engine anti-ice pipes and remove the throttle cable. Up top we would disconnect the intake and exhaust of the cabin compressor and remove the P7 pipe (the P7 system provides the flight engineer with an indication of thrust). Now all we needed to do was to remove the four mounting bolts and winch it down . . . which was the fun bit. The winches – which were manual, may I add – were not long enough to lower the engine all the way to the floor; just halfway down. Someone would have to 'ride' the engine down and insert four 'steady cables' which would suspend the engine halfway. Once the steady cables had taken the weight of the engine, the guy or girl on the engine would disconnect the winch cables and insert a pair of extension cables. These extension cables would provide sufficient extra length to lower the engine to the ground once the steady cables had been removed. Health and safety? Well, let's just say that doing an engine change outside in the wet was interesting!

If you had an experienced bunch of lads and lasses, there was no reason you couldn't have an engine change completed in a 12-hour shift; however, normally this wouldn't happen as you would be pulled off to do other jobs on other jets and it was commonplace that an engine change was completed by several shifts.

The refitting of the engine was simply a reverse of the remove . . . well, close enough! Engine changes were also carried out around the world. I was involved in one such engine change in Brazil following a turbine failure. The equipment was shipped out to us on a Hercules and we changed it much like we would at Brize Norton, apart from there being fewer people and some suspect maintenance stands from the airport! An engine change down-route normally entailed lots more work, as you only received a basic engine from Brize Norton. This meant that you needed to swap components between the old and new engine, including the exhaust section. At Brize Norton, the engine bay used to supply you with an engine that was prebuilt for a specific engine location – so much easier!

FAR LEFT The port main undercarriage on ZD241 required the oleo shock to be recharged with nitrogen following a leak over the winter. Here Ollie Pallett fits an adaptor, which allows the nitrogen rig to connect to the charging point. *(Keith Wilson)*

LEFT Once the adaptor is fitted to the charging point at the bottom of the oleo, the nitrogen-charging hose is connected and charging can commence. The four blue inline flexible pipes in the picture are hydraulic pipes for the braking and undercarriage systems. *(Keith Wilson)*

BELOW Ollie Pallett moves away from the undercarriage leg and alongside the nitrogen supply truck. The pressure of the nitrogen is slowly increased and the leg starts to extend. The strut is charged until the correct extension-versus-pressure is achieved based on the aircraft weight – in this case around 8in (of exposed oleo) is the required from the pressure. *(Keith Wilson)*

RIGHT The undercarriage strut after reinflation. The extent of the exercise can be seen from the oily witness marks on the exposed oleo, which are visible in this view. *(Keith Wilson)*

Changing an engine on XR808

An engine was probably one of the most regularly changed major components on the VC10 during its RAF service. Where possible, engines were changed during scheduled maintenance to minimise downtime, but often they were replaced out on the line, owing to failures.

An engine change was not the most complicated of tasks, rather it was time-consuming. It involved the removal of all panels and the disconnection of engine services before it could be lowered out of its nacelle. Fitting an engine was almost a reversal of the removal, although you did need to run and check the functionality of the new engine once it was installed.

The following sequence of images was taken during a double engine change on XR808 while the aircraft was undergoing her last primary servicing in Base Hangar during December 2009. XR808 was due to be removed from service in 2010 (although this later changed) and the decision had been made to remove two serviceable low-hour engines that could usefully be used to keep the remaining fleet running. Two high-hour engines were refitted into XR808. These were engines that had sufficient life on them to see her through to retirement. This kind of requirement became commonplace towards the end of the VC10s' RAF service life. The engine changes were carried out by a team from the 101 Squadron Heavy Rectification Flight.

TOP In order to change the engine, you would first need to open/remove the engine access panels. In this view you can see the No 1 engine with the thrust reverser panels removed, the upper rear hinged panels open and the lower aft cowl also open. The detachable part of the 'beaver tail' has yet to be removed. *(Ollie Pallett)*

RIGHT Here the lower forward and aft cowls are open. These provide access to the lower part of the engine where the majority of disconnections take place. For example, you would uncouple the fuel, hydraulic and HP air pipes, all electrical plugs, HP cock rod and the throttle cable. *(Ollie Pallett)*

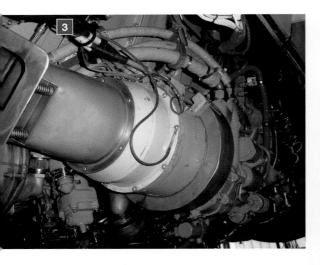

ABOVE When changing an engine you need to swap the generator from the old to the new engine. In this view the generator is still connected. In order to gain access to the generator mounting bolts, you first need to remove the cooling shroud (the gunmetal-grey shroud positioned around the generator). Once this is done and all of the electrical cables have been disconnected, the generator can be slid forward from the spines inside the constant speed drive unit (CSDU) and removed. *(Ollie Pallett)*

ABOVE This view shows the forward face of the CSDU with the generator removed. To the top of the picture one can see where the engine electrical cables have been disconnected from the airframe. In the plastic bag to the top right of the picture are the generator cables. *(Ollie Pallett)*

BELOW Once the engine has had its services disconnected, the lifting beam and winches are fitted. The lifting beam fits into two lugs on the rear engine beam and front engine beam. Two adaptors have to be fitted before the lifting beam is secured in placed by a number of 'pip-pins'. Once the lifting beam is in place, the winches can be lifted on. *(Ollie Pallett)*

BELOW The blue frame in the picture is the lifting beam, which is located into the two lugs on the rear of the aft engine beam. Below this are the two pins which hold the engine in place at the rear. Located in between the two mounting bolts is a lug on the engine mount. This is where the aft cable winch connects. Once the winches are connected, the four mounting bolts (two forward and two aft) can be removed. *(Ollie Pallett)*

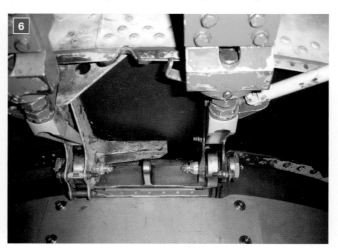

ABOVE The winches are not of sufficient length to lower the engine all the way to the ground. Here, a technician is fitting one of the four steady cables which allow the engine to hang in place halfway down, while extension cables are fitted to the winch cables. Note, on the right-hand side of the picture the three hydraulic pipes are tied out of the way and the throttle cable stowed on its 'keeper'. *(Ollie Pallett)*

BELOW Here a technician watches the engine down to ensure it is clear of any obstructions. The Conway was a tight fit within the engine bay and a careful eye was needed on removal to ensure it didn't damage the airframe on the way down. However, one of the checks conducted when fitting a replacement was to carry out a thorough inspection for any damage. *(Ollie Pallett)*

ABOVE Looking down from above the engine, you can see the four 'steady' cables have been disconnected while the engine is being lowered down to the ground with the aid of the winch extension cables. Note the adaptors that allow the lifting beam to be mounted to the forward engine beam. Where the engine steady cables are bolted, is also where the engine is normally mounted to the forward engine beam. *(Ollie Pallett)*

BELOW Finally the engine can be lowered and fixed into the transportation stand – then it's time for a cup of coffee! This image provides a good view of the left-hand side of the engine where the cabin compressor is mounted on the top. *(Ollie Pallett)*

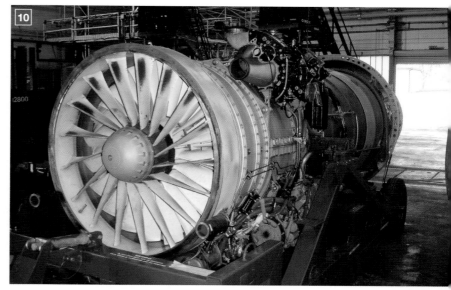

So much noise!

Most of the work we did on the Conway required testing afterwards and this nearly always involved running the engines. Ground-running the Conway was a fairly straightforward and laborious task; 90% of the time it just involved running them at ground idle – for maybe a leak check – however, sometimes the tests called for high-power runs, or much more noise! At Brize Norton we had a large metal building which we backed the jet up to called a 'detuner'. This sort of helped to dampen some of the noise, but whenever we had to do checks down-route, it was the raw noise that could be heard.

During the post-installation checks following an engine change, one of the tests conducted was to check the acceleration time of the engine from ground idle to 1.5% below maximum rpm. This involved 'slamming' the throttle from minimum to maximum in less than one second and recording the time taken

to gain maximum rpm minus 1.5%. This is something that wouldn't happen during normal engine operations and it was a confidence test of the engine set-up. From the outside of the aircraft it was a sight to behold as you watched the stub wings twist under the power and listened to the roar of the Conway as it quickly spooled up from minimum to maximum in around five seconds! However, it could sometimes go wrong. During one such test, while I was conducting the ground run, the engine surged during spool-up. This is the effect when the engine spools up too quickly and the pressure inside the engine becomes too great. As a consequence, the flow reverses and comes out the front of the engine! Cue me sheepishly calling my chief to explain that I needed another new engine. . . .

I used to love ground-running the Conways; this was probably the ultimate task for a 'sumpie'. While sitting in the flight engineer's seat, you would be in sole control of four roaring Conways and this came with much responsibility. The Conway had few inbuilt protection systems and while it was hard to over-stress it, if you did something wrong it could bite you.

The flight engineer's panel is a myriad of gauges, lights and switches. As a panel it was daunting at first but it is well thought out and once you have learned, it becomes second nature (although you still get neck ache constantly watching over everything to make sure all the systems are behaving as they should). In order to overcome the need for scanning all the dials and gauges, I'm sure many of us learned to operate our eyes independently. Everybody who ran the Conway had to be checked out and approved by a competent person after conducting a minimum of eight live supervised ground runs; you certainly couldn't just turn up and have a go. Every person had their own way of conducting the pre-start checks; I was no different. I used to go through my checks in the same set manner every time, ensuring that I'd missed nothing. Checks would include things like walking around the outside of the jet to ensure all was ready; checking inside that all systems and switches were in the correct configuration; paying particular attention to testing the fire-detection system and ensure the warning bell went off (irritatingly, it sounded

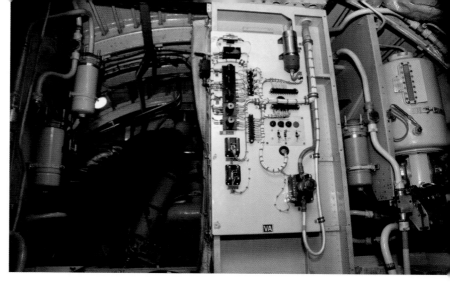

much like a doorbell going off constantly!). Once you had completed all of the checks, you would don a headset and call 'Ground' on the radio to get permission for the ground run.

On the flight deck with you would be another ground runner who sat in the pilot's seat to cover the brakes and to operate the radios while also being of assistance if and when required. After first starting the APU (auxiliary power unit) and ensuring it was running at the correct speed, you would select 'bleed air' on the APU and you would be ready to start. On the engineer's panel you would then lift the Perspex cover adjacent to the throttle quadrant and select 'LP start' on the rotary switch. Once you had clearance to start from the safety man outside, you would push forward and hold the start switch for the required engine. At this point you would hear a whoosh of air as the starter spun into life and the bleed air pressure would drop off. On the start panel the igniters, starter valve open and correct rotation lights would come on, the HP rpm gauge would spring into life and the hydraulic pressure would begin to rise. Once the outside man confirmed the engine was turning, you would open the HP cock, allowing fuel into the engine. When the HP rpm gauge indicated around 11%, you would get ignition and you would see the EGT gauge start to rise; you watched this like a hawk, while also monitoring all the other required gauges like oil pressure, shaft speeds, and so on, ensuring it didn't run over 690°C. At 26% HP rpm you would release the start switch and let the engine continue to spool up until it reached its idle speed – around 56–58% – while all of the time having your hand on the HP cock in case you needed to rapidly shut the engine down. From pushing the start switch to achieving idle speed, all happens in about a minute. It's a lot to watch and monitor but, as I said, it soon became second nature.

Not maintainer-friendly

The VC10 certainly wasn't designed with the maintainer in mind. There were many jobs which would send shivers down the spines of people. Mention the brake control valve or toilet gate valve to the 'riggers' and they would run to all corners of the hangar to avoid changing it. Ask a 'sumpie' to refit the stone guards in the

undercarriage bay and they would do their best to find an excuse not to do it; this due to the fact they would never line up. As a 'techie' on the VC10, you would learn the skill to be able to locate, replace and wire-lock components just by feel, as more often than not, you couldn't see and feel the item that needed changing at the same time. Many a time I've ended up with cuts up and down my arm from being elbow-deep in an access hole, blindly feeling around while trying to find what I actually need.

Hydraulic fluid

One thing I have to mention is the hydraulic fluid used on the VC10 – 'Skydrol'. This was used as it had excellent properties at low operating temperatures. However, it is

ABOVE The hydraulics bay on K.4 ZD241 at Bruntingthorpe. The hydraulic system uses a fluid called 'Skydrol' – probably one of the most horrific fluids known to man. It had a repugnant taste and you could 'taste' it in the air! (Keith Wilson)

LEFT Regular maintenance is carried out to the hydraulic system and includes checking the hydraulic levels. Here the 'B' system reservoir and sight glass can be seen, along with a can of Skydrol in the drip tray ready to replenish the system.
(Keith Wilson)

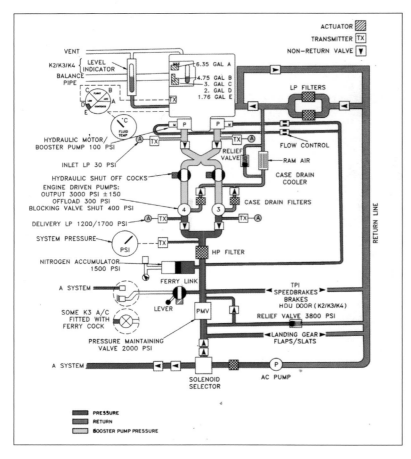

Schematic diagram of the hydraulic system on the VC10 labels:

VENT
K2/K3/K4 { LEVEL INDICATOR
BALANCE PIPE
6.35 GAL A
4.75 GAL B
3. GAL C
2. GAL D
1.76 GAL E
ACTUATOR
TRANSMITTER TX
NON-RETURN VALVE
LP FILTERS
FLUID TEMP °C
HYDRAULIC MOTOR/ BOOSTER PUMP 100 PSI
RELIEF VALVE
FLOW CONTROL
INLET LP 30 PSI
RAM AIR
HYDRAULIC SHUT OFF COCKS
CASE DRAIN COOLER
ENGINE DRIVEN PUMPS: OUTPUT 3000 PSI ±150 OFFLOAD 300 PSI BLOCKING VALVE SHUT 400 PSI
CASE DRAIN FILTERS
DELIVERY LP 1200/1700 PSI
SYSTEM PRESSURE PSI
RETURN LINE
HP FILTER
NITROGEN ACCUMULATOR 1500 PSI
FERRY LINK
A SYSTEM
LEVER
TPI SPEEDBRAKES BRAKES HDU DOOR (K2/K3/K4)
SOME K3 A/C FITTED WITH FERRY COCK
PMV
RELIEF VALVE 3800 PSI
PRESSURE MAINTAINING VALVE 2000 PSI
A SYSTEM
LANDING GEAR FLAPS/SLATS
SOLENOID SELECTOR
AC PUMP

PRESSURE
RETURN
BOOSTER PUMP PRESSURE

ABOVE Schematic diagram of the hydraulic system on the VC10. *(via Andy Townshend)*

probably one of the most horrific fluids you will ever come across. It would eat the paint on the aircraft, melt plastic and generally cause havoc with whatever it came into contact with. It was contact with people, though, that caused the issues! It had a repugnant taste and you could 'taste' it in the air, especially in hot and cramped conditions like the rear of the aircraft where the hydraulic reservoirs are located! However, the taste was the least of your problems – and this is from personal experience. If you got it in your eye, it was a very painful experience. In my case, it meant the nurse having to remove my contact lenses which were slowly melting to my eyes. Safety glasses or gloves wouldn't protect you, mainly because it just destroyed them!

Overseas flexibility

Much of what I have written describes the activities at the relatively comfortable location of RAF Brize Norton. However, we operated the VC10 all over the world – from the Middle East to the Falklands, and from -40ºC to +50ºC. Doing many of the tasks at Brize Norton was hard enough, even using the specialist equipment we were provided with. Down-route we often had to adapt and utilise what was

BELOW With the engines located high up on the rear fuselage, access without specialised equipment would be impossible. Here, a technician from 101 Squadron can be seen replacing engine covers on to a VC10 after landing from its mission during Operation Herrick in October 2010. *(Crown Copyright/ Air Historical Branch image AUAB-10-255-OUT-UNC-042/Sergeant Corrine Buxton)*

BELOW However, if you don't have the specialist equipment, you have to make do! When Ollie Pallett and his 101 Squadron engineering team were required to change an engine on ZD241 that had suffered a turbine failure while at Recife, Brazil, in December 2008, they had to use what was available, including this luggage conveyor. *(Ollie Pallett)*

available at the location. I've seen and done engine changes with belt loaders, baggage carts and forklifts. I've seen people working at the very top of the tail in cherry pickers that look as flimsy as paper. I've even seen people get on to the engines without assistance from any ground equipment – and I will leave how they did that up to your imagination. Wherever we went it was normally a challenge to explain to your local hosts what you required; very often the language barrier meant you would have to come up with sign language to describe what you needed, although it could all be quite amusing!

Scrapheap challenge

Towards the end of my time on the VC10, the old girl started to become more and more unreliable. Coupled with the lack of spares and reduction in manpower, it made for a tough time, which was lovingly referred to by many as 'scrapheap challenge'. Spares were a big issue. Many supply contracts had expired as the original 'out of service' date had kept slipping to the right and they were not renewed. Some spares became so worn that reconditioning them became impossible and we also started to need spares which had never previously been ordered. The project teams worked hard to source spares and renew contracts, but in the world of aviation, nothing is quick.

One way we got around this problem was to 'rob' parts from one VC10 to service another. 'Robbing' is a military term for removing parts from one airframe to keep another airframe flying. This solution only moved the problem around, but meant we could keep jets in the air. Working in the hangar, it was commonplace to come in on a Monday morning and find a mound of job cards on the desk showing the host of parts that the line had robbed over the weekend. This pleased us immensely as we would then have to refit the spares when they came into stock.

Spares recovery from the jets that started to be scrapped at Bruntingthorpe provided a valuable source of spares; no sooner had a VC10 landed, a team would be removing core and critical spares and returning them into the supply system. One of the main issues with a jet that was effectively hand-built is that fitting

parts becomes an art. Rarely could you remove parts like panels and flying controls and simply fit them to another aircraft. Each panel had been adjusted and fettled at the factory simply to make it fit; so much time would have to be spent doing the very same thing to get it to fit on to another aircraft. It wasn't unknown to get a 'new' part from stores and it would have been annotated by previous engineers to say which aircraft it *hadn't* fitted. The most frustrating part of working VC10s was the lack of spares, as it often prevented you from doing your job.

Life on the line

Ollie continues with his time on the 'line at RAF Brize Norton:

The line was split into four shifts which could provide 24-hour cover, 365 days a year. Each shift worked a pattern of days and nights on a 28-day rota and we each worked for 14 of those. The shift was run by a Rectification 'Rects' Controller. His job was to prioritise the work and manage the flying programme to ensure we could provide aircraft for the tasks that had been planned by the squadrons. Alongside the 'Rects' Controller sat the Line Controller, whose job was to manage a number of small line teams who dealt with aircraft 'see-ins', 'see-offs' and flight servicing. The shift was then split into the four trade desks – 'sumpies', 'riggers', 'fairies' and 'leckies'. At the beginning of each shift you would be tasked with either working the line or working the trade desk . . . or if it was busy, both!

If you were blessed with working the line, you would be spilt down into teams of four or five people. Your tasks would include seeing off aircraft ('see-offs'), seeing in aircraft ('see-ins') and carrying out flight servicing.

LEFT When an American DC10 was taxiing out from the adjacent stand at Al Udeid, Qatar, on 25 January 2009, it unfortunately blew a maintenance stand into ZA147 as she powered around the turn. The resultant skin damage had to be repaired on site and was completed by a specialist repair team flown in from RAF St Athan. *(Ollie Pallett)*

'See-off'

A 'see-off' would entail preparing the aircraft for flight. You would remove all bungs and blanks, then take out the landing gear and RAT (ram air turbine) safety pins. Each member of the team would conduct their relevant trade BF (before flight) servicing. A BF servicing consisted of essential checks – like fluid and gas levels – along with the inspections of critical parts. You would refuel the aircraft based on the aircrew and task requirements. You could put anything up to 100,000 litres (82 tonnes) into the aircraft, which could take up to an hour. Once the aircrew had accepted the aircraft, the team NCO would be on the headset communicating with the crew while keeping a good lookout around the outside of the aircraft, and giving the 'start' clearance when asked. The other team members would remove the chocks, remove the ground power unit (GPU) when signalled and provide a wingtip clearance from obstacles. Finally, one member of the team would marshal the aircraft away from the stand.

'See-in'

A 'see-in' would start by marshalling the jet on to the stand after its arrival at Brize Norton and, once stationary, the NCO would connect their headset and talk to the flight crew while the aircraft was chocked and ground power applied. Depending on the task the aircraft had just completed (and what it was going to do next), the appropriate flight servicing to be carried out would be decided.

If the aircraft was on an operational turnaround (i.e. it was needed back in the air as soon as possible) the team would carry out a ContOps (continuous operations) servicing. This consisted of the minimum requirements to get it safely back into the air. Oil would be put in the engines, only inspections of vital components would be carried out and the aircraft refuelled and sent on its way again.

If the aircraft was on the ground for around four hours between sorties, the team would carry out a TR (turnaround) servicing. This is similar to the 'ContOps' servicing and also included some additional in-depth inspections, especially if the AAR pods had been used. These would be trailed out to inspect the hoses and baskets for damage and then wound back

into their pods. A turnaround also satisfied the requirements of a BF servicing.

Lastly, if the aircraft was to be on the ground for a longer period of time, the team would carry out an AF (after flight) servicing. An AF servicing consisted of all work that is done on a TR or ContOps, but includes many more inspections, top-ups and checks. Checking tyres, hydraulic levels, airframe inspections, engine inspections, internal inspections, safety equipment, AAR systems (wing-mounted POD and fuselage-mounted HDU), hose inspections (if the aircraft had been on an AAR sortie) were just a few of the items covered. An AF was a thorough check, although as a general rule, it was done using the naked eye, without the need for specialist tools or equipment. After an AF, when the aircraft next flew it would still require a further BF before it could fly!

All-weather luxury!

You would be out in all weathers and could expect to spend up to four or five hours out on the line; all without a break if there were several aircraft movements during the day. While working the line, you wouldn't be expected to fix 'snags' unless they were simple. More often than not you would radio in and one of the guys on the trade desk would come out and rectify it.

Trade desk

If you were working on the trade desk you would be involved in the fault-finding and rectification of faults, along with any scheduled maintenance tasks that were required to be carried out on the aircraft. The VC10 had a scheduled maintenance programme that required thousands of tasks to be carried out at various different intervals. For example, every 60 flight hours you had to change the magnetic detector plug on the Rolls-Royce Conway engine. This detector was essential as it checked for and detected early failure of the engine. Another scheduled task meant cleaning the onboard sinks in the toilets and galleys every seven days. Other regular tasks included the changing of components which had become life-expired, lubrication of many moving parts and checks of a raft of systems to ensure they all still worked correctly.

The scheduled maintenance was there both to prevent failure and/or to detect faults before they posed a flight risk. Unscheduled faults were either found during the flight servicing on the line, or were reported by the flight crew post flight. After a flight, the crew would debrief with the relevant trades and all pertinent information would be taken down to assist with the fault diagnosis.

The trade work on the line was varied and you never really knew what you were coming in to face each day. Jobs ranged from simple tasks like bulb changes, right though to major component changes – including engines and flying controls. You could be tasked with fixing several faults across a number of jets or you could equally spend 12 hours fault-finding and fixing one fault. You could also be called out to 'crew in snags' where the flight crew may have started their pre-flight checks and found a problem. Here you would be under extreme pressure to rectify the fault as quickly as possible, in order that the aircraft could depart on time.

Very often you might not be able to complete your task and would have to hand it over to the next shift to complete. This was where it was vital your paperwork was both accurate and up to date, otherwise the following shift could end up repeating work already done, or completely missing something.

MOD700 paperwork

All work from servicing right though to major rectification work was recorded using a system known as the 'MOD700'-series paperwork. At the heart of all this was a book called the 'MOD Form 700', simply referred to by most engineers as the '700. The '700 was a black folder which contained a variety of numbered forms, recording all of the maintenance conducted on the aircraft. This book always flew with the aircraft and was the main source of information to both flight crews and engineers alike.

Alongside the '700 was an electronic system where we also recorded all the work that had been completed. This system was known as LITS and while I won't bore you with the details, I guarantee the mere mention of LITS will have any VC10 engineers reading this shuddering with hatred for it!

The line was a fluid environment to work in and things were constantly changing. The plan at 07:00 was probably on version 4 by 07:30! It provided a wealth of variety but certainly kept you on your toes, and was always full of surprises!

Refuelling and defuelling . . .

The fuel on a VC10 was stored in a number of different tanks across the wings, depending upon the particular variant; it could also be stored in the tailfin and/or fuselage tanks. Let's first consider an RAF C.1K. The fuel was housed in eight integral wing tanks – numbered 1A, 1, 2, centre, 3, 4, 4A, along with the fin – providing a total capacity of just over 70 tonnes.

Refuelling

Refuelling was normally carried out using a control panel located on the right-hand lower wing just outboard of the main gear (see below). Each aircraft was fitted with two pressure refuelling points – one on either side – that, if required, could be used at the same time, as often was the case. The refuelling bowser would be connected to the pressure refuelling points and would pump fuel into the tanks at the rate of around 2,500 litres per minute (a rate that would fill your average car in around a second). Refuelling could be carried out in two modes, automatic or manual. On the underwing control panel, each tank had its own gauge and associated refuel switch, apart, that is, from the fin, which had two gauges for redundancy purposes due to the critical nature of needing to know exactly how much fuel was contained in the fin.

In automatic mode, each tank gauge had two needles on it, white and yellow. The white

BELOW The refuelling and defuelling control panel on K.4 ZD241, located behind a cover underneath the inboard rear starboard wing. The gauge for the fin tank was tucked away at the bottom. At the time of the photograph, most of the fuel was contained in tanks 2 and 3, while tanks 1, 4 and the centre only contained small quantities. Tanks 1A and 4A were empty, as was the fin tank.
(Keith Wilson)

ABOVE The fin tank fuel quantity gauge on ZD241, tucked away in the bottom of the fuel control panel. The gauges indicate the tank is empty.
(Keith Wilson)

needle indicated how much fuel was in the tank while the yellow needle could be manually changed to pre-select a required level of fuel. Once you had pre-selected each tank with the fuel level required, you would open the refuel valves and each tank would – in theory, that is – automatically stop filling when it reached its pre-selected level.

In manual mode you would have to monitor the fuel load as it was being pumped into the aircraft and then close the refuel valves as and when the tanks reached the required levels.

Refuelling itself was a relatively easy and simple task to complete, but it did require

you to think about what you were doing. The automatic system didn't always shut the fuel off at the right quantity and you could end up with too much in one tank, or – worse still – have the fuel incorrectly distributed.

The fin tank on a C.1K held up to 5,000kg. Any fuel in the fin would have the effect of moving the centre of gravity (CofG) rearwards [although please see the photograph of XR806 on p. 157 to visualise what *could* go wrong]. However, if the jet was fuelled correctly, the fuel in the wing tanks would counter this effect.

When refuelling, you would be given an overall figure to fuel the aircraft to and you would then distribute the fuel into the various tanks in accordance with a table from the maintenance manual. This would ensure that the aircraft's CofG would be in the correct place.

One of the most important things we had to watch for was that during the refuelling process, the ratio of fuel between the centre tank and the fin stayed around 3.5:1. This would ensure that there was always enough in the centre tank to keep the CofG within limits. Similarly, tanks 1A and 4A also had the effect of moving the CofG rearward but, as with the fin tank, if it was loaded correctly, it was not a problem.

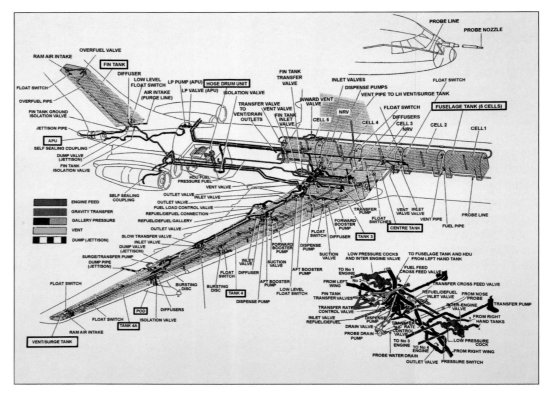

RIGHT Schematic diagram of the fuel system on a VC10 K.3, including the five additional fuel tanks located in the fuselage.
(via Andy Townshend)

Defuelling

Sometimes we would be required to defuel the aircraft, usually because maintenance requirements dictated it. The aircraft was to be jacked up and needed to contain less than 4 tonnes to ensure the correct CofG and weight distribution. Defuelling could be carried out using two different methods – either suction or pressure. With both methods the bowser would connect to the same points as used for a refuelling. Suction defuelling would be accomplished by the bowser producing a negative pressure and then the refuel/defuel valves would be selected to 'open' and the bowser would effectively 'suck' the fuel out of the tanks that were selected 'open'. Pressure defuelling used the aircraft's own fuel pumps to pump the fuel out of the tanks and into the bowser.

Pressure defuelling was the usual method used at Brize Norton as the fuel was pumped back into the underground ring main which served the parking bays. It was also the preferred method of the 'liney' as you would carry this function out from the warmth and comfort of the flight engineer's station on the flight deck. There was no provision to operate the fuel pumps from outside the aircraft.

One of the issues that had to be carefully considered when defuelling an aircraft was that the fin tank had no internal pumps and was emptied into the centre tank via gravity alone. During the defuelling process you could pump fuel out of the centre tank at a quicker rate than the fuel would be gravity-fed from the fin tank; this could, if not carefully monitored, result in the ratio between the tanks becoming less than 3.5:1, with the CofG moving aft as a consequence. This fact was drummed into all technicians by their instructors during initial VC10 training as the unfortunate incident with XR806 had clearly demonstrated the dangers of not doing it correctly. The incident led to XR806 being written off!

'Roadrunner'

At RAF Brize Norton we have an underground ring main arrangement that provides fuel to most, but not all, parking areas. Alternatively, or when operating at locations without a ring main, we use a fuel bowser, which brings the fuel with

it and is able to pump it directly into the aircraft.

Generally, we prefer to use the ring main and when we need to refuel the jet we order a fuel truck, known locally as a 'roadrunner'. It contains a series of fuel filters but has no fuel on board; it is primarily a means of connecting the fuel in the ring main to the aircraft and then it provides the pressure to pump it in.

When defuelling, however, the ring main has no pressure or suction capability. If we use the fuel bowser, it has its own onboard pumps to provide the suction to remove the fuel from the aircraft and pump it back into the bowser. However, the preferred method at Brize is to connect a rig to the aircraft and the ring main. We then use the aircraft's own onboard fuel pumps to remove the fuel by pumping it directly into the ring main.

QRA

In order to support the National QRA (Quick Reaction Alert) programme, a VC10 was held in readiness 24 hours a day, 365 days a year, and ready to launch at a moment's notice, if required.

From an engineering perspective, QRA was one of the top priorities and all efforts were made to support it – not just at squadron level but station-wide as well. Day to day, the QRA would not normally take up too much manpower. For the technicians on the shift, it would be a case of 'business as usual'.

However, if the QRA 'shout' came, it was a very different matter. All available people would go straight to the aircraft and start to prepare it for flight. A fuel truck would be connected, just in case the crew required any additional fuel.

ABOVE Refuelling and defuelling the VC10 was a relatively simple process, as long as you followed the plan. If not, the results could be disastrous! On 18 December 1997, XR806 was damaged beyond economic repair in a ground defuelling accident at Brize Norton as a result of not draining fuel from the tailfin first. *(Crown Copyright/ Air Historical Branch image AHB-F540-BZN-19971218-02)*

ABOVE Two technicians from 101 Squadron changing the centreline refuelling drogue (basket) on the ramp at Brize Norton, 29 July 2009. Not a particularly difficult job but one made all the more unpleasant on this occasion as heavy rain and strong winds added to the task. *(Crown Copyright/Air Historical Branch image Drogue-Change-in-the-rain/Stephen Lympany)*

ABOVE With the left gull wing panel open on the Mk. 32 air-to-air refuelling pod, the 'Tensator' spring (which helps to prevent hose whip when a receiver aircraft plugs into the basket during AAR) and the 'Logic box' (the central control unit of the pod) can be inspected. *(Keith Wilson)*

BELOW Schematic drawing of the flight refuelling Mk. 32 AAR pod. *(via Andy Townshend)*

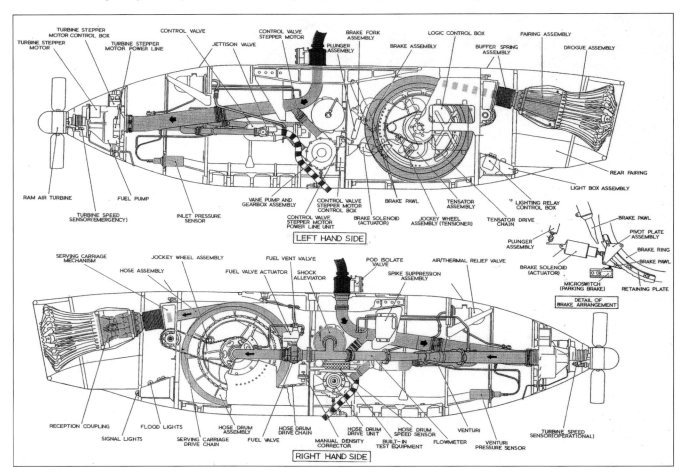

LEFT The centreline Mk. 17B AAR pod on K.4 ZD241. At the time this photograph was taken, the access panel was down and the hose and drogue had been removed for service, leaving the remaining operational parts on view. *(Keith Wilson)*

ABOVE Access to the fuel components can be gained through the bottom panel of the Mk. 32 AAR pod. In the middle of the picture is the control valve which diverts fuel to either side of a vane pump and which, in turn, is connected through a gearbox to the hose-drive system. *(Keith Wilson)*

The aircraft was already pre-loaded with a set quantity of fuel so it could just launch if required, and the aircraft would be powered up with the flight servicing completed.

Once the flight crew had arrived and passed a final fuel figure, the aircraft would be closed up and then dispatched on to its task. On return from the task, the aircraft would have to be serviced; any faults would need to be rectified and the aircraft refuelled in the shortest possible time so that it could be declared back 'on readiness'.

Hats off to the VC10 engineers

Over the life of the VC10, so many people have been involved in keeping her flying. The operational success and world-renowned reputation of the VC10 is due in very large part to the people who maintained her. From the RAF point of view, thousands of engineers have worked on her from both military and civilian backgrounds. There were those on the line, those who worked on 'Minors' and 'Majors' teams – whether in Base Hangar at Brize Norton, Abingdon or St Athan – the civilian working parties that were part of the squadron, or the project teams at locations

such as Abbeywood. The list is endless and I apologise to those I may have omitted in error. I worked with many of those people during my time and without doubt the VC10 would not have flown for so long without their hard work and dedication. Very often their dedication was never noticed or recognised.

I'm often asked if I would do it all again. Yes, I would, in a heartbeat. I remember with great fondness the time I spent on VC10s. It made me the engineer I am today. I travelled the world while working on the 'old girl' and saw places that the general public just don't know about. Perhaps, more importantly, I worked with some fantastic people and made many friends for life. We still talk about many of the stories we shared and it all goes to show what a great time we all had on the VC10. I loved my time on VC10s and all good things must come to an end. That said, she certainly will never be forgotten. Not if I can help it anyway!

ABOVE Another view of the Mk. 17B centreline AAR pod on ZD241, seen here without the hose and drogue installed. The traffic lights either side of the pod can be clearly seen. *(Keith Wilson)*

Chapter Eight

Almost, but not quite – the unbuilt VC10 projects

The VC10's basic design was so over-engineered, and its power ratings so high, that it was relatively easy for the Vickers design team to develop airframes that were highly advanced for their time. Although these ideas did not become a reality, some of them reappeared many years later, underlining not only the depth of talent at Vickers, but emphasising just what an advanced and efficient design the VC10 really was.

OPPOSITE Vickers artwork showing the 'poffler' version of the VC10. Shown with six air-launched ballistic missiles (ALBMs), the VC10 was designed to carry up to eight Skybolt missiles on underwing pylons and operate at very high take-off weights, although jet-assisted take-off (JATO) options were also planned to facilitate this. It was from this study that the true multi-role military version of the VC10 was later conceived. *(BAE SYSTEMS/Brooklands Museum)*

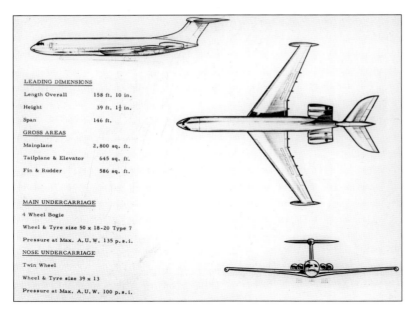

LEADING DIMENSIONS	
Length Overall	158 ft. 10 in.
Height	39 ft. 1½ in.
Span	146 ft.
GROSS AREAS	
Mainplane	2,800 sq. ft.
Tailplane & Elevator	645 sq. ft.
Fin & Rudder	586 sq. ft.
MAIN UNDERCARRIAGE	
4 Wheel Bogie	
Wheel & Tyre size 50 x 18-20 Type 7	
Pressure at Max. A.U.W. 135 p.s.i.	
NOSE UNDERCARRIAGE	
Twin Wheel	
Wheel & Tyre size 39 x 13	
Pressure at Max. A.U.W. 100 p.s.i.	

ABOVE The original plans for the Super VC10 included wingtip or 'slipper' fuel tanks. *(BAE SYSTEMS/ Brooklands Museum)*

Civilian projects

When the British Overseas Airways Corporation (BOAC) required a stretched version of the standard VC10 to provide a competitive platform for the airline's transatlantic routes, Vickers were able to complete the proposal with ease. In fact, their first attempt at a Super VC10 was not the aircraft that finally went into production. Their first creation was a 212-seat aircraft that offered the range required for non-stop transatlantic operations and a very respectable seat-per-mile cost projection that would have provided BOAC with a very profitable aircraft for the various transatlantic routes. Unfortunately, BOAC were ultra-conservative with their projections, concerned that they would not meet the required load factors.

In hindsight, had BOAC taken a chance with the 212-seat variant, they may have had a pleasant surprise. When the 139-seat (16 first class and 123 economy) Super VC10 entered service on the transatlantic routes, a very high level of passenger appeal was immediately apparent. They achieved an average load factor on the routes of 71.6% when the market average was just 52.1%. Anecdotal evidence has indicated that over the years, passenger appeal remained high and many passengers elected to fly on the VC10 even in preference to the Boeing 747 'Jumbo Jet'.

The following are some of the proposals offered by Vickers-Armstrong (Aircraft) Ltd and their successors, the British Aircraft Corporation (BAC).

The VC10-265 Superb

This proposal featured a stretched version of the VC10 – with a difference. Long before Boeing had considered the concept with the 747, Vickers offered a 265-seat version with a double-bubble fuselage, known as the

RIGHT An initial model of the Super VC10 in early BOAC colours. It featured the wingtip fuel tanks and would have been a beautiful aircraft. *(BAE SYSTEMS/ Brooklands Museum)*

'Superb'. It featured uprated engines and major structural changes including a reshaped nose. Unfortunately, like the advanced VC10-based triple-fuselage flying trimaran-style 450-seat airliner that Vickers offered in 1964, funding was not forthcoming and neither project was proceeded with.

Pan American Super VC10 proposal

In 1960, the Civil Aircraft Development Group of Vickers-Armstrong (Aircraft) Ltd offered a proposal to Pan American World Airways on a Super VC10 proposal in both passenger and freighter versions. It was a brave move, especially considering the limited success that both British and European manufacturers have enjoyed with US airlines! However, buoyed by the fact that Vickers had just sold a number of their Viscount turboprop-powered airliners to North American-based airlines including Capital Airways, Continental Airways, Northeast Airlines and Trans-Canada Airlines, Vickers made the offer.

For the Pan Am proposal, Vickers came up

ABOVE A retouched image of the proposed Super VC10 200-seat model. Note that all four engines featured thrust reversers. *(BAE SYSTEMS/ Brooklands Museum)*

LEFT The Vickers VC10-265 'Superb'; a 265-seat, double-deck proposal featuring reshaped nose contours. *(BAE SYSTEMS/ Brooklands Museum)*

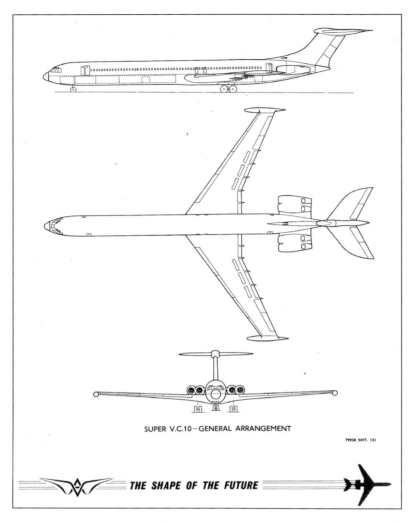

SUPER V.C.10 – GENERAL ARRANGEMENT

79938 SHT. 131

THE SHAPE OF THE FUTURE

ABOVE The shape of the Super VC10 for Pan American Airways, which was proposed to them in 1960. Missing from this drawing are the extended root fillet leading-edge areas that were added to the proposal. *(BAE SYSTEMS/Brooklands Museum)*

with a concept that featured the extra power of the Rolls-Royce Conway 7 engine, producing 24,000lb of thrust. Cleverly, Vickers offered an American-designed cabin, with an interior designed by Butler of New York.

Perhaps the most innovative piece of the design was the leading edge of each wing featuring a root extension fillet to provide an increase in wing area as well as additional space for fuel. It also included wingtip fuel pods. The total fuel capacity was now 20,625 Imperial gallons (24,750 US gallons).

Vickers came up with a novel idea of a small underfloor compartment that could be used as a passenger lounge or a crew rest area, with a small staircase providing access, which was later replicated on the Boeing 747.

Sadly, the Pan American VC10 design never left the drawing board. However, negotiations continued with United Airlines leading to a letter

of intent for a fleet of all-cargo VC10 T4s, while similar letters were signed by Eastern Airlines and TAA of Australia. Once again, they were never progressed beyond the paper stage.

Freight study

During the early 1960s, BAC undertook a major study into North Atlantic freight operations, with particular emphasis on the DC-7F Freighter Conversion, the Britannia 312 Freighter Conversion and the proposed VC10F-3 aircraft.

It appeared that BOAC intended to operate the Britannia Freighter aircraft from 1963. Using an assumed daily freight service, three aircraft would be required. As a result of the anticipated build-up of freight traffic, five aircraft would have been required from 1968, and ten by 1970.

By mid-1967, the VC10F-3 aircraft would become more economical on the route. More importantly, with a significantly improved capacity, three VC10F-3 aircraft could operate the route with the anticipated freight levels of 1970, compared with ten Britannia Freighters required to carry the same load.

As a consequence of the study, BAC offered the freight business two new variants of the VC10: the VC10F-4 side-loading freighter and the CPF-4 combined passenger and freight aircraft.

VC10F-4 side-loading freighter

Initially designed for BOAC purely as a passenger jet, the VC10 design was modified for use with British United Airways (BUA) with the addition of a large forward freight door, still with the same all-up weight as the standard VC10. This permitted BUA to operate in a combined passenger/freight configuration, allowing the most economical arrangement for each route.

When the RAF ordered the second batch of aircraft, they also specified the side-loading freight door. However, they added a strengthened floor to military standards capable of carrying bulk freight and tracked vehicles. The aircraft also featured an increased all-up weight to 322,000lb, providing a maximum civilian payload of 64,000lb.

The VC10F-4, designed in 1962, was the next logical development. It proposed a side-

RIGHT At the same time, the British Aircraft Corporation also offered the VC10 in the F-4 Freighter configuration. The VC10 F-4 and CPF-4 were serious proposals. If they had gone ahead with these, the VC10 would have had a major influence on, if not effectively created, the market that is today's cargo scene. *(BAE SYSTEMS via PRM Aviation)*

loading door of similar dimensions to the BUA and RAF aircraft, with an all-up weight of 330,000lb, a freight hold of 7,850cu ft, and a maximum payload of 80,000lb with the standard floor (78,200lb with the heavy-duty floor). The payloads could be carried over a range of 3,600 statute miles, while operating from some of the most exacting airfields in the world. The design also offered a further alternative – a swing-nose version.

VC10 CPF-4 'combi' freighter

The combined passenger/freight version was similar to the F-4 variant described above. However, its design philosophy took into account the need for maximum flexibility by some airlines, particularly those developing freight routes. BAC recognised that many airlines would need a transitional period when freight traffic alone would be uneconomical

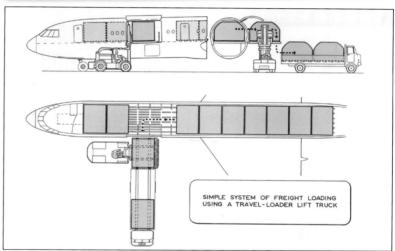

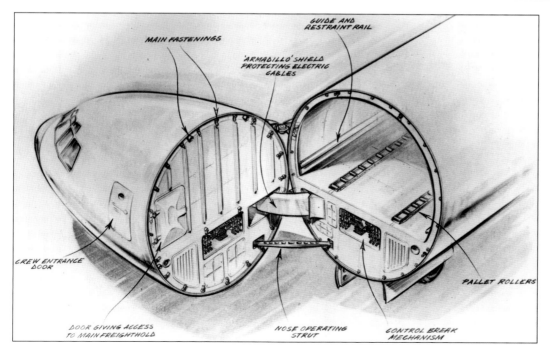

ABOVE One of the unique features of the VC10 F-4 Freighter was the innovative but simple system of freight loading. *(BAE SYSTEMS via PRM Aviation)*

LEFT An early drawing of the hinged-nose facility, available on both the F-4 and CPF-4 versions. It was particularly useful for the straight-in loading of bulky cargo. *(BAE SYSTEMS/Brooklands Museum)*

to operate. The VC10 CPF-4 was offered as a composite passenger/freighter version and could be operated in any of seven different configurations. Conversion from the all-passenger role to the all-freight role could be accomplished in two to three hours.

The CPF-4 side-loader had a proposed all-up weight of 330,000lb, a freight hold of 7,180cu ft and a maximum payload of 75,350lb with the standard floor. With the heavy-duty floor, this was reduced to 73,550lb. The payloads could have been carried over a range up to 3,600 statute miles. Maximum seating at 34-inch pitch was 152 in the passenger-only configuration. It too offered the additional option of a swing-nose variant.

A freight-handling system, which had been designed to accommodate most of the existing or proposed pallet plan-forms, was available for both the side-loading and swing-nose version of the CPF-4. This was designed to be opened and closed hydraulically via an inboard-mounted jack-arm strut slide.

Once again, the design offered the payloads and range while operating from some of the most exacting airfields in the world, outperforming any contemporary jet freighter.

The VC10 F-4 and CPF-4 were serious proposals. If they had gone ahead they would have captured, if not created, the market that is today's current cargo scene. Sadly, BAC were prevented from progressing these ideas through a lack of support.

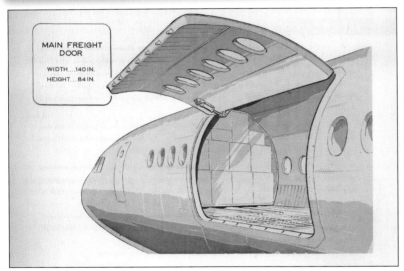

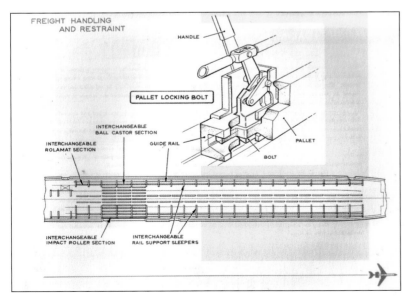

Short-haul VC10

In June 1966, the BAC project office at
Weybridge proposed the short-haul version
of the VC10, although some confusion still
surrounds this variant. Actually, there were two
versions of short-haul proposals during the life
of the VC10. The first was a 221/230-seat long-
bodied version featuring clipped wings, which
curtailed range but improved passenger payload.

The proposal was for 221 seats at a
comfortable 34-inch pitch, or 230 seats in a
one-cabin class with 32-inch pitch. The aircraft
was to be powered by Rolls-Royce Conway 43s
and also featured a Bristol Siddeley Artouste 520

ABOVE An artist's impression of a Super VC10 in British European Airways
colours. A short-haul version of the VC10 was also proposed to this airline.
(BAE SYSTEMS)

APU. The main payload/range market was the
400–1,000-mile sectors, ideal for the European
airlines. This version was prepared for British
European Airways and a model in the airline's
colours was produced, although no further
commercial progress was made with the project.

VC11

The second short-haul version was the
VC11, an 80- to 120-seat aircraft that bore a

LEFT An artist's
impression of the
proposed VC11 – an
80- to 120-seat aircraft
that had similarities
with the Vanjet from a
decade earlier.
*(BAE SYSTEMS/
Brooklands Museum)*

significant resemblance to the earlier Vanjet from a decade earlier. The VC11 was proposed to Trans-Canada Airlines (TCA) in Canada and National Airways Corporation (NAC) in New Zealand during 1966.

Military concepts

The background to 'poffling'

Having made the decision in 1960 to acquire the Skybolt missile system in preference to the Blue Streak, there was the question of its deployment. The options were considered by the Air Staff and the British Nuclear Deterrent Study Group (BNDSG). The BNDSG comprised senior officers, civil servants and scientists who were charged with developing the most efficient use of Britain's nuclear weapons to create the creditable deterrent the country required.

Skybolt was an American ballistic missile that had grown out of the Douglas GAM-77 Hound Dog project. Eventually, after a number of iterations, the final Skybolt version offered to the RAF was the GAM-87. Eventually, 140 rounds were ordered and these were to arm the 72 remaining Vulcan B.2S aircraft.

Skybolt operations, whether on a 'scramble' (later named Quick Reaction Alert – QRA) basis, or airborne alert, followed a set of fairly rigid rules. To achieve maximum range, the missile had to be launched on a track directed at the target. Off-track launches, while possible, incurred a significant range penalty. The preferred launch altitude was 40,000ft, something the Vulcan could exceed. To hit a target with any level of accuracy, a ballistic weapon needed to know its launch point. The launch sequence involved the inertial navigation system being updated from the astro-navigation star-tracker, to provide the point of origin on launch. While this could be conducted on the ground before take-off, the accuracy of the launch system deteriorated with time and in the 1960s one hour after take-off was considered the maximum permissible delay.

One of the vulnerabilities of the system was that you faced the prospect of being destroyed on the ground by a pre-emptive strike. As a consequence, it was deemed necessary to keep fully armed aircraft on constant airborne alert and the USAF continued this practice with their force of Skybolt-equipped B-52 bombers. The Air Staff and Ministry of Aviation looked at these operations in 1960 and considered airborne alert, for which they coined the phrase 'poffler', to be a viable option for the survival of the deterrent force.

When the Air Staff considered this problem, it soon became obvious that the Vulcan was not suited to such tasking. They lacked the endurance required for the role, while anticipating very serious consequences on aircraft servicing. Under existing servicing programmes, Vulcan B.2S aircraft could only mount patrols for four to six weeks before being forced to stand down for heavy maintenance.

As a consequence, the Air Staff approached both Avro and Handley Page in 1960 with requests for a 'poffler' that could perform a mission of at least 12 hours, carry an adequate weapon load and keep the British nuclear forces safe from a pre-emptive strike. Avro offered what would have become the Vulcan Phase 6, while Handley Page offered the HP.114. Unfortunately, both designs had one major weakness.

The V-bombers were designed for war and intended for discreet missions. They were not designed for the repeated take-off and landings (cycles) of the 'poffler' role. As such, the V-bombers had an airframe life of 10,000 hours. 'Poffling' would eat into that life, using up the V-Force's valuable airframe life in under five years, even considering a fairly conservative sortie rate. It was not a viable option.

On the other hand, airliners were designed with cycles in mind, as an aircraft on the ground is not making money. The Air Staff had already been in discussions with Vickers for the VC10 as an Air Transport (AT), Casualty Evacuation (Casevac) and Trooping aircraft and were close to placing an order. The VC10 had a fatigue life in the region of 30,000 hours, making the type more suitable for the 'poffler' role. Vickers were keen to expand the capabilities of their VC10 and also offered an air tanking version, but the contract for that went to Valiant. Sustaining the 'poffler' role, however, would also use up the Valiant's fatigue life.

Classified files accessed

Thanks to access granted under the Freedom of Information Act 2000, to requests made specifically for this book, files previously considered 'Classified' have revealed an interesting picture.

As early as 19 February 1960, the Chief of the Air Staff (CAS) wrote to the Deputy Chief of the Air Staff (DCAS):

I think the time has come for us to tell the Ministry of Aviation that we have serious ideas of introducing the VC.10 as a follow on to Comet and also as a carrier for Skybolt. I think we should request them to study this problem and advise us when they think we can have the advanced version of this aircraft in service and what would be the performance when carrying Skybolt. Do they think for example that we should have the first few as purely passenger cum freight carriers or could we from the very start fit them up for carrying Skybolt? If we can, I think we should.

The DCAS's response was interesting:

We have already had discussions with the Ministry of Aviation about the VC10, both as a successor to the Comet and as a Skybolt carrier. With regard to the latter, Vickers is doing a feasibility study to determine how many weapons could be carried and the most suitable points of attachment. Wind tunnel tests will probably be necessary at a later date when we have more information on the weapon.

Pending further information on the modifications required to make the VC10 into a Skybolt carrier, I think we should assume that the first few aircraft to replace the Comets will be purely passenger and light freight aircraft.

With the existing V-Force aircraft expected to be maintained until 1970, the pressure to identify a replacement was intense. Vickers soon responded with the following:

- A VC10 tanker version modified to carry two 138A weapons could be available for RAF use in 1964.
- A 1st Stage Development (of the above) VC10 containing extra fuel tanks in the fuselage and uprated engines to 26,000lb could be available in 1966. This variant was capable of carrying four Skybolt missiles, with an endurance of 11½ hours and capable of operating from existing runways.
- A 2nd Stage Development (of the above) VC10 with an all-up weight of 450,000lb, with strengthening, would require developed engines of 40,000lb and would be available in 1968.

Air Staff planning saw the need for at least 60 '1st Stage Development' VC10 aircraft. These would fulfil the new role, including the Airborne Alert Concept, with an introduction into service date of 1967/68. A stockpile of 240 0.5 megaton-yield Skybolts was also required. All of this was at an estimated cost of £198 million. However, further inter-departmental 'negotiations' reduced the number of aircraft to 50 and the number of warheads to 120.

At the request of the Scientific Adviser to the Air Ministry, an investigation was completed (probably by the Atomic Weapons Research Establishment – AWRE – at Aldermaston) into the actual size of the warhead to be carried by the Skybolts. Previous estimations had indicated that a warhead delivering a 0.5 megaton yield was required, while others had felt that 0.8 would provide a better solution. The study also analysed the size of the fleet, number of warheads required and their effectiveness and reliability.

What is most interesting from the one-time top secret memo dated October 1961, are the parameters considered and how they impacted on the eventual planned outcome. These parameters included:

- The force required was based on the BNDSG requirement to attack 40 large cities in western Russia, and to achieve an expected damage level of 50% against each.
- The number of warheads necessary to ensure that aircraft were always fully equipped when on patrol depended on the

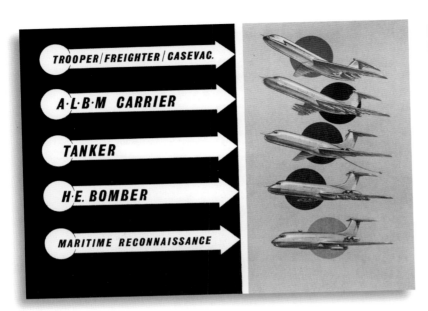

ABOVE **The cover of the first brochure for the true multi-role VC10 for the RAF.** *(BAE SYSTEMS/Brooklands Museum)*

- A missile range of 1,000nm was assumed.
- The US had estimated that the delivery error under ideal range conditions would be 3,000ft but this would have degraded to around 7,000ft under operational conditions. The latter figure was used.
- The US estimated that the launch/flight reliability of Skybolt would have been 80% in service.
- It was assumed that the weapon would be ground-burst, so a fall-out would have been obtained as a bonus effect.

The final study concluded that 0.5 megatons was the appropriate warhead and those previous assumptions made on the fleet size and warhead numbers were correct.

A true multi-role design

By May 1961, Vickers was well advanced in their radical design of a true multi-role VC10 platform. Their first brochure was delivered by Sir Geoffrey Tuttle to the Air Marshal R.B. Lees (the DCAS) on 18 May 1961. It was followed up on 21 November 1961 with a more detailed proposal from Sir George Edwards to the Controller of Aircraft at the Ministry of Aviation. In the letter, Sir George Edwards outlined:

- A flight refuelling tanker.
- An air-launched ballistic missile (ALBM) carrier carrying eight Skybolts.
- A conventional bomber (with eight 1,000lb bombs to be carried in each of the eight cocoons slung from the Skybolt attachment points).
- A Coastal Command aircraft to Scheme MR. 1 (with the weapons carried in cocoons suspended from two of the Skybolt attachment points).

Not included in the list, but later developed by the RAF Staff College at Henlow, was the 'Red Barrel' version. Fitted with AI (Air Interception) radar, an operations room and armed with up to 18 air-to-air missiles (AAMs), it was proposed for patrol use over the North Atlantic and Norwegian Sea. It would have been the largest 'fighter' aircraft ever developed!

ability to switch missiles between carriers. Since the missile carrier would have been on patrol for around four months of the year, it should have been practical to transfer or 'switch' its warheads to another missile carrier for at least part of the remaining eight months.

- It was assumed that each patrolling VC10 would carry six missiles.
- It was assumed that the average sortie length against the BNDSG target list was about seven hours (it was also assumed that the force would operate without tanker support).
- The aircraft was designed to have a fatigue life of 30,000 hours.
- An average utilisation per year per aircraft was assumed as 3,200 hours (based on aircraft fatigue life and serviceability considerations).
- An engine overhaul life of 2,000 hours was assumed.
- The in-flight reliability would fall to about 85% in the first hour of flight and then by 2% for each subsequent hour.
- It was assumed that one aircraft would be written off every 100,000 flying hours on average.
- The designed fatigue life of the missile was 25,000 hours.

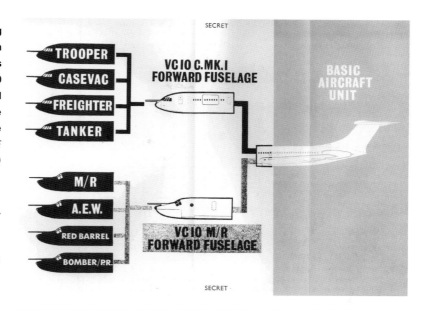

Sadly, all to no avail

A succession of test failures and the development of submarine-launched ballistic missiles (SLBMs) eventually led to the cancellation of the Skybolt programme in December 1962. The UK had decided to base its entire 1960s deterrent force on Skybolt, and its cancellation led to a major disagreement between the UK and US, referred to today as the 'Skybolt Crisis'.

This was resolved through meetings leading to the Royal Navy gaining the UGM-27 Polaris missile and construction of the Resolution-class submarines to launch them.

Without an order for the VC10 in the 'poffler' role, no further orders were forthcoming for any of the other multi-role VC10 proposals, except the tanker version which came at a much later stage. That conversion programme proved the VC10 tanker to be a world beater.

So much good money was subsequently wasted on projects such as the Nimrod AEW.3 programme, while the conversion of ancient Shackleton Maritime Reconnaissance platforms into AEW aircraft ahead of the *eventual* Boeing Sentry project would not have been required; the multi-role VC10 could and would have satisfied all of those roles.

All of the creative and innovative thinking from Vickers-Armstrong and, later, BAC, came to absolutely nothing. The VC10 was a great aircraft in its lifetime . . . but it could have been so much better . . . in so many roles.

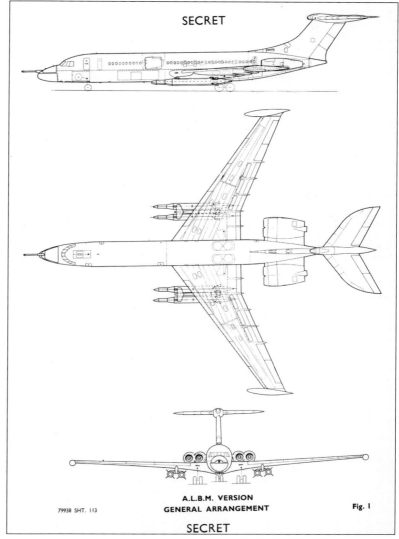

A.L.B.M. VERSION
GENERAL ARRANGEMENT

Fig. 1

Chapter Nine

VC10 survivors

Sadly, of the 54 VC10 aircraft produced at Weybridge, not a single example is still flying anywhere in the world. The bureaucracy and red tape preventing one ever flying again is unlikely to change the current situation, while the sums of money required to fund a flying VC10 are probably too vast to even contemplate.

However, at least two examples – K.3 ZA150 at Dunsfold and K.4 ZD241 at Bruntingthorpe – are back in a 'live' ground-running condition. This allows the public the opportunity to witness the sight and sound of a VC10 with four Rolls-Royce Conway engines running at almost full power.

OPPOSITE After having spent time with 1312 Flight on the Falkland Islands, VC10 K.4, ZD241, made its final flight into Bruntingthorpe on 12 March 2013. Thanks to GJD Services and a small group of volunteers from the ZD241 Bruntingthorpe Preservation Group who have brought the aircraft back up to a ground-running 'live' condition, the aircraft is still able to occasionally demonstrate the amazing Conway roar, complete with smoke during high-speed taxi runs, up and down the runway at Bruntingthorpe. *(Philip Stevens)*

Ground-running examples

At the time of writing, two airframes (ZA150 and ZD241) are maintained in a ground-running 'live' condition. A third example – ZA148 with the Cornwall Aviation Heritage Centre – is undergoing work that should see her taxi at Newquay under her own power sometime in the future.

Vickers VC10 K.3 ZA150/J

ZA150 was the very last VC10 of the 54 built at Brooklands in the 1960s and was one of the last two VC10 aircraft to fly with 101 Squadron at RAF Brize Norton.

Originally, it was the fifth aircraft ordered by East African Airways (EAA) as a Type 1154. It made its maiden flight at Brooklands on 16 February 1970, before entering service later in that month as 5H-MOG. EAA ran into financial difficulties in January 1977 and the aircraft was parked at Embakasi Airport, Nairobi, until the British Aircraft Corporation (BAC) repossessed the aircraft in August of the same year. It was then flown back to Filton where it was stored.

Four of the five Super VC10 aircraft delivered to EAA were repossessed by BAC and all were flown to Filton. Shortly afterwards, they were purchased by the RAF for conversion into VC10 K.3 tanker aircraft. This process was completed in late 1984 and ZA150 was delivered to 101 Squadron on 1 February 1985, where it remained for the entirety of its military life.

ZA150 was withdrawn from use and acquired by Brooklands Museum when it was flown into Dunsfold Aerodrome on 24 September 2013. Here, a team of dedicated volunteers maintain it in running order. It was open for visitors during the 'Wings & Wheels' events of 2014 and 2015. At the latter event it completed a fast-taxi demonstration on the Sunday. It is hoped this performance can be repeated at events in 2016 and beyond.

Vickers VC10 K.4 ZD241/P

This aircraft started life as a Type 1151 Super VC10 ordered by BOAC as G-ASGM. It made its first flight at Brooklands on 26 February 1968 and was delivered to the airline on 9 March of the same year. In 1975, BOAC and BEA merged with the new airline – British Airways – coming into being on 1 April 1974. Shortly afterwards, the aircraft was painted in the new British Airways livery.

It remained in service with British Airways until withdrawn in July 1980 before being stored at Abingdon. It was acquired by the RAF and the serial number ZD241 allocated. Later, it was flown to Filton where it was converted to a K.4 tanker. When the conversion work was completed, ZD241 joined 101 Squadron at Brize Norton.

The aircraft was withdrawn from service and flown to Bruntingthorpe on 21 March 2013 where it was subsequently decommissioned in accordance with the disposal contract, and made ready for her eventual parting-out and scrapping by GJD Services.

Gary Spoors, the managing director of GJD

BELOW VC10 K.3, ZA150/J, is owned by the Brooklands Museum but is based at nearby Dunsfold, where it is lovingly maintained by the ZA150 Volunteer Support Group. The aircraft is still able to taxi under the power of its own Rolls-Royce Conway engines and the occasional high-speed run down the Dunsfold runway may be something to look forward to in the future? *(Keith Wilson)*

LEFT Having joined BOAC in September 1964, G-ARVF was sold to the United Arab Emirates in 1974 where it was operated in a VVIP configuration. After being withdrawn from service in the UAE, G-ARVF has been preserved at Flugausstellung Hermeskeil in Germany since 1981. *(Lee Barton)*

Services, is a former RAF VC10 engineer. He had decided that he would like to preserve a VC10 in live condition and had originally selected XR808 for that role. However, XR808 was then allocated to the RAF Museum for their collection at Cosford. Following a technical study of those airframes available at Bruntingthorpe, it was decided that ZD241 would be the most suitable to recommission and preserve.

Later in 2013, Gary Spoors put out a call for experienced former VC10 engineers and volunteers to help out with the recommissioning of ZD241. A small team was formed and the name 'ZD241 Bruntingthorpe Preservation Group' adopted. This team has been working on ZD241 ever since and the aircraft has frequently demonstrated its ground-running and fast-taxi capabilities at Bruntingthorpe. Gary hopes to keep the aircraft running so that the 100th anniversary of the type's first flight can be celebrated in style.

More information on the 'ZD241 Bruntingthorpe Preservation Group' is available in Appendix 5.

Complete aircraft

Vickers VC10 Type 1101 G-ARVF

G-ARVF was the fifth aircraft in the original order from BOAC for the Type 1101. It made its first flight at Brooklands on 6 July 1963 and was delivered to the airline on 4 September 1964. This aircraft was actively involved in the earliest route-proving trials, particularly to the African destinations.

It was sold to the United Arab Emirates in July 1974 where it was converted and subsequently operated in a VVIP configuration until being withdrawn from UAE service in 1981. It was then flown to Germany and has been preserved at Flugausstellung Hermeskeil since 1981.

Vickers VC10 Type 1103 A4O-AB

This aircraft was ordered by British United Airways (BUA) and made its first flight at Brooklands on 17 October 1964. It was delivered to BUA at Gatwick on 31 October and immediately entered service. BUA was later acquired by British Caledonian Airlines (BCAL) and G-ASIX adopted the new colours. It was

BELOW This standard Type 1103 VC10 was delivered to BUA as G-ASIX on 31 October 1964 and features a large forward freight door on the port side of the fuselage. When BUA was acquired by British Caledonian Airways (BCAL), G-ASIX adopted their colours until sold to the Omani Royal Flight as A4O-AB. Here, it underwent a major interior upgrade to a VVIP interior fit. When the aircraft was eventually retired from service, the aircraft was flown into Weybridge via Heathrow on 6 July 1987, for preservation with the Brooklands Museum. It retains the spectacular VVIP interior and is open to visitors of the museum. It is well worth a visit. *(Keith Wilson)*

later sold to the Omani Royal Flight as A4O-AB and was converted to a VVIP role, very much in keeping with its royal duties as the personal jet of the Sultan of Oman. It was a regular visitor to the UK during this time.

When the aircraft was finally withdrawn from service in 1987, it was offered to the Brooklands Museum at Weybridge. The aircraft was initially flown to Heathrow before continuing its journey to Brooklands where it made its final landing on to the runway from which it had made its very first flight.

The aircraft is open to the public at the Brooklands Museum where guided tours are available. It is displayed in its Omani Royal Flight colours, with its regal interior available for public viewing.

Vickers VC10 C.1K XR808

XR808 was the third VC10 C.1 ordered by the RAF. It made its first flight at Brooklands on 9 June 1966 and was delivered to 10 Squadron at RAF Fairford on 7 July that year. The squadron moved to Brize Norton shortly afterwards and the aircraft remained at Brize until the decision was taken to convert all of the RAF's remaining 13 VC10 C.1 aircraft to C.1K tanker configuration.

The conversion was undertaken at Bournemouth/Hurn and was completed in February 1997, after which the aircraft returned to Brize Norton. However, it joined 101 Squadron and continued to serve in its new tanker/transport role until the decision was taken to withdraw the type from service. On 29 July 2013, XR808 was flown to Bruntingthorpe as part of the Spares Recovery Programme. There were 43,865 hours on the airframe.

Before that process could start, XR808 (or 'Bob', as the aircraft is known, because of the tail number) was gifted to the RAF Museum. However, when it became apparent that a VC10 could not be flown into Cosford because of the short runway, many believed that the last chance to get an example of the aircraft into a museum had gone. However, behind the scenes planning continued and arrangements were made for the aircraft to be dismantled at Bruntingthorpe and moved in pieces, by road, to the RAF Museum site at Cosford.

The dismantling, shipping and reassembly task was undertaken by GJD Services, who were no strangers to dismantling a VC10 as they had already performed this task on several of the RAF's retiring VC10 fleet. It was not an easy task, though, as thousands of wing bolts had to be removed from inside the structure and special cradles had to be constructed to hold the separated components.

Moving an almost 50m-long aircraft, even in pieces, by road is not a simple matter and the specialist haulier required dispensation from the Highways Agency as well as the removal of various bits of street furniture and, at certain points, a police escort. Getting through some of the bridges and towns along the route was also tricky and there were sometimes only inches to spare.

Reassembly was no small challenge either, but the team rose to it magnificently and the aircraft has been on public display at the RAF Museum, Cosford, since 2015.

This move was an expensive operation with sponsorship funding coming from the RAF Charitable Trust, Rolls-Royce, BAE Systems and GJD Services.

Vickers VC10 Type 1151 G-ASGC

G-ASGC was the third Super VC10 ordered by BOAC. It made its first flight at Brooklands on 1 January 1965 and was delivered to BOAC at London Airport on 27 March carrying 'BOAC Cunard' titles in which it operated for a number of years. It was repainted in British Airways colours after the merger in 1974. It remained with BA until 1980, when it was withdrawn from service.

It was flown to Duxford on 15 April 1980 for preservation with the Duxford Aviation Society (DAS) as part of their excellent British Airliner Collection. Visitors to Duxford are able to take tours inside the aircraft, which has been returned to its original 'BOAC Cunard' livery by DAS.

Vickers VC10 K.3 ZA147

This aircraft was the second ordered by East African Airways (EAA) as a Type 1154. It made its first flight at Brooklands on 12 October 1966 and was delivered to the airline on 31 October that year as 5H-MMT. It remained in service with EAA until the airline's financial collapse and was parked at Embakasi Airport, Nairobi, by 28 January 1977. It was repossessed by BAC, flown back to the UK and stored at Filton.

The airframe was later acquired by the RAF for conversion to a K.3 tanker, which was undertaken at Filton by BAE Systems. The work was completed and the aircraft was flown to Brize Norton on 9 August 1985 as ZA147/F, when it joined 101 Squadron.

It remained in service with 101 Squadron until being withdrawn from use on 25 September 2013, making the very last VC10 flight from Brize Norton to Bruntingthorpe for the Spares Recovery Programme. The aircraft is currently

ABOVE Having made its first flight at Weybridge on 1 January 1965, Super VC10, G-ASGC, spent the first six years of its working life in BOAC colours before the airline's merger with BEA to form British Airways (BA) in April 1974. G-ASGC was repainted in BA colours and remained with them until retirement to Duxford in April 1980. Visitors to Duxford will be able to take tours inside the aircraft, which was recently returned to its original BOAC Cunard livery by the DAS. (Keith Wilson)

complete but engineless. It had been earmarked for display at Duxford but its future is currently uncertain. The aircraft may now be broken with the cockpit section going on loan to the Moravia Collection from GJD Services, while the remainder may be used as spares for ZD241.

BELOW Having made its last flight into Bruntingthorpe on 25 September 2013, VC10 K.3, ZA147/F, has remained almost complete since – although the engines and in-flight refuelling probe have been removed. Sadly, the future of ZA147 is not now secure. It had been intended to move the complete aircraft to Duxford but, at the time of writing, this seems unlikely to happen. It is more likely to be broken up, with the cockpit section being loaned to the Moravia Collection. (Keith Wilson)

Vickers VC10 K.3 ZA148

This was the third aircraft ordered by East African Airways (EAA) as a Type 1154. It made its first flight at Brooklands on 21 March 1967 and was delivered to the airline just ten days later as 5Y-ADA. It remained in service with EAA until the airline's financial collapse and was parked at Embakasi Airport, Nairobi, by 28 January 1977. It too was repossessed by BAC, flown back to the UK and stored at Filton.

The RAF acquired the airframe for conversion to a K.3 tanker, which was undertaken at Bristol by BAE Systems. After work was completed, the aircraft was flown to Brize Norton on 4 July 1984 as ZA148/G, when it joined 101 Squadron.

It remained in service with 101 Squadron until being withdrawn from use on 28 August when it was flown from Brize Norton via Bristol Airport before landing at Newquay for display with the Classic Air Force Collection. That arrangement soon fell through and GJD Services have adopted ZA148, which is currently on loan to the Cornwall Aviation Heritage Centre. Incidentally, GJD Services are also the principal shareholders in the Cornwall Aviation Heritage Centre.

The aircraft is currently on static display with good access to the public, but a small team of enthusiasts are endeavouring to return ZA148 to a 'live' state, enabling it to taxi under its own power. Hopefully, four Conway engines will soon be heard roaring in Cornwall!

Fuselage and cockpit sections

Vickers VC10 Type 1101 G-ARVM

G-ARVM was the last of the 12 Type 1101 standard VC10s built at Brooklands for BOAC, making its first flight on 6 July 1964. It was delivered to the airline just eight days later where it operated both as a passenger carrier as well as a crew trainer with BOAC and, later, British Airways.

In 1974 the British Airways standard VC10 fleet was retired from service, apart from 'VM, which remained in service as a training aircraft while also being retained as a 'standby aircraft' for the airline's Super VC10 and Concorde fleets.

G-ARVM was finally retired in October 1979 when it made its final flight to the RAF

Museum at Cosford and became the first VC10 to be preserved.

In 2006 the aircraft was broken up at Cosford although British Airways did offer the fuselage to the Brooklands Museum, where it arrived in October 2006 in two pieces. The two halves were soon rejoined and it is now the only surviving VC10 Type 1101 preserved in the UK.

In 2012 the interior was refurbished to commemorate the 50th anniversary of the first flight of the VC10. Currently, the fuselage is on display at the Brooklands Museum and is open to the public with a comprehensive VC10 exhibition housed in the rear cabin.

Vickers C10 C.1K XV104

XV104 was the ninth VC10 C.1 built for the RAF. It made its first flight at Brooklands on 14 July 1967 and was delivered to 10 Squadron at Fairford on 3 August. No 10 Squadron moved to Brize Norton where XV104 continued to serve until the decision was taken to convert all C.1 aircraft into C.1K Tanker/Transports. XV104 was converted at Hurn in 1998 and returned to Brize Norton with 101 Squadron where it continued to serve until the type was withdrawn from service.

XV104 made its last flight to Bruntingthorpe on 4 July 2012 where it joined the Spares Recovery Programme. Shortly afterwards it was broken up, although the fuselage section was retained by GJD Services and is currently held in storage at Bruntingthorpe.

Vickers C10 C.1K XV106

XV106 was the eleventh VC10 C.1 built for the RAF. It made its first flight at Brooklands on 17 November 1966 and was delivered to 10 Squadron at Fairford on 1 December. No 10 Squadron moved to Brize Norton where XV106 continued to serve until the decision was taken to convert all C.1 aircraft into C.1K Tanker/Transports. XV106 was converted at Hurn and returned to Brize Norton with 101 Squadron where it continued to serve until the type was withdrawn from service.

XV106 made its last flight to Bruntingthorpe on 7 November 2012 where it joined the Spares Recovery Programme. Shortly afterwards it was broken up, although

ABOVE Stored within a secure compound at Bruntingthorpe are three VC10 C.1K cockpit sections, along with around a dozen Rolls-Royce Conway engine assemblies – plus a Sea King cabin and another unidentified cockpit. The three VC10 C.1K cockpit sections are (from left to right) XV104, XV106 and XV109. *(Keith Wilson)*

the fuselage section was retained by GJD Services and is currently held in storage at Bruntingthorpe. It is expected that the forward fuselage will be loaned by GJD Services to the BAE Collection at Woodford.

Vickers C10 C.1K XV108

XV108 was the thirteenth VC10 C.1 built for the RAF. It made its first flight at Brooklands on 7 June 1968 and was delivered to 10 Squadron at Fairford just 11 days later. No 10 Squadron moved to Brize Norton where XV108 continued to serve until the decision was taken to convert all C.1 aircraft into C.1K Tanker/Transports. XV108 was converted at Hurn in August 1995 and returned to Brize Norton with 101 Squadron where it continued to serve until the type was withdrawn from service.

BELOW When VC10 C.1K, XV108, was withdrawn from service it was flown into Bruntingthorpe on 7 November 2012 for parting out. The forward fuselage section was carefully separated from the rest of the airframe during the dismantling process and by 20 September 2013 it was mounted on wooden blocks ahead of a road journey and display at the East Midlands Aeropark. *(Gary Spoors)*

RIGHT After a
successful road
journey, the nose
section of XV108 was
installed at the East
Midlands Aeropark
and is now available
for public inspection.
(Ken Williams/East
Midlands Aeropark)

BELOW VC10 K.3,
ZA149/H, made
its final flight into
Bruntingthorpe on
18 March 2013 to join
the Spares Recovery
Programme. After
being broken up,
the forward fuselage
section was retained
and transferred
to another part of
the airfield, where
it underwent a
restoration programme
led by Martin Slater
into the colours of
Gulf Air. Recently, the
aircraft was moved
by road and sea to
Sharjah, where it is
now on display.
(Keith Wilson)

XV108 was withdrawn from service and
made its last flight into Bruntingthorpe on
7 November 2012 for the Spares Recovery
Programme. The forward fuselage section was
carefully separated from the rest of the airframe
during the dismantling process undertaken by
the GJD Services team and by 20 September
2013 it was mounted on wooden blocks
ahead of a road journey and display at the East
Midlands Aeropark.

After a successful road journey, the nose
section of XV108 was installed at the East
Midlands Aeropark, where it is on loan to the
museum from GJD Services. It is expected to
be available for public inspection by the time of
this book's publication.

Vickers C10 C.1K XV109

XV109 was the fourteenth and final VC10
C.1 built for the RAF. It made its first flight at
Brooklands on 18 July 1968 and was delivered
to 10 Squadron at Fairford on 1 August.
No 10 Squadron moved to Brize Norton
where XV109 continued to serve until the
decision was taken to convert all C.1 aircraft
into C.1K Tanker/Transports. XV109 was
converted at Hurn in August 1995 and returned
to Brize Norton with 101 Squadron where it
continued to serve until the type was withdrawn
from service.

XV109 made its last flight into Bruntingthorpe
in June 2010 for the Spares Recovery
Programme. Shortly afterwards it was broken
up, although the fuselage section was retained
by GJD Services and is currently held in storage
at Bruntingthorpe.

Vickers VC10 K.3 ZA149/H

This was the fourth aircraft ordered by East
African Airways (EAA) as a Type 1154. It made
its first flight at Brooklands on 19 April 1969
and was delivered to the airline 11 days later
as 5X-UVJ. It remained in service with EAA until
the airline's financial collapse and was parked at
Embakasi Airport, Nairobi, by 28 January 1977.
It was repossessed by BAC, flown back to the
UK, and stored at Filton.

The airframe was later acquired by the RAF
for conversion to a K.3 tanker, which was

undertaken at Bristol by BAE Systems. The work was completed and the aircraft was flown to Brize Norton on 25 March 1985 as ZA149/H, when it joined 101 Squadron.

It remained in service with 101 Squadron until being withdrawn from use on 18 March 2013 when it was flown into Bruntingthorpe for the Spares Recovery Programme. After being broken up, the forward fuselage section was transferred to another part of the airfield, where it underwent a restoration programme led by Martin Slater, into the colours of Gulf Air.

The aircraft has since been moved by road and sea to Sharjah and is now on display at the Mahatta Aviation Museum.

Structural test section

The structural test section was built by Vickers-Armstrong (Aircraft) Ltd at Weybridge and allocated the construction number 801A. Initially it was tested in the stratosphere chamber before being tested in the Aircraft Laboratories' water tank where it was ultimately pressurised to destruction, leading to damaged roof panels. It was later donated to the Brooklands Museum in 1986.

In 1992, British Airways repainted the fuselage into 1960s BOAC colours and it was placed back on display.

In 1996, RAF St Athan borrowed it for VC10 front bulkhead replacement trials and, in return,

made the fuselage completely weatherproof, fitted new Perspex viewing panels and cabin windows and supplied a new support trailer before the fuselage section was returned to Brooklands for display.

BELOW VC10 K.2, ZA144, was withdrawn from service and flown to RAF St Athan in August 2000 where it was initially stored. Later, the decision was taken to scrap the airframe. The forward fuselage section was stored at St Athan until at least 2010 (where this image was taken on 4 December 2007) before being transported by road to Boscombe Down, where it joined the Joint Aircraft Recovery and Transport Squadron (JARTS). In this 'new' role the aircraft section was occasionally seen on the back of a trailer being moved around the UK. The current whereabouts and status of the fuselage is unknown. (Kev Slade)

Appendix 1

VC10 production list

Construction number	Model number	Registration or serial	Date of first flight	Customer/operator	Fate	Location/date of final flight
801A				Forward fuselage section only constructed – without main cargo door – for ground test purposes only	Preserved at Brooklands Museum in BA colours	
801B				Forward fuselage section only constructed – with main cargo door – for water tank testing purposes only	Not known	
802				Airframe, excluding cockpit, manufactured for structural testing purposes	Not known but probably scrapped	
803	1103	G-ARTA	29-Jun-62	Prototype series 1100 aircraft. Purchased by Freddie Laker and leased to Middle East Airways from 1968–1969. Sold and delivered to British United Airways April 1969. Later operated in British Caledonian colours	Written off after a heavy landing at Gatwick on 28-Jan-1972. Broken up at Gatwick during 1973	Gatwick 28-Jan-1973
804	1101	G-ARVA	8-Nov-62	BOAC d/d 08-Dec-1964. Sold to Nigerian Airways as 5N-ABD on 29-Sept-69	Written off in accident 14km from Lagos 20-Nov-69. 11 crew and 76 passengers – no survivors	Crashed 20-Nov-1969
805	1101	G-ARVB	21-Nov-62	BOAC d/d 06-Feb-1965. Merged with British Airways on 01-Apr-1974 and painted in BA colours	Withdrawn from use and stored at Heathrow in July 1974. Scrapped at Heathrow in October 1976.	Heathrow July 1974
806	1101	G-ARVC	21-Feb-63	BOAC d/d 01-Dec-1964. Leased to Nigerian Airways in 1967. Leased to Gulf Air in February 1974. Acquired by Gulf Air in October 1974 as A40-VC	Withdrawn from Gulf Air use in 1977 and placed into storage. Converted to K.2 tanker as ZA144/D in 1982. Withdrawn from use and stored at St Athan in August 2000. Later scrapped. Forward fuselage transferred to the JARTS at Boscombe Down	St Athan August 2000
807	1101	G-ARVE	15-Apr-63	BOAC d/d 01-Oct-1964. Merged with British Airways on 01-Apr-1974 and painted in BA colours	Withdrawn from use and stored at Heathrow October 1974. Scrapped at Heathrow October 1976	Heathrow October 1974
808	1101	G-ARVF	6-Jul-63	BOAC d/d 04-Sept-1964. Merged with British Airways on 01-Apr-1974 and painted in BA colours. Sold to United Arab Emirates 19-July-1974.	Withdrawn from use and later preserved at Flugausstellung Hermeskeil, Germany, since 1981	
809	1101	G-ARVG	17-Oct-63	BOAC d/d 12-June-1964. Merged with British Airways on 01-Apr-1974 and painted in BA colours. Leased to Gulf Air in June 1974, then acquired by Gulf Air as A40-VG	Withdrawn from Gulf Air use in 1977 and placed into storage. Converted to K.2 tanker as ZA141/B. Withdrawn from RAF use and broken up St Athan 2000	St Athan 2000
810	1101	G-ARVH	22-Nov-63	BOAC d/d 02-July-1964. Merged with British Airways on 01-Apr-1974 and painted in BA colours	Withdrawn from use and stored at Heathrow October 1974. Scrapped at Heathrow in October 1976	Heathrow October 1974
811	1101	G-ARVI	20-Dec-63	BOAC d/d 22-Apr-1964. Merged with British Airways on 01-Apr-1974 and painted in BA colours. Leased to Gulf Air in March 1974, then acquired in 1975 by Gulf Air as A40-VI	Withdrawn from use by Gulf Air in December 1977 and placed into storage. Converted to K.2 tanker as ZA142/C and delivered to 101 Squadron 18-Apr-1984. Withdrawn from RAF use in 2001 and stored at St Athan. Broken up in 2003	St Athan 2001
812	1101	G-ARVJ	25-Feb-64	BOAC d/d 23-Apr-1964. Merged with British Airways on 01-Apr-1974 and painted in BA colours. Leased to Qatar Amiri Flight from 1975–1981. Acquired by RAF in September 1982 as ZD493	Wfu at Brize Norton and broken up by 1991	Brize Norton
813	1101	G-ARVK	28-Mar-64	BOAC d/d 02-May-1964. Merged with British Airways on 01-Apr-1974 and painted in BA colours. Leased to Gulf Air in 1974, then acquired in June 1975 by Gulf Air as A40-VK	Withdrawn from Gulf Air use in 1977 and placed into storage. Converted to K.2 tanker as ZA143/D. Withdrawn from RAF use in February 2000 and stored St Athan. Later broken up	St Athan
814	1101	G-ARVL	2-Jun-64	BOAC d/d 16-June-1964. Leased to Nigerian Airways in 1969 and later returned. Merged with British Airways on 01-Apr-1974 and painted in BA colours. Acquired by Gulf Air in February 1975 as A40-VL	Withdrawn from Gulf Air use in December 1977 and placed into storage. Converted to K.2 tanker as ZA140/A. Withdrawn from RAF use in May 2000 and stored St Athan. Broken up by 2001	St Athan

Construction number	Model number	Registration or serial	Date of first flight	Customer/operator	Fate	Location/date of final flight
815	1101	G-ARVM	6-Jul-64	BOAC d/d 22-July-1964. Merged with British Airways on 01-Apr-1974 and painted in BA colours	Withdrawn from use and preserved at the RAF Museum, Cosford. Broken up in 2006 and forward fuselage moved to Brooklands, arriving 19-Oct-2006	Cosford October 1979
819	1103	G-ASIW	30-Jul-64	BUA British United Airways d/d 30-Sept-1964. Later served in British Caledonian Airways colours. To Air Malawi in November 1974 as 7Q-YKH	Withdrawn from use and stored (at Bournemouth/Hurn) October 1979. Transferred to Blantyre, Malawi, in 1981. Broken up by 1994	Blantyre, Malawi, 1981
820	1103	G-ASIX	17-Oct-64	BUA d/d 31-Oct-1964. Later served in British Caledonian Airways colours. To Oman Royal Flight as A4O-AB	Withdrawn from use and preserved at Weybridge in July 1987	Weybridge 06-07-1987
823	1102	9G-ABO	14-Nov-64	Ghana Airways d/d 27-Jan-1965	Withdrawn from use in December 1980 and stored at Prestwick. Broken up in 1983	Prestwick December 1980
824	1102	9G-ABP	21-May-65	Ghana Airways d/d 18-June-1965. Leased to Middle East Air Airlines (MEA) 01-Apr-1967	Destroyed on ground when Israeli commandos attacked 14 aircraft at Beirut International Airport on 28-Dec-1968	Beirut 28-Dec-1968
825	1102	9G-ABQ	18-Jun-65	Order cancelled and registration ntu. Sold to BUA as G-ATDJ d/d 01-July-1965. Later operated in British Caledonian colours. Withdrawn from use and acquired in March 1973 by the Royal Aircraft Establishment as XX914	Withdrawn from use and initially stored at RAE Thurleigh. Tailfin donated to ZA141. Aircraft broken up in 1984 although two large fuselage sections delivered to the RAF Air Movements School at Brize Norton as 8777M in July 1983	RAE Thurleigh 06-May-1975
826	1106	XR806	26-Nov-65	10 Squadron, RAF d/d 07-July-1966. Named George Thompson VC. Converted to C.1K in 1995 and delivered to 10 Squadron in February 1996	Dbr in defuelling accident at Brize Norton on 18-Dec-1997 and broken up	Brize Norton
827	1106	XR807	25-Mar-66	10 Squadron, RAF d/d 17-Nov-1966. Named Donald Garland VC. Converted to C.1K in September 1994. Transferred to 101 Squadron in October 2005	Wfu and flown to Bruntingthorpe for Spares Recovery Programme 04-June-2010. Broken up by 28-July-2010	Bruntingthorpe 04-June-2010
828	1106	XR808	9-Jun-66	10 Squadron, RAF d/d 07-07-1966. Named Kenneth Campbell VC. Converted to C.1K in 02-1997. Transferred to 101 Squadron in October 2005	Wfu and flown to Bruntingthorpe for Spares Recovery Programme 29-July-2013. TT 43,865 hours. Later dismantled and moved by road to Cosford before being reassembled for display	Bruntingthorpe 29-July-2013
829	1106	XR809	28-Jul-66	10 Squadron, RAF, d/d 31-Aug-1966. Named Hugh Malcolm VC. Transferred to Rolls-Royce as an engine test bed in July 1969. The aircraft flew with a single RB211 on the port side and a pair of Conway engines on the starboard side	After discounting the possibility of returning the aircraft to RAF service due to the uneconomical costs, the aircraft was wfu at Kemble and broken up in 1982	Kemble
830	1106	XR810	29-Nov-66	10 Squadron, RAF, d/d 21-Dec-1966. Named David Lord VC. Converted to C.1K in 1998. Transferred to 101 Squadron	Wfu 2005 and scrapped at St Athan in September 2006. Flight deck initially retained by GJD Services but has since been reduced to scrap	St Athan 2005
831	1106	XV101	11-Jan-67	10 Squadron, RAF, d/d 31-Jan-1967. Named Lance Hawker VC. Converted to C.1K in 1997. Transferred to 101 Squadron	Wfu 20-Nov-2011. Broken up by June 2012	Bruntingthorpe 20-Nov-2011
832	1106	XV102	5-May-67	10 Squadron, RAF, d/d 25-May-1967. Named Guy Gibson VC. Converted to C.1K in 1998. Transferred to 101 Squadron	Wfu 12-Dec-2011. Broken up by June 2012	Bruntingthorpe 12-Dec-2011
833	1106	XV103	14-Jun-67	10 Squadron, RAF, d/d 05-July-1967. Named Edward Mannock VC. Converted to C.1K in 1998. Transferred to 101 Squadron	Wfu 2001 and broken up at St Athan by 2003	St Athan 2001
834	1106	XV104	14-Jul-67	10 Squadron, RAF, d/d 03-08-1967. Named James McCudden VC. Converted to C.1K in 1998. Transferred to 101 Squadron.	Wfu and flown to Bruntingthorpe for Spares Recovery Programme. Cockpit section retained.	Bruntingthorpe 04-07-2013
835	1106	XV105	3-Oct-67	10 Squadron, RAF, d/d 20-10-1967. Named Albert Ball VC. Converted to C.1K in 1995. Transferred to 101 Squadron.	Wfu and flown to Bruntingthorpe for Spares Recovery Programme.	Bruntingthorpe 31-08-2011
836	1106	XV106	17-Nov-67	10 Squadron, RAF, d/d 01-Dec-1967. Named Thomas Mottershead VC. Converted to C.1K. Transferred to 101 Squadron	Wfu and flown to Bruntingthorpe for Spares Recovery Programme. Cockpit section retained and may be loaned by GJD Services to the BAe Collection at Woodford	Bruntingthorpe 07-Nov-2012
837	1106	XV107	22-Mar-68	10 Squadron, RAF, d/d 17-Apr-1968. Named James Nicholson VC. Converted to C.1K in June 1996. Transferred to 101 Squadron	Wfu and flown to Bruntingthorpe for Spares Recovery Programme. Broken up by January 2012	Bruntingthorpe 12-Dec-2011

Construction number	Model number	Registration or serial	Date of first flight	Customer/operator	Fate	Location/date of final flight
838	1106	XV108	7-Jun-68	10 Squadron, RAF, d/d 18-June-1968. Named William Rhodes-Moorehouse VC. Converted to C.1K in August 1995. Transferred to 101 Squadron	Wfu and flown to Bruntingthorpe for Spares Recovery Programme. Broken up by June 2010. Cockpit section on loan from GJD Services, displayed at East Midlands Aeropark	Bruntingthorpe 07-Nov-2012
839	1106	XV109	18-Jul-68	10 Squadron, RAF, d/d 01-Aug-1968. Named Arthur Scarf VC. Converted to C.1K in August 1995. Transferred to 101 Squadron	Wfu and flown to Bruntingthorpe for Spares Recovery Programme. Broken up by June 2010	Bruntingthorpe 31-Mar-2010
840	1102	9G-ABU		Allocated to Ghana Airways but construction never completed		
851	1151	G-ASGA	7-May-64	Prototype Series 1151. BOAC d/d 31-Dec-1965. Merged with British Airways on 01-Apr-1974 and painted in BA colours. Transferred to RAF in April 1980 and converted to K.4 as ZD230. 101 Squadron	Withdrawn from use 2006 and broken up at St Athan. Flight deck initially retained by GJD Services but has since been reduced to scrap	St Athan 16-Dec-2005
852	1151	G-ASGB	29-Sep-64	BOAC d/d 30-Apr-1965. Merged with British Airways on 01-Apr-1974 and painted in BA colours. Transferred to RAF in April 1980 as ZD231. Stored at Abingdon	Withdrawn from use and broken up for spares at Abingdon in April 1987	Abingdon
853	1151	G-ASGC	1-Jan-65	BOAC d/d 27-03-1965. Also carried 'Cunard' titles. Merged with British Airways on 01-04-1974 and painted in BA colours.	Withdrawn from use in April 1980 and flown to Duxford for preservation.	Duxford 15-Apr-1980
854	1151	G-ASGD	11-Feb-65	BOAC d/d 01-Apr-1965. Merged with British Airways on 01-Apr-1974 and painted in BA colours. Transferred to RAF in May 1981 as ZD232. Stored at Brize Norton	Broken up 1982	Brize Norton
855	1151	G-ASGE	6-Mar-65	BOAC d/d 27-Mar-1965. Merged with British Airways on 01-Apr-1974 and painted in BA colours. Transferred to RAF in May 1980 as ZD233. Stored at Brize Norton	Withdrawn from use and broken up 1982	Brize Norton
856	1151	G-ASGF	24-Mar-65	BOAC d/d 02-Apr-1965. Merged with British Airways on 01-Apr-1974 and painted in BA colours. Transferred to RAF in May 1981 as ZD234. Stored at Brize Norton	Withdrawn from use and broken up 1982. Nose section converted to flight simulator and allocated maintenance serial 8700M	Brize Norton
857	1151	G-ASGG	17-May-65	Used for development of automatic landing trials. BOAC d/d 21-June-1967. Merged with British Airways on 01-Apr-1974 and painted in BA colours. Transferred to RAF in May 1981 and converted to K.4 as ZD235. 101 Squadron	Withdrawn from use and broken up for spares at Abingdon	Abingdon
858	1151	G-ASGH	2-Oct-65	BOAC d/d 04-Nov-1965. Merged with British Airways on 01-Apr-1974 and painted in BA colours. Transferred to RAF in April 1980 as ZD236. Stored at St Athan	Withdrawn from use and broken up at St Athan in April 1987	St Athan
859	1151	G-ASGI	28-Jan-66	BOAC d/d 12-Feb-1966. Merged with British Airways on 01-Apr-1974 and painted in BA colours. Transferred to RAF in April 1980 as ZD237. Stored at Abingdon	Withdrawn from use and broken up at Abingdon in March 1987	Abingdon
860	1151	G-ASGJ	22-Feb-67	BOAC d/d 07-Mar-1967. Merged with British Airways on 01-Apr-1974 and painted in BA colours. Transferred to RAF in April 1980 as ZD238. Stored at Abingdon	Withdrawn from use and broken up at Abingdon 04-1987.	Abingdon
861	1151	G-ASGK	1-Sep-67	BOAC d/d 27-Oct-1967. Merged with British Airways on 01-Apr-1974 and painted in BA colours. Transferred to RAF in March 1980 as ZD239. Stored at Abingdon	Withdrawn from use and broken up at Abingdon 1987	Abingdon
862	1151	G-ASGL	22-Dec-67	BOAC d/d 25-Jan-1968. Merged with British Airways on 01-Apr-1974 and painted in BA colours. Transferred to RAF in April 1981 and converted to K.4 as ZD240. 101 Squadron	Withdrawn from use and broken up at St Athan 2005. Flight deck initially retained by GJD Services but has since been reduced to scrap	St Athan 04-Aug-2005
863	1151	G-ASGM	26-Feb-68	BOAC d/d 09-Mar-1968. Merged with British Airways on 01-Apr-1974 and painted in BA colours. Transferred to RAF in July 1980 and converted to K.4 as ZD241/P. 101 Squadron	Withdrawn from use and flown to Bruntingthorpe for Spares Recovery Programme. However, the aircraft will now be preserved at Bruntingthorpe as a ground-running example by GJD Services	Bruntingthorpe 21-Mar-2013
864	1151	G-ASGN	1-May-68	BOAC d/d 07-May-1968	Written off at Dawson's Field, Jordan, after hijacking by PFLP terrorists along with Swissair DC-8 HB-IDD and TWA Boeing 707 N8715T	Dawson's Field, Jordan 12-Sept-1970
865	1151	G-ASGO	11-Sep-68	BOAC d/d 27-Sept-1968	Written off after being set alight by hijackers at Amsterdam Schiphol Airport on 03-Mar-1974. Some parts were retained for exhibition at Amsterdam	Amsterdam Schiphol 03-Mar-1974

Construction number	Model number	Registration or serial	Date of first flight	Customer/operator	Fate	Location/date of final flight
866	1151	G-ASGP	20-Nov-68	BOAC d/d 06-Dec-1968. Merged with British Airways on 01-Apr-1974 and painted in BA colours. Transferred to RAF in April 1981 and stored at St Athan from 1981 to 1987 when it was converted to K.4 as ZD242. 101 Squadron	Withdrawn from use in 2005 and used for airframe testing at Boscombe Down. Broken up by February 2011	Boscombe Down
867	1151	G-ASGR	12-Feb-69	BOAC d/d 31-May-1969. Merged with British Airways on 01-Apr-1974 and painted in BA colours. Transferred to RAF as ZD243 in May 1981 and stored at Abingdon until 1987	Broken up at St Athan in 1987	St Athan
868	1151	G-ASGS			BOAC. Order cancelled, aircraft not built	
869	1151	G-ASGT			BOAC. Order cancelled, aircraft not built	
870	1151	G-ASGU			BOAC. Order cancelled, aircraft not built	
871	1151	G-ASGV			BOAC. Order cancelled, aircraft not built	
872	1151	G-ASGW			BOAC. Order cancelled, aircraft not built	
873	1151	G-ASGX			BOAC. Order cancelled, aircraft not built	
874	1151	G-ASGY			BOAC. Order cancelled, aircraft not built	
875	1151	G-ASGZ			BOAC. Order cancelled, aircraft not built	
876	1151	G-ASHA			BOAC. Order cancelled, aircraft not built	
877	1151	G-ASHB			BOAC. Order cancelled, aircraft not built	
878	1151	G-ASHC			BOAC. Order cancelled, aircraft not built	
879	1151	G-ASHD			BOAC. Order cancelled, aircraft not built	
880	1151	G-ASHE			BOAC. Order cancelled, aircraft not built	
881	1154	5X-UVA	3-Sep-66	East African Airways (EAA) d/d 30-Sept-1966	Destroyed during take-off accident at Addis Ababa 18-Apr-1972	Addis Ababa 18-Apr-1972
882	1154	5H-MMT	12-Oct-66	East African Airways (EAA) d/d 31-Oct-1966. Parked at Embakasi upon collapse of EAA 28-Jan-1977. Flown back to UK and stored at Filton. Acquired by RAF as ZA147/F and converted to K.3 on 09-Aug-1985. 101 Squadron. Named Arthur Scarf VC in April 2010. Also named Albert Ball VC in August 2011. Other names also added later	Withdrawn from use 25-Sept-2013, making the very last VC10 flight from Brize Norton to Bruntingthorpe for Spares Recovery Programme. Aircraft is currently complete but engineless. It had been earmarked for Duxford but its future is currently uncertain. The aircraft may now be broken up, with the cockpit section going on loan to the Moravia Collection from GJD Services	Bruntingthorpe 25-Sept-2013
883	1154	5Y-ADA	21-Mar-67	East African Airways (EAA) d/d 31-Mar-1967. Parked at Embakasi upon collapse of EAA 28-Jan-1977. Flown back to UK and stored at Filton. Acquired by RAF as ZA148/G and converted to K.3 on 04-July-1984. 101 Squadron. Named George Thompson VC. Also named Guy Gibson VC in December 2011. Other names also added later	Withdrawn from use 28-Aug-2013 and flown from Brize Norton via Bristol Airport before landing at Newquay. Aircraft on loan from GJD Services to Cornwall Aviation Heritage Centre	Newquay 28-Aug-2013
884	1154	5X-UVJ	19-Apr-69	East African Airways (EAA) d/d 30-Apr-1969. Parked at Embakasi upon collapse of EAA 28-Jan-1977. Flown back to UK and stored at Filton. Acquired by RAF as ZA149/H and converted to K.3 on 25-Mar-1985. 101 Squadron. Named Edward Mannock VC in January 2001. Also named James Nicholson VC in February 2012. Other names also added later	Withdrawn from use on 18-Mar-2013 and flown from Brize Norton to Bruntingthorpe for Spares Recovery Programme. Forward fuselage retained	Bruntingthorpe 18-Mar-2013
885	1154	5H-MOG	16-Feb-70	East African Airways (EAA) d/d 27-Feb-1970. Parked at Embakasi upon collapse of EAA 28-Jan-1977. Repossessed by BAC on 03-Aug-1977 and flown back to UK; stored at Filton. Acquired by RAF as ZA150/J and converted to K.3 on 01-Feb-1985. 101 Squadron. Named Donald Garland VC and Thomas Gray VC in April 2001. Also named Lance Hawker VC in November 2011	Withdrawn from use on 24-Sept-2013 and flown from Brize Norton to Dunsfold for preservation with the Brooklands Museum	Dunsfold 24-Sept-2013

Abbreviations:	
BAC	British Aircraft Corporation
Dbr	Damaged beyond repair
d/d	Delivery date
JARTS	Joint Aircraft Recovery and Transport Squadron
Ntu	Not taken up
Wfu	Withdrawn from use

Appendix 2

───(●)───────────────────

VC10s extant

Model	Serial/ registration	Code	Construction number	Squadron/airline markings	Location	Condition	Remarks
United Kingdom							
Vickers VC10 EMU			801A	BA colours	Brooklands Museum, Brooklands	Test shell, cockpit	
Vickers VC10 K.2	ZA144		806	101 Squadron	Joint Aircraft Recovery and Transport Squadron (JARTS), Boscombe Down	Forward fuselage	Ex-A40-VC, G-ARVC
Vickers VC10 Srs 1101	G-ARVM		815	BA colours	Brooklands Museum, Brooklands	Fuselage	Ex-BA and BOAC, arrived 19-Oct-2006
Vickers VC10 Srs 1103	A40-AB		820	Sultan of Oman colour scheme	Brooklands Museum, Brooklands	Complete	Ex-G-ASIX, BCAL and BUA, last flight into Brooklands 6-July-1987
Vickers VC10 C.1K	XR808	R	828	101 Squadron	RAF Museum, Cosford	Complete	Kenneth Campbell VC, last flight into Bruntingthorpe 29-July-2013
Vickers VC10 C.1K	XV104	U	834	101 Squadron	GJD Services, Bruntingthorpe	Cockpit section	James McCudden VC, last flight into Bruntingthorpe 4-Nov-2012
Vickers VC10 C.1K	XV106	W	836	101 Squadron	GJD Services, Bruntingthorpe	Cockpit section	Arthur Scarf VC, last flight into Bruntingthorpe 7-Dec-2012
Vickers VC10 C.1K	XV108	Y	838	10 Squadron	East Midlands Aeropark, East Midlands Airport	Forward fuselage	William Rhodes-Moorhouse VC, last flight 7-Nov-2012
Vickers VC10 C.1K	XV109	Z	839	101 Squadron	GJD Services, Bruntingthorpe	Cockpit section	Thomas Mottershead VC, last flight into Bruntingthorpe 31-Mar-2010
Vickers Super VC10	G-ASGC		853	BOAC Cunard livery	British Airliner Collection, Duxford Aviation Society, Duxford	Complete	Last flight into Duxford 15-Apr-1980
Vickers VC10 K.4	ZD241	N	863	101 Squadron	Gary Spoors, Bruntingthorpe	Complete, taxiable	Ex-BA and BOAC G-ASGM, last flight into Bruntingthorpe 12-Mar-2013
Vickers VC10 K.3	ZA147	F	882	101 Squadron	GJD Services, Bruntingthorpe	Complete but engineless	Ex-EAA A/W 5H-MMT, last flight into Bruntingthorpe 25-Sept-2013
Vickers VC10 K.3	ZA148	G	883	101 Squadron	Newquay Cornwall Airport	Complete	Ex-EAA A/W 5Y-ADA, last flight into Newquay 28-Aug-2013
Vickers VC10 K.3	ZA149	H	884	101 Squadron	GJD Services, Bruntingthorpe	Forward fuselage	Ex-EAA A/W 5X-UVJ, last flight into Bruntingthorpe 25-Sept-2013
Vickers VC10 K.3	ZA150	J	885	101 Squadron	Brooklands Museum, Dunsfold	Complete, taxiable	Ex-EAA A/W 5H-MOG, last flight into Dunsfold 24-Sept-2013
Germany							
Vickers VC10 Srs 1101	G-ARVF		808	United Arab Emirates	Flugausstellung Hermeskeil, near Trier	Complete	

Appendix 3

Technical specifications

	Standard VC10 Type 1101	RAF VC10 C.1 Type 1106	Super VC10 Type 1151
Dimensions			
Overall length	159ft 8in	159ft 8in	171ft 8in
Wingspan	146ft 2in	146ft 2in	146ft 2in
Height	39ft 6in	39ft 6in	39ft 6in
Tailplane span	43ft 10in	43ft 10in	43ft 10in
Tailplane area	638ft²	638ft²	638ft²
Gross wing area	2,851ft²	2,932ft²	2,932ft²
Aspect ratio	7.5	7.3	7.3
Cabin dimensions			
Length	92ft 4in	92ft 4in	105ft 0in
Maximum width	11ft 6in	11ft 6in	11ft 6in
Maximum height	7ft 5in	7ft 5in	7ft 5in
Luggage volume	1,490ft³	1,490ft³	1,930ft³
Accommodation	up to 151 seats	up to 150 seats	up to 174 seats
Weights			
Maximum take-off weight	312,000lb	323,000lb	335,000lb
Maximum landing weight	216,000lb	235,000lb	237,000lb
Typical operating weight	147,000lb	146,000lb	156,828lb
Maximum payload	40,420lb	57,400lb	58,172lb
Total fuel capacity	17,925 Imp galls	19,365 Imp galls	19,340 Imp galls
Performance			
Maximum payload range (no reserves)	4,380nm	3,390nm	4,100nm
Maximum fuel range (no reserves)	5,275nm	–	6,195nm
Maximum cruise speed	502kts	494kts	505kts
Economical cruise speed	480kts	369kts	478kts
Initial rate of climb	1,920ft/min	3,050ft/min	2,300ft/min
Take-off distance	8,280ft	8,400ft	8,750ft
Landing run (at Max landing weight)	6,380ft	6,500ft	6,850ft
Service ceiling	38,000ft	38,000ft	38,000ft
Powerplants	Four Rolls-Royce Conway RCo42 turbofans of 21,000lb each	Four Rolls-Royce Conway RCo43 turbofans of 22,500lb each	Four Rolls-Royce Conway RCo43 turbofans of 22,500lb each

Appendix 4

VC10 type designations

Type number	Details
Standard VC10	
1100	Prototype standard VC10
1101	BOAC production version (12 built)
1102	Two built for Ghana Airways, one with main deck cargo door, both with 4% wing chord extension
1103	Three built for BUA with main deck cargo door and wing chord extension
1104	Nigerian Airways version (none built)
1105	Original designation for the RAF Transport Command as VC10 C.1. This was changed when the RAF decided to incorporate the main deck freight floor
1106	RAF Transport Command C.1 variant. Modifications included folding hatracks, machined cargo floor, Rolls-Royce Conway RCo.43 engines and fin fuel tank (14 built)
1107	RAF tanker (none built)
1109	Prototype converted to airline standard for Laker Airways, with Type 1106 wing
1110	Generic designation for VC10A (none built). Vickers later used this as an internal designation for the Sultan of Oman's VC10
1111	Version of VC10A for BOAC (none built)
1112	VC10 K.2, tanker conversion for RAF of Type 1101 (5 converted)
1125	Standard (could be a hybrid standard/Super design) VC10 for Aerolineas Argentinas (none built)
Super VC10	
1151	BOAC production version of the Super VC10 which included the wing chord extension, Rolls-Royce Conway RCo.43 engines and fin fuel tank (17 built)
1152	BOAC Super VC10 version with main deck freight door (none built)
1153	Not built. Some sources have claimed that this variant was designed for EAA, but this was not the case
1154	Super VC10 for EAA with main deck freight door (5 built)
1157	Super VC10 for Varanair Siam (none built)
1158	Super VC10 for CSA (none built)
1161	Super VC10 for Nigerian Airways (none built)
1162	Super VC10 for Tarom (none built)
1163	Allocated to a specification for Super VC10s for China. Specification shows both full passenger and mixed passenger/freight layouts, indicating that this version would have incorporated a main deck freight door (none built)
1164	Super VC10 K.3, tanker conversion for the RAF of Type 1154 (4 converted)
1166	Proposed conversion to RAF tanker VC10 K.3A (none converted)
1170	Super VC10 K.4, tanker conversion for RAF of Type 1151 (5 converted)
1180	Proposed double-deck version with 295 economy seats (none built)
1181	Proposed double-deck version with improved passenger amenities, 286 economy seats (none built)
1180	VC10 C.1K, tanker conversion for RAF of Type 1106 (13 converted)
1191	Proposed short-haul version for BEA (none built)
'Specials'	
G-AXLR	Delivered as a Type 1106 to the RAF, this aircraft was leased to Rolls-Royce for airborne testing of the RB211 engine. To accomplish this, the Nos 1 and 2 engines were removed and the pylon modified to accept the larger RB211 engine, thereby creating a three-engined VC10. After the completion of test flying with Rolls-Royce, the aircraft was flown to RAF Kemble. It was inspected and found that the airframe was distorted, so never returned to squadron service. After considering a major rebuild, which proved to be uneconomical, it was struck off charge and cannibalised for spares. For several years afterwards it served as a training aid for Special Air Services training before being eventually scrapped

Appendix 5

ZD241 Bruntingthorpe Preservation Group

ZD241 and her Bruntingthorpe rebirth

On 13 March 2013, VC10 K.4 ZD241 was retired from RAF service and made her last flight to Bruntingthorpe. She was handed over to the disposal agent, GJD Services, and was subsequently decommissioned in accordance with the disposal contract, ready for her eventual parting-out and scrapping.

Gary Spoors, the managing director of GJD Services, is a former RAF VC10 engineer. He had decided that he would like to preserve a VC10 in live condition and had originally selected XR808 for that role. However, the RAF Museum decided to take a VC10 for their collection at Cosford and XR808 was earmarked.

This left Gary Spoors with a difficult decision on which airframe to select. Following a technical study of those available at Bruntingthorpe, it was decided that ZD241 would be the most suitable to recommission and preserve.

Later in 2013, Gary Spoors put out a call for experienced former VC10 engineers and volunteers to help out with the recommissioning of ZD241. A small team was formed and the name 'ZD241 Bruntingthorpe Preservation Group' adopted. That small but dedicated team consisted of four former RAF VC10 engineers, along with two keen and willing volunteers. Work soon started on the task before them.

After 241's arrival at Bruntingthorpe and as part of the earlier decommissioning process, the engines had been removed, the hydraulics and fuel systems drained, engine fire extinguisher bottles removed, along with the removal of various other components as part of the spares recovery process. In addition, certain 'sensitive' pieces of military equipment had already been taken out by the RAF, prior to her being handed over to GJD Services.

In March 2014 the new team commenced the process that would eventually take several months: to reconnect ZD241's systems ready for her debut in the forthcoming Cold War Jets Day at Bruntingthorpe in the following May. GJD Services had helped start the process by refitting the engines prior to the team's arrival, making them ready for the team to reconnect them.

Following an overview of what work was actually required to return ZD241 to a 'live' condition, the team commenced the task of reconnecting the engines, replenishing the hydraulics and fuel systems and refitting all of the parts that were missing. Many of the required parts came from other already-disposed airframes on the site, along with parts obtained from K.3 ZA147 – the other complete airframe in GJD's possession.

The work was carried out over several maintenance days in March and April 2014 and the team methodically worked their way through the jet, ensuring she was fully rebuilt, until all systems were ready to be checked. However, it was not all straightforward and the team encountered a number of problems.

During the earlier spares recovery, some of the removed parts had not been correctly accounted for and following an inspection of the bleed air system it was found a flame detector had been removed from a pipe in the rear of the aircraft.

Following these checks, power was then applied to the airframe using an external ground power unit and all of the aircraft's systems were systematically powered up and checked for correct operation. These tests included – among many – operating the flying controls, moving the flaps and slats throughout their ranges, operating the TPI (tailplane incidence – the large all-moving control surface on the top of the fin) and operating the aircraft fuel and hydraulics systems. Perhaps somewhat surprisingly, most systems powered up were 100% serviceable and only a few snags were required to be fixed. These included the engine

fuel flow indication and the No 3 engine EGT (exhaust gas temperature) system.

Once the team were satisfied, they proceeded to start the engines for the first time since her retirement the previous March. Initially, the engines were operated only at idle power and all ran perfectly. After shutting down, all four engines were inspected for leaks and faults; the airframe was then prepared for later high-power engine runs, eventually leading to her moving under her own power.

In late April the team embarked on the final part of the jigsaw puzzle and ran each engine at high power – checking all of the operating parameters. Once they declared themselves happy, the resident pilot released the parking brake and once again, she moved under her own power. A slow-speed taxi was carried out to ensure the brakes and steering operated as required. Once the team had undertaken a finish inspection and was satisfied that all was in order, ZD241 was taxied out to the runaway and all four Rolls-Royce Conway engines were wound up to maximum – around 99–100% HP rpm – and a high-speed run was conducted. To say the team was chuffed with their achievements would be something of an understatement!

In May 2014, ZD241 made her public debut in the Cold War Jets event at Bruntingthorpe to great acclaim. All four Conway engines roared and she thundered down the 3,000m runway at around 100kts (around 110mph) – setting off a number of car alarms in the process! Maximum reverse thrust was then selected and she came to a noisy stop, before conducting a 180° turn and back-tracking down the runway before returning to her parking slot and shutting down in front of the crowd. ZD241 is now a firm favourite at the Cold War Jet events.

Over time, the team has added new recruits and this has helped to spread the workload during the year while conducting the continuing maintenance programme. The team regularly meet and conduct a variety of anti-deterioration tasks (the regular tasks carried out to maintain an aircraft in the best possible state while in a static condition). These tasks include the regular running of the engines at idle, exercising all movable surfaces and greasing as required, rotating the tyres to prevent flat spots, applying

ground power and running up systems while internal heating is applied to blow any moisture out. The aircraft is always inspected thoroughly to detect any issues so they can be rectified at the earliest opportunity.

Where possible the team try to schedule tasks each time they are at Bruntingthorpe, in order to preserve the longevity of the airframe. This includes the removal of any corrosion and reapplication of the protective finishes. Although many of the systems are not necessary for the ground-running and taxiing, the team try to maintain all systems on ZD241 to the same high standard and preserve the legacy of the airframe for people to admire. They also wash the jet to remove dirt and contaminates, but the sheer size of the airframe means this is usually carried out over several weekends.

All of the work conducted on ZD241 is done by technical and non-technical volunteers who give up their free time to work on her. This support and dedication is fundamental and the key to the long-term preservation of ZD241.

The team is currently made up of former VC10 pilots, engineers and volunteers. The former VC10 engineers are Ollie Pallett and Mark Wollage who are currently serving in the RAF, along with Gary Farrar (retired composite engineer), Steve Jones (aircraft maintenance contractor), John Kite (machine engineer) and Phil Juffs (Rolls-Royce), who are all former RAF maintenance personnel. The team's volunteer base is made up of Bill Rowe, Richard Faint, David Simmonds, Mark Taylor, Stewart Weller and Neil Brooks, all of whom have a diverse reason for loving the VC10.

Team pilots Andy Townshend and Chris Haywood (both former VC10 flight crew and currently serving pilots in the RAF) make up the team, but are just as happy getting dirty as they are on the flight deck.

Mention must also be made of another team based at Bruntingthorpe and that is the 'T-Baggers'. They are also a small group, but they operate a pair of Blackburn Buccaneer aircraft. Their help and guidance over the last two years has been invaluable to ZD241's team set-up.

Lastly, massive thanks must go to Gary Spoors of GJD Services. Without his continued support none of the above would have been possible and the team would not be able to do

OPPOSITE VC10 K.4, ZD241, parked on the ramp at Bruntingthorpe. On the starboard wing are some of the team's committed volunteers, along with the aircraft's benefactor Gary Spoors (standing fourth from right of image). *(Keith Wilson)*

191

what they do. The man is a living legend in the world of VC10 preservation.

The plan

Although the ZD241 Preservation Group at Bruntingthorpe has achieved their first goal of returning ZD241 to a 'live' condition, their attention has now turned to her long-term future. The ultimate goal is to preserve the legacy of the VC10 for the new generations to admire and learn from. The immediate task still remains to keep ZD241 in a live condition and show her off twice-yearly at the Cold War Jet days; however, they are now planning her long-term opportunities.

ZD241 made her first flight at Brooklands on 26 February 1968 as G-ASGM. Now the team are looking for a special way to celebrate the 50th anniversary of her first flight – February 2018. Longer-term they are looking to continue their work and hopefully still be in a position to show her off to the public for the 75th anniversary of the VC10's first flight, on 29 June 2037.

This will all require some form of financial backing. Currently, the team operates on a shoestring. They rely heavily on the goodwill and kindness of both Mr Dave Walton, the owner of Bruntingthorpe Airfield, who allows them to keep the aircraft at Bruntingthorpe free of charge; and to GJD Services who very kindly supply them with out-of-date lubricants, loan them ground equipment and provide waste fuel, while allowing them to run the aircraft on their insurance.

In order to move forward, the ZD241 Preservation Group would like to get themselves into a position where they are self-sufficient. This would require an average annual income of around £5,000. Currently, they are trying a number of different ways to raise income. If any would-be sponsors are out there, please get in touch via the ZD241 Preservation Group's Facebook page.

Facebook page:
ZD241 Bruntingthorpe Preservation Group

Bibliography and sources

Andrews, C.F. and Morgan E.B., *Vickers Aircraft since 1908*, 2nd edition (Putnam, 1988)

British Aviation Research Group, *British Military Aircraft Serials and Markings*, 2nd edition (BARG/Nostalgair/The Aviation Hobby Shop, 1983)

Cole, Lance, *Vickers VC10* (Crowood Press, 2000)

Ellis, Ken, *Wrecks & Relics*, 24th edition (Crécy Publishing, 2014)

Flintham, Victor, *Air Wars and Aircraft – A Detailed Record of Air Combat, 1945 to the Present* (Arms and Armour Press, 1989)

Gibson, Chris, *Vulcan's Hammer – V-Force Projects and Weapons since 1945* (Hikoki Publications Ltd, 2011)

Hedley, Martin, *Modern Civil Aircraft: 1 Vickers VC10* (Ian Allan Ltd, 1982)

Jefford Wing Commander C.G., MBE, RAF, *RAF Squadrons* (Airlife, 1988)

Robertson, Bruce, *British Military Aircraft Serials 1878–1987* (Midland Counties Publications, 1987)

Skinner, Stephen, *British Aircraft Corporation – A History* (Crowood Press, 2012)

Thetford, Owen, *Aircraft of the Royal Air Force since 1918*, 8th edition (Putnam, 1988)

Trevenen James, A.G., *The Royal Air Force – The Past 30 Years* (McDonald and Jane's Publishers Limited, 1976)

Trubshaw, Brian with Edmondson, Sally, *Test Pilot* (Sutton Publishing, 1998)

Wynn, Humphrey, *The RAF Strategic Nuclear Deterrent Forces: Their Origins, Roles and Deployment 1946–1969: A Documentary History* (HMSO 1994)

Putnam Aeronautical Review: Issue Number One (Conway Maritime Press Ltd, May 1989)

Various editions of *Air Clues* magazine, issued monthly for the Royal Air Force by the Director of Flying Training (MoD)

Various editions of the *Airplane* partwork (Orbis Publishing Limited, 1990)

Various editions of *Flight International* magazine, published weekly by IPC

Index